BEHIND THE BADGE IN RIVER CITY:
A PORTLAND POLICE MEMOIR

ADVANCE PRAISE FOR *BEHIND THE BADGE*

Don Dupay takes his reader to a Portland few of us would recognize in his fascinating and gritty Behind The Badge in River City: A Portland Police Memoir. *It's the ultimate ride along; you follow him to the darkest reaches of the city where vice is nice and truth has consequences. Strap yourself in, it's going to be a bumpy ride!*

—Kathy Smith
Portland Broadcast Journalist and Anchorwoman,
with KGW and KATU

This book is not only historically accurate it is also extremely personal. Dupay shows us what it was like to be a cop at a particular time in this particular city. It is a rare achievement. Mr. Dupay's voice is wonderful as he tells his story. I think it should be turned into a TV show.

—JD Chandler, author of *Murder and Scandal in Prohibition Portland; Sex, Vice and Misdeeds in Mayor Baker's Reign*

I knew Don - the author and I worked for the same enforcement agency - and he sure tells it like it was.

—Bob Peschka, retired Lieutenant with Portland Police Bureau

As you turn the pages of Behind the Badge in River City, *you can almost smell the stale cigarettes and bourbon breath in the Police precinct, as you read chapter after chapter of Don Dupay's firsthand experiences on the force. Dupay draws us deep into what would otherwise be a beautiful picture of 1970s Portland and forces us to see the dirty corners and the skeleton-filled closets. Just like a good friend, to truly know a city you must also accept it flaws. Reading this book and getting to see behind the curtain of how we policed our town is an opportunity you shouldn't pass up.*

—Sean Davis, author of *The Wax Bullet War*

A fine book, accessible and touching as it follows Don Dupay's career arc. It traces the author's beginnings as a newly minted Portland Police officer. Along the way see how Dupay's career was a lot like

everyone's: occasional exciting moments punctuated by long pauses, paperwork and office politics. Throughout the vignettes that form the structure of Behind the Badge *its clear Dupay serves honorably and well. Some of the events portrayed (I'll let you discover them) are plainly disturbing and pulse with verisimilitude. They had a cumulative effect on this good cop. That and Dupay's reluctance to bend to expedience limited his career prospects within the Bureau. The Portland Police Bureau performs a necessary public safety function. It was never easy on either side of that thin blue line.* Behind the Badge in River City: A Portland Police Memoir *makes that clear. This is a valuable historical document from a man who lived through the events. Buy this book. It's the best way to honor Don Dupay's 17-year career.*

—Mark Sanchez, retired KOIN journalist

This is a book that you won't want to put down (but if you must, you can, as each chapter is complete unto itself), a book filled with the history of the Portland Police Bureau from the 1960s into the 1970s. DuPay's steady, articulate, honest voice fills his memoir of his time on the police force with the integrity of the good cop he was, as he maneuvered his way through just about every despicable or heart breaking situation imaginable for one in that role. And he has a soft spot for dogs. No cats are allowed on the tavern cutting board, though; that will bring the Board of Health. This is a very good read that sheds light on the inner workings, at that time, of an agency we all depend heavily upon, officers we hope we can trust. The reader can trust Don DuPay to tell good stories very well, with great command of language, of scene. This is a wonderful read. I love knowing more about Portland. This shows the truth of our police department and includes appalling corruption and crime both inside and outside the force, but also provides ample heroes and humor.

—Susan Reese, Portland State University English professor

Behind the Badge in River City: A Portland Police Memoir *is a gritty, exciting, true account of what police work was really like in the early 1960s and 1970s. Reading the book, I was reminded of Joseph Wambaugh and Robert B. Parker's fiction about police work, which was often autobiographical. DuPay's authentic, often brutally honest, page-turner grabbed me right away and would not let go. If I were to return to the job of being a cop, I'd be proud to have Detective DuPay "have my back" as I'd be inspired to do my very best work. Maintaining integrity as he did, he walked the same kind of fine line I had to, and he did it very well. In fact, he did it better than most. The book is worthy of a read by anyone interested in the history and realities of real police work, and as it reveals much of the angst and stress that an honest police officer can go through, it is not for the faint of heart.*

—John T. MacF. Mood
Retired Motor Officer, Charleston City PD

Former Detective Don DuPay tells stories that make the hair rise up on the back of your neck. In seventeen years with the department, he worked jail duty, East Precinct, traffic division, vice squad, morals, and North Precinct until spending his last few years with the department as a detective, working the burglary and homicide details. We are allowed to almost intimately know DuPay and the men he worked with. In addition to his fellow officers, he introduces us to pimps, prostitutes, safe-crackers, drug addicts, thieves and thugs. But we are never left to choose between the "good guys" and the "bad guys." Don keeps it real.

—Timothy Martin Flanagan
Editor, *Portland Alliance Newspaper*, Portland, Oregon

Don Dupay's book, Behind the Badge in River City *should be read by ever citizen, voter and taxpayer in Portland. It is a classic work, truthfully told. It has the feel of rightousness, the ring of justice. It tells us exactly how we got to where we are today on the Portland Police Force, with a lot of work still to do. Not a rant, not a kiss and tell, but just good, solid, important story-telling. As someone who has been watching Portland police and politics closely for 48 years, I admire it very much.*

—Ron Buel
Journalist and original publisher and editor of *Willamette Week*

BEHIND THE BADGE IN RIVER CITY

A PORTLAND POLICE MEMOIR

— SECOND EDITION —

DON DUPAY

OREGON GREYSTONE PRESS
PORTLAND, OREGON

Behind the Badge in River City: A Portland Police Memoir, Second Edition
© 2016 Don DuPay
Edited by Theresa Griffin Kennedy

All rights reserved. This book or any portion thereof may not be reproduced or used in any manner whatsoever without the express written permission of the author, except for the use of brief quotations in a book review.

Oregon Greystone Press
Portland, OR

Cover Design: Claire Flint Last
Printed in the United States of America

Cover Photograph: Wes and Dotty Weber
www.westdotphotography.com

LCCN: 2015931225
ISBN: 978-0692709771

Contents

Foreword	xv
Introduction	xvii
Prologue	1
Central Precinct 1961	5
The Good Old Days	8
Cars and Queers	11
The Keeper of the Prison	13
Keep Your Mouth Shut	18
Paddy Wagons and Shotguns	20
East Precinct	22
Invitation Only	25
Learning the Rules	28
Police Academy	31
Traffic Division	33
The Probationary Year	36
Partners and Friends	38
Bus's Kill	43
The Stinker	46
Officer Gump	48
Upturned Cars and Onlookers	51
Movers and Violators	53
Street Racing	56
The Low Speed Chase	62
Columbus Day Storm	68
Losing a Friend to Vice	75
Finding a New Partner	82
Ambushes and Triple Fatal's	88
Vice Squad	93
Van's Olympic Room	103
Fool's Errand in Old Town	107
More Trouble at Van's	110

North Precinct...114
Headstones and Traffic Tickets.......................123
New Blood..125
A Troubled Teen..127
Going Back to the Ghetto..............................129
Walking the Alleys...135
Tying up Loose Ends.....................................137
Blood and Spit...141
Self-Defense...144
Behind Opperman's Store..............................147
Fat Mary and Sergeant Rich..........................150
Animals on the Night Shift...........................152
Killing the Animal of Another......................155
Assault with an Electrical Cord.....................163
The Watts Riots...166
Instant Extradition..171
Thelma and the Trick....................................176
Perspective...179
More Perspective...181
The .25 Caliber Semi-automatic Pistol.........183
Man Down: Clarence's Sidewalk Demise......187
Captain Jim Purcell Junior............................191
Interlude..196
Some St John's Families; a Retrospective......213
The Detectives, Fall, 1967.............................216
The Initiation..219
From Behind a Desk......................................221
The Stardust and the Strip............................226
Working Morals...228
Accidental Death...231
Auto Theft in Portland..................................233
A Sense of Violation......................................236
Getting Noticed...240
The Heavy Squad..245

The Homemade Surveillance Truck	248
The Professionals	254
Boreascope Benny	260
The Little Old Plumbing Store	263
Luncheon Appointments Before Police Work	265
The Instructor at the Academy	269
An Avalanche	273
Sitting in the Van	276
Losing Another Cop	279
The Crook	282
The Secret Snitch	290
Homicide Detail, summer of 1975	293
Murder on the Riverbank 1975	300
Pals No More	307
The Roof Top Assassin	312
The Convenience Store Murder	320
Another Dead Body	325
Bessie Staley and the Canary	329
The Zebedee Manning Death	338
Epilogue	350
Authors Note	355
Final Editors Reflection	360
About the Editor	369
Acknowledgements	370
About The Author	375

*To my former partner Frank Jozaitis,
who for some reason or another couldn't make it.
And to Leo Miller, my friend and mentor,
who for some reason or another couldn't make it either.*

Foreword

In 1975, Don DuPay was a Portland homicide detective who knew too much. For one thing, he knew that Zebedee Manning, the 15-year-old black kid lying on his bed with a .22 rifle resting on his chest and a bullet hole in his forehead, was *not* a suicide. In the first place, there were two other bullet holes in the bedroom besides the one in Zebedee's forehead – one in the ceiling and one in the wall behind the bed. And secondly, as DuPay quickly realized, the kid couldn't have reached the trigger and held the muzzle of the gun against his forehead at the same time. His arms just weren't long enough. It was murder.

Downstairs on the kitchen table was a nearly empty whiskey bottle and four glasses. If Zebedee had committed suicide, he'd certainly had a lot of company at the time. The way DuPay saw it, the whole thing had been staged, and he proceeded to investigate the case as a homicide. After about a week, DuPay's boss called him into his office and told him to drop the case. "Don," the lieutenant said, "he's a nigger junkie. And we're too busy. Go do something else."

Even making allowances for the prevalent racism in the bureau at that time, that didn't make sense either. So, DuPay kept poking around on his own. As he would learn, Zebedee's "uncle," a big time Portland drug dealer, had recently been arrested. DuPay figured someone was looking for the uncle's stash, and whoever it was was trying to get Zebedee to tell them where it was hidden.

After a few drinks failed to loosen Zebedee's tongue, they'd taken him upstairs to his bedroom and started to play a game of chicken with him, holding the muzzle of his .22 rifle against his forehead. One shot goes off to the left. Another into the ceiling. The third time something goes very wrong – maybe they'd all been drinking too much – and Zebedee gets a bullet in the head. Whoever the shooters are lay Zebedee's body back on the bed, put the rifle on his chest, and get the hell out of there.

DuPay is starting to suspect it's some of his fellow cops when the lieutenant, who's just learned that DuPay has been investigating the case in defiance of his orders, calls him into his office and tells him he's been transferred out of homicide and back to burglary.

For a look at the Portland Police Bureau as you've never seen it before, don't miss Don DuPay's excellent memoir, *Behind the Badge in River City. A Portland Police Memoir.*

—Phil Stanford, Feb 10th, 2013
Author of Portland Confidential; Sex, Crime and Corruption in the Rose City.

Introduction

When I first became aware that my dear friend, Don DuPay, had written a personal memoir, while in his middle fifties, from 1991 to 1992, detailing his time as a Portland police officer and detective, I was skeptical his manuscript would exceed more than about seventy or one hundred pages. I wasn't certain the writing would be something I could help craft into anything more substantial than a short memoir or remembrance for family and friends to enjoy. When Don brought out a fat binder, with exactly 235 typed pages, I was nearly exultant with hope and excitement at the possibilities I knew existed.

I knew with his natural, direct and humorous writing, the task of editing the manuscript and collaborating with him had the potential to become something special and indeed effortless. I knew that assisting in his process of telling what it was like to work as a police officer in Portland Oregon, during a special time in the city's history was an important task that demanded my involvement to ensure its completion. After getting the only copy scanned and saved electronically, I performed two preliminary edits, alone. Once we could sit down with the saved file, Don and I began eight, laborious, line-by-line edits. This included taking out unneeded words and repetitive phrases along with adding richer detail, while I encouraged Don to elaborate on memories he'd rather have forgotten. This fleshing-out of the stories sometimes required pertinent clarification, and was a difficult process of continuous fact checking.

Don, like many men who've worked long-term, in law enforcement careers, was diagnosed, several years after leaving the force, with Post Traumatic Stress Disorder. Remembering the horrible violence and death he witnessed in his seventeen-year career with the Portland Police Bureau was challenging and painful. He was sometimes overcome with the raw emotion of revisiting unwanted memories and grotesque details. The memories of what he was able and unable to do to procure justice for crime victims who still haunt his memory was not an easy task. This, I believe, is a typical pattern many law enforcement officers face: a complex and difficult feeling of responsibility to those victimized by crime and a nagging feeling of guilt at not being able to solve the dilemmas crime victims experience as a result of crimes they've survived or *not* survived.

However, going over the manuscript was a labor of love for both of us. For Don, because recalling his successful career and the incidents he'd written about previously and remembering the uniqueness of his time with the bureau gave him a renewed sense of self-worth and validation for a profession he was always proud to be a part of. And for me, because as a writer, I felt thrilled to be involved in such an historically relevant text, and I knew that this process, though painful, was also very healing for Don.

Part of this process of recollection and creative collaboration was aided when, in early August of 2013, I gained access to Don's complete personnel file with 166 pages of records, documents and detailed performance evaluations. These documents provided key insights into Don's career and conduct as an officer and later as a detective. They were invaluable in providing accuracy with regard to promotions, transfers, health issues and other statements Don has made concerning his career. The documents detail the chronology of memorable events and also detail his eventual resignation from the Portland Police Bureau April 11, 1978.

When Don spoke with me about the crime victims he was not able to save, the blood and gore he witnessed, the beatings, elderly rape victims, battered wives, abused children, the knifings and gunplay, the ambush and murder, his empathy was still deep and extremely complex. Don is and was a man with a clear sense of right and wrong. He has an acute sense of simple truth and a highly developed empathy for those less fortunate. Don was a police officer who went against the popular grain of many law enforcement officers of his time and what they were willing to do to fit in. He was a police officer who was dedicated, as much as he could be, to excellence, truthfulness and accountability.

Some of the stories in this book are tragic and moving, others are comic, while retaining a certain pathos within that comedy. All show a man who cared deeply for the simple, everyday people he came across. It is with pleasure and pride, that I present this memoir to you, detailing some very complex human dynamics. This is a book about the life and times of one law enforcement man, who has always called River City his home.

—Theresa Griffin Kennedy
2013

Prologue

APRIL 6, 1961, I was sworn in as a brand new police officer in a ceremony held in the office of Ray Smith, the city auditor, in City Hall. I was nervous, proud of myself for passing all the tests, not least of all surviving the interview with the shrink, and now I stood with my hand up, swearing to serve the citizens in an honorable manner. I was sworn in wearing a dark blue, pin-stripe suit and a tie. Uniforms were not yet available and for about ten days I continued to wear it; jumping out of the police car, trailing my coach, with my tie flapping in the wind, and my six inch barrel Smith and Wesson revolver resting within a holster on my hip. I felt a little like Elliot Ness, and I wondered, because of the curious looks I got, if folks thought the guy in the suit was supervising the guy in the uniform.

After ten days, the sergeant finally gave me the necessary vouchers to buy my uniforms and I hurried to Nudelman's Men's Store on SW Fourth and Washington, now the site of Portland Luggage. The store was in the basement and they sold uniforms to police, sheriffs, firemen, postmen, and private security guards. I was issued three pairs of blue pants, waist size 30, length 33, three blue shirts with darker blue epaulets and "Bureau of Police" patches sewn on both shoulders, long sleeves, size 15 ½ 34, three black clip-on ties, and a police cap with a patent leather bill, size 9. The coat was what they called an "Eisenhower," with brass buttons up the front, size 44 long.

Next came the leather gun belt, with extra bullet loops, attached swivel holster, full snap-down top, and the call-box key I would need to contact the precinct while out in the field. When the holster was snapped shut, you couldn't see the gun inside, and though those old fashioned holsters have been criticized for being awkward and clumsy, my colleagues and I never had any problems with them. I was issued a big, beautiful, shiny, brass buckle for the gun belt. This came along with a black leather belt to hold up the trousers, also with a shiny brass buckle. The clerk finally handed me a ten-inch sap, filled with powdered lead and covered with heavy black leather. I later learned they worked well for smashing out front teeth.

With all my new things in tow I rushed home to try everything on. God, I was excited! I dressed in the bathroom in front of the big mirror. First the trousers, a heavy durable twill, the kind of cloth that got shiny in the butt after six months of sitting in a police car. I snaked the belt through the belt loops. The belt and pants fit perfectly. In the mirror, an entirely new person was emerging. I took the shirt off the hanger and put it on. I buttoned it up the front and buttoned the long sleeves, at the wrists. I tucked the shirt into the trousers and fastened the belt. A moment later, I fastened the collar and snapped on a tie. The cap with the shiny bill fit perfectly, too. Next, I removed the new leather gun belt from the hook on the bathroom door. The belt was heavy with my revolver and handcuffs in place and already snapped down. The new leather squeaked as I hooked the big buckle in front.

Now fully dressed, I stepped back to look at the person in the mirror, staring back at me. Man, did I look sharp. *Who in the hell is that?* I remember thinking to myself. I practiced making stern faces in the mirror and adjusting the bill of the cap to different angles. Satisfied that my stern face would work, I introduced myself to the mirror image. "Hi, I'm Officer DuPay! I have badge number 354, a loaded gun, and a letter from the chief of police, to prove it!" I was just twenty-five years old.

It was still several hours before I went to work but I stayed suited up, looking in the mirror as much as possible, and waiting for the time when it would be roll call at the precinct. Later, that night, while I was sitting among all the other officers, I looked like a new copper penny in a room full of old coppers. Have you ever heard the old saying, once a Marine, always a Marine? It's the same with cops. Once a cop, always a cop. Once you put on the uniform, you never really take it off.

The Safety Patrol and the Coffey Brothers

I have often wondered how my early life experiences led to my career as a Portland Police officer. Back in the seventh grade, at Rose City Park grade school, in 1948, I was appointed to the safety patrol. Every morning I reported early to the homeroom teacher, to get my official flag and safety patrol belt. The belt was a Sam Brown style and all white. It went around my waist and over my shoulder. On the shoulder strap was a big, shiny, silver badge that read "Portland Public School Safety Patrol." I was assigned a street corner, and I remember standing there with pride. When I put my flag down, the cars *stopped*. The white belt and silver badge reinforced my authority over all passing cars that might endanger my classmates as they walked across the street heading home. In the afternoon, I was allowed to leave class a few minutes early to get my flag and belt with the impressive badge and protect the same crossing. I loved the feeling of authority the badge gave me and looking back now, I can honestly say that I never got over that feeling.

In later years, around the time I began attending Grant High School, I worked for my parents at our popular DuPay's Drive-in Restaurant, as a bus boy and soda jerk. Portland police officers taking advantage of our policy of giving officers free coffee, would stop by more than once a shift for a cup of hot Java. They liked to chat with the cute girl carhops who worked for us, this being the early 1950s when drive-in restaurants were all the vogue in Portland. The officers got free coffee and we got the secure feeling of having a police presence at our restaurant nearly all the time. It seemed a fair trade-off.

Two of my favorite cops were Donald and Clayton Coffey, who worked District 18. They were brothers who worked out of East Precinct, working in the East Moreland and Sellwood districts. It was a standing joke with us, at DuPay's Drive-in, that, "The Coffey brothers are here for their coffee."

I was always happy to see them. They made me feel welcome and would frequently let me sit in the back seat of their car to listen to the radio, while they sat in the restaurant drinking coffee and chatting with my parents. Sometimes they would let me sit in the car with them, and I was thrilled, while we talked, to be able to look at their gold badges with the numbers on the bottom. As a kid growing up in 1950s Portland, Oregon, a police officer was someone you looked up to, someone decent, who held a high place of prestige in the community and the Coffey brothers personified that decency and prestige. I learned their radio number, 18, and what 10-8 and 10-7 meant, in service and out of service. When they stopped by our restaurant, they always said they were "10-10 at DuPays." That meant they were occupied (drinking coffee at DuPay's) but available for calls. I asked them about their guns and how much extra ammunition they carried and if they had ever had to shoot anyone. They were both very accommodating, nice guys, and always answered my questions. Sometimes a call would come over the radio and they would put their caps back on, hand me the coffee cups and take off, looking serious. Sometimes they would have to turn on their siren and take off in a hurry.

Later in life, when I was discharged from the United States Navy, I often remembered the good times I'd had with the Coffey brothers, and I knew deep down that I wanted to be a police officer. My folks were sorely disappointed because they wanted me, when I got out of the Navy, to take over the family restaurant. I had other plans though and I never forgot the Coffey brothers or being able to sit in their police car and how nice and accommodating they were, taking the time to talk to me and answer my questions about police work. They always appeared confident and in-charge with their guns and badges and I admired them. Yes, I wanted to be a *policeman!* As soon as I was able, I started taking all the tests and getting my body in good condition for all the push-ups and sit-ups I knew I would have to do to prove my physical agility. I was discharged from the Navy in April 1959, and was sworn in as a Portland Police officer two years later in April 1961.

Central Precinct 1961

EARLY TO BED, EARLY TO RISE

It was about three in the morning and my partner, Lud Bernardinelli, former Gael star football tackle and I were sitting in the Sun Sang restaurant at SW Second and Oak drinking coffee and writing reports. I was new on the job, being trained as a street policeman, and we had just arrested a scruffy, sour smelling, urine stained wino who crossed our path in front of the police car. It was the spring of 1961 and as it was a violation of the city ordinance to be drunk on the street, drunks went to jail. I was later to learn they were an important part of the police overtime pay system. I finished the hand-written report on an eight-by-ten, officer's report sheet, carefully setting my coffee cup away from the report, to avoid any potential stains. Just about all reports went on one form, which made it easier to complete reports. I knew that I'd better not drink too much coffee or I'd be out pissing and keeping my partner awake all night. This guy wasn't my regular training coach. He was one of the old timers who worked a full-time day job and used the police graveyard shift as a place to sleep and manipulate the overtime system. Most of the guys on graveyard slept in their cars at night. Bernardinelli was no exception and it used to piss me off.

The Sun Sang was just across the street from police headquarters. Central Precinct was located at 209 SW Oak Street, and we walked back and put the finished report in the sergeant's in-box. Then we returned to the police car and resumed patrol. Except we didn't. Lud drove to a friend's service garage in the downtown area, located on SW 10th Avenue. He opened the overhead door with his key and we drove inside closing the door behind us. "Isn't this great?" he asked, "We're inside out of the weather, nobody can see us and hopefully the radio won't bother us. You be sure and answer up if they call for car number seven, but don't volunteer for nothin!" Lud got out from behind the driver's seat and took off his gun belt, put it in the trunk and then retrieved a pillow and blanket. Climbing into the back seat, he was asleep in twenty minutes. I was flabbergasted, to say the least. Is this what police work was going to be about? I felt angry, then disgusted, then bored. Praying for a radio call didn't help either, and so the night dragged on.

Our police car was a black and white '59 Ford sedan, with a gumball type red light on top. The heater didn't work very well, there were no seat belts and I was afraid to turn on the engine for heat, afraid of waking up old Lud. But that's the way it was in 1961. Brand new police officers were as low as dirt, not entitled to an opinion, and could be fired immediately for any reason. Our job was to write reports and answer the radio. There was no civil service protection until after one year of employment had been earned, so I kept my mouth shut, waiting not only for the night to pass but the first year as well. I told myself that in a year I'd be making over a hundred bucks a week and would have a secure civil service job. Still, I wondered why Lud presumed I wouldn't complain to the Sergeant about his sleeping on the job. I wanted to, but I never did. I knew better.

Slowly, daylight came and at about 7:30 a.m. old Lud woke up. After putting his bed back in the trunk, we were off to Sun Sang's for hot coffee and breakfast. As we walked in the restaurant, I heard the plaintive notes of *Angel Baby* by Rosie and the Originals playing on an old box radio. I reached for my wallet after giving my order and Lud just laughed at me while the waitress looked amused, with her hand on her hip and a big smile on her face. I put my wallet back in my pocket feeling confused and slightly embarrassed. I found out early in my career that policemen were rarely if ever charged for what they ate or drank. I enjoyed the coffee. It warmed my bones from the long night sitting in the cold car. The breakfast of scrambled eggs, bacon and toast never tasted so good and I was grateful for the nourishment, cupping my hands over the hot cup of coffee.

After getting off duty, we went to the second floor city attorney's office and signed a complaint against the wino for the crime of "being drunk on the street." By now it was 8:30 a.m. and municipal court, where we would testify against the wino, would start at 9:00 a.m. Both the municipal court and city traffic court were on the second floor of police headquarters. We sat in Judge Joe Labadie's court room waiting for him to appear. Judges always seemed to be ten minutes late. When our case was called by the bailiff, Lud testified that the wino jaywalked across the street about fifty feet from the corner, directly in front of the police car, and "the man smelled strongly of an alcoholic beverage and was unsteady on his feet." The wino was arrested for being drunk in public and issued a citation for jaywalking. Actually he hadn't jaywalked at all, but he was too hung-over to know that. Lud stuffed a citation in his pocket and the wino was sentenced to a few days in jail, at which time we were free to go home. It was ten a.m. Two hours overtime had been earned, for both Lud and myself. As I walked to my car, the sun was out. It was going to be a beautiful day. I wondered if people were meant to stay awake all night and sleep all day. They told me I'd get used to it. I never did.

The Good Old Days

THE TOOLS WE USED

I THINK THE EARLY 1960s WERE the "good old days," that some retired officers, nowadays may lament. We had a lot of tools in the form of laws and ordinances that are unconstitutional by today's standards. Adultery was a felony and a three year penitentiary offense, if you can believe it. Even back then, that law seemed absurd, when I realized that half the police department was committing adultery. Loitering, just standing around could put you in jail. And we actually had an adult curfew called the After Hours Law. An adult could go to jail just for being on the street after 3:00 a.m. without a good reason. The good reason was determined by the cop. That law always bothered me and I never abused it. But I did use it at the right times, when necessary, to get dangerous people off the streets.

Another city ordinance was Lewd Cohabitation, which meant any couple living together while not married, and it was actually against the law. We called it "Lewd Co-hab," and though it was not a misdemeanor, it was a city ordinance and we could arrest people for violating it. We got a call one night, working the graveyard shift out of central precinct, to go to the South End of downtown Portland. A Gypsy family was having a big fight; some kind of a domestic disturbance involving a man and a woman and some possible acts of infidelity. The South End of downtown was a tenderloin district then, with ramshackle houses, sleazy bars, after-hours clubs, and numerous prostitutes roaming the streets. The neighbors had called about the noise and the "screaming." My partner that night wasn't my regular coach, but an officer who had about five years on the job. They called him "Cowboy," because he wore black, shiny cowboy boots with his blue PPB uniform. His black hair was always slicked back with Brilliantine hair grease, and he wore his police cap perched on the back of his head, rather than have the brim over his forehead. He didn't want his police cap to mess up his perfectly coiffed hair, which he was very vain about.

I asked him once, "Can you *wear* cowboy boots? Isn't that against dress code?" and he replied, "They're black—they're shiny and I like em' so I wear em'. You could too, if you wanted, DuPay." When we got to the call, near Lair Hill Park, and despite our inability to understand the Romany language they were speaking, we determined that the couple were fighting over some accusation of cheating. Frustrated by our inability to calm the couple down and stop their fighting, Cowboy determined they were not married and so we resolved it by arresting the couple for "lewd cohabitation." It was against the law in the city of Portland, in 1961, to live with someone you weren't married to. After finishing up the paperwork, Cowboy asked, with a smile,

"Have you been to the Mural room yet?"

"Not yet," I said.

"Well, let's go listen to a little music and have some coffee."

"Okay, sounds good."

We drove to Johnny's Mural Room on Jefferson Street, a hangout for the fast crowd. "We'll be 10-10 for a bar check," Cowboy told the dispatcher. We went in and watched the small-time, local

Photo courtesy of Theresa Griffin Kennedy

crooks circulating around the bar, socializing and trying to do business. The music was fast and professional and the patrons were dancing and having a good time listening to a local black group, Ira Mumford and His Boys. Longtime Portland resident and nationally ranked professional drummer, Dick Hall, was beating out a spectacular drum solo while the band played *Caravan*. My partner, Cowboy, knew the bartender, who poured us two cups of black coffee. We sipped the coffee and watched the people interact. Cowboy nodded towards a few known heavies, telling me their names, which I jotted down in my notebook. This was fun I remember thinking. Checking bars and watching people, it was all part of the job.

The following night, when roll call was over, I was back to working with my regular training coach. He had bright red hair and we called him *Red*. Red was a veteran of over ten years with a reputation for being a good cop. He was friendly and I was comfortable working with him. Red and I never slept on the job. When we weren't answering calls we were checking alleys, looking for break-ins and talking to people. That night it was raining hard. The water came down in heavy torrents, making it difficult to see through the car windshield. The radio cracked, "Car # 3, check on a man down on Fourth Avenue near Flanders." I reached in the back seat to get my rain coat. Red answered the radio and we didn't take long to get there, red light and siren blaring. Red cursed the rain but didn't let it slow him down, as we flew through the streets. We saw the man down, as soon as we pulled up. He was laying on the rain-soaked sidewalk with his head and chest in the gutter. Blood was gushing from his mouth as he vomited. Huge quantities of blood. I couldn't believe it. Blood and rainwater mixed together running into the gutter. The man's dirty baseball cap had come off and was floating away in the bloody mixture. Red called an ambulance but the man died right in front of my eyes. It was the first time I'd ever seen someone die and it was horrible. I've never forgotten it. The deceased was a wino. The alcohol had eaten away the lining of his stomach.

Cars and Queers

THE CHERRY PATCH

ALTHOUGH THEY ALWAYS DENIED IT, the police department administrators had a traffic ticket quota. Prowl officers, whose jobs were primarily non-traffic, had to write a minimum of twelve moving traffic violations per man, per month. Speeding, running a red light or traffic sign were all moving violations. So was jaywalking, I was soon to learn. In the early 1960s gay people were called queers and faggots and were the target of extra police attention by both uniformed officers and vice officers. There was a gay bar at 735 SW First, now the site of Dragonwell Bistro, and my coach would park the police car about a block up the street. He'd position the car so as to have a clear view of the bar. Shortly after closing time, after 2:30 am, the bar patrons would crowd out onto the sidewalk and jaywalk across SW Yamhill. We would write two or three jaywalking tickets, check their records for any warrants and fill out "FIR" cards. Field Interrogation Reports.

We called the area a "cherry patch," because so many jaywalkers were available. This helped get us our quota. After writing out citations we cruised the tenderloin area and drove by an especially sleazy bar called The Old Glory, at 118 SW Madison Street. My coach and I were keeping our eyes peeled for a suitable drunk to arrest. "Hey, it's for the overtime pay!" my coach joked good naturedly. The graveyard shift routine was clear. Be sure to get a traffic "mover," and if any arrests were made we had to sign a complaint. Overtime pay was a necessity for survival, if you were a cop. At that time police officers were underpaid and struggled financially; $420 a month was not a lot to live on. This is not to say that people shouldn't have gotten traffic tickets when they violated the law, but the problem with the quota system was that it often resulted in citizens getting traffic tickets they wouldn't otherwise receive. And officers were punished if they didn't comply with the quota system. Punishment was usually a week working desk-duty at the precinct, which no engaged, hardworking cop ever wanted. I went along with this at the time, but it never sat well with me. It wasn't the kind of work I'd envisioned from the back of the Coffey Brothers squad car. Traffic safety aside, citations are now and always have been an important source of revenue for any city. But law enforcement should be about truth and justice, not about revenue or manipulating the system.

The Keeper of the Prison

JAIL DUTY

New officers were transferred around the Police Bureau for training purposes and I was sent to work in the city jail on the four p.m. to midnight shift. The jail was located on the top floor of the Police Headquarters building on SW Oak, accessible only by a single elevator from the lobby or basement parking area. The Chief of Police was also called the keeper of the city prison. I don't use the term to be humorous: there was actually a question on the civil service exam, asking who the keeper, was. Regardless of the proper answer on the exam, the jail was actually run by an abrasive, cigar smoking sergeant and two or three older patrolmen, who'd signed on in the 1940s. These were guys who were tired of outside street duty and its dangers, and had opted for cozy inside jobs. The boss-sergeant had a full-time job building houses and was normally two hours late for work each day.

Because police cars didn't have roll-bars or secure back seats at that time, officers were generally not allowed to transport their own prisoners. So, a jail cop would drive a paddy wagon to the scene of each arrest and pick up the prisoners. The paddy wagon's radio number was 99. It was a big, black, squarish vehicle, like a delivery van, but with reinforced steel plates and no way for the back holding compartment to connect to the front, where the drivers were. This ensured the driver's safety. 99 was the *only* paddy wagon for the entire city of Portland at that time. Occasionally, if an officer couldn't wait for 99, they would transport the prisoner in their vehicle to a holding cell at the precinct. Many officers preferred this because they disliked having to wait around for 99 to finally get there. I enjoyed going on runs in number 99. It gave me an opportunity to get away from the jail which always had an oppressive feeling and a bad smell: a combination of sweat and Pine Sol cleaning fluid. Jail houses are full of heavy, negative vibrations and it would just get to me, till my skin itched and the back of my throat felt tight.

The wagon driver and I would pick up prisoners from the holding cells at both East and North Precinct and when we rolled into the basement parking area of headquarters building, we'd open the back door of the vehicle. There, the prisoner would see a wide yellow line complete with directional arrows painted on the concrete leading to the jail elevator. Once on the jail floor you entered a glass-enclosed secure area. On duty jailers would then activate the electrical door lock and book the prisoner in at the booking counter. Just down the hall was the boil-up room. Filthy prisoners would be given a hot bath, willing or not, and their clothing placed into the "steam cabinet," that killed vermin, like head lice, body crabs, fleas and ticks. All the dirty boil-up work was done by jail trustees. A trustee was a prisoner on good behavior, usually a drunk in jail to sober up for a few days. They received one half-day off their sentences for each boil-up and they earned it. Sometimes they had to wrestle with an unwilling prisoner, to get their clothing off; the kind of winos who didn't enjoy regular bathing. It was smelly, dirty work. Trustees also washed all the police cars and manned the shoeshine stand in the officers' lounge. The prisoners were all generally well taken care of, by the jailers, and there was no abuse or brutality by jail officers, as far as I knew.

Chaplain Ed Stelle had been hired in the early 1960s, by the bureau, to counsel and assist prisoners and was generally available to them at all hours. Ed visited the jail every shift and was always very protective of prisoners' well-being, providing a watchful eye on their treatment. Ed was a wonderful person and soon became my friend and mentor. He was a slight man, with thinning grey hair and had compassion written all over his face. Ed became a beloved part of the bureau and our only source of counsel. At that time officers were not encouraged to share their troubles and we were expected to suck it up and not complain about anything, be it work-related or personal.

I got along with everyone at the jail, except the old timer sergeant. His name was Cunningham, and we just naturally clashed. He was middle-aged, heavyset and not too bright. Despite a fat beer-belly, he looked like he could bench press a bear. Cunningham always had a nasty cigar chomped in the corner of his mouth and was always about two hours late for work each day. His full time contracting job kept him from getting to work on time, but nobody said a thing. Watch *me* come to work two hours late and we'd see what might happen. Such was the beauty of civil service. Fatso could come to work late every day and nobody would complain, but rookies were not entitled to an opinion, or even an innocent mistake.

Visiting hours at the jail were once a week for families and friends. Other than this, we were constantly kept busy assisting identification officers with mug shots, making prisoners available for detectives to interview, and assisting bail bondsmen in releasing prisoners. Joe Levy Bail Bonds Company was located directly across the street from the jail and did a brisk business. Joe was a short older man, a little stooped over, with a few wisps of silver hair combed over his bald spot. He showed up at the booking desk two or three times a shift getting people out. He always smiled and was always polite and patient. A nice guy for a bail bondsman and a sharp businessman.

The summer of 1961 resulted in one of the biggest murder investigations of the time. On June 8, 1961, Portland Police received a phone call from a local housewife. She was upset and concerned because her dog had brought home a human foot in a tattered brown paper bag. When detectives arrived to question the woman at her home, and examine the foot, the dog arrived home again, this time carrying a severed hand in its mouth. This would begin a hunt that would end in the murder conviction of Richard "The Butcher" Marquette, a local Portland man from St. Johns, aged twenty-six.

The body parts belonged to Mrs. Joan Caudle, a local wife and mother of two, only 24-years old. Marquette had murdered and then dismembered Caudle, June 6, 1961, with a 100-year-old, steel butcher's knife that was so sharp, it could cut through bone. They had met at a tavern and Caudle recognized Marquette from a grade school they'd both attended as children. They continued to drink, visiting several other bars and ended up at Marquette's home at 314 SE 27th, where they had sex. Sometime during the night, Marquette strangled her with his arm, and claims to have woken up in the morning to her dead body lying next to him and no memory of having killed her. Marquette claims to have "panicked" trying to think of how to dispose of the body.

Some of Caudle's body parts were found in Marquette's home and the detectives were continuing to hunt for her severed head. It would later be found along the edge of the Willamette River. The horror story was all over the media. After the butchering, Marquette fled Oregon. He ran as far as Tijuana but eventually came back to California from Mexico, where he was arrested by the FBI for unlawful flight to avoid prosecution, the day after they'd placed him on their Most Wanted list. The feds located him in Santa Maria, California, working in a junkyard. Marquette was back in the Portland city jail only a couple of days after that, and had just been booked in by the transporting FBI when I got my first look at him. Richard Marquette was the first murderer I'd ever seen. He was unkempt, dirty and needed a shave. At just under six feet tall, he was thin and unsavory looking. I was reluctant to touch his dirty body and clothes when I had to search him. Though I knew he'd been searched by the FBI, I was fearful of sticking my hands in his pockets, not knowing what I'd find, but I was required to search him and so I did.

There was a very intense look in his eyes that I'll never forget. A look of pure hatred, directed at everyone. Sergeant Cunningham had assigned me the duty of giving Marquette a safety razor, which didn't make sense to me. I had to guard this killer while he shaved? Marquette kept glancing at me, through the mirror, as I stood behind him with those intense, glaring eyes. I stood to the side, to have a full view of him, in case he tried to slash me with the razor and he must have known that I was hyper vigilant. He was 26-years old, thin, malnourished looking and unprepossessing. I was 25-years old but at six feet tall and 190 pounds he was no match for me. Marquette had to have known, I'd knock him on his ass if he tried anything. Here was a man who had butchered the mother of two children and he was trying to keep from cutting himself shaving. How could he have cut off her head? Marquette was the first murderer I had ever seen but would certainly not be the last.

Keep Your Mouth Shut

IS THAT CLEAR OFFICER?

ONE HOT EVENING AT ABOUT six p.m. the two regular jailers and I were sitting behind the booking counter. We had an electric fan going and the outside windows were open to let in some air for the prisoners. It was an unusually slow day. No one had been booked in since we went to work at four p.m. Then suddenly, the jail elevator doors opened and an officer appeared. He had one of our regular winos in custody. Because the wino was Swedish, we called him "Swede," and he wore a wooden peg-leg. His other nickname was Peg leg Pete. Swede looked like something right out of a 1940s pirate movie.

Sergeant Cunningham was also in the elevator just coming to work. We were all sitting down but he yelled at *me*, "Hey son, get off your lazy ass and get this prisoner booked in!" I flashed anger. "I'll take care of it," I said, "But I don't wanna hear much of anything from somebody who's two hours late for work every day!" Sergeant Cunningham just about bit his ever present cigar in two as he glowered at me in shock and disbelief, saying nothing. Of course the very next morning at nine o'clock sharp I was ordered to be in the captain's office. Captain Glen Harms was a grey-haired old timer who had come up through the ranks in the 1940s and 1950s. He wasn't wearing a uniform and had on a sloppy suit jacket that didn't match his pants and his paunch showed almost above the table he was sitting behind. Captain Harms was friendly but his message was clear. He said I had "the makings of a good policeman," but if I didn't learn to keep my "mouth shut," about what I saw and heard at work, I wouldn't make it past my probation year.

"Is that clear, officer?"
"Yes Sir."
"You may go now."

I was out of his office at 9:10 a.m. Years later, I would reflect back on that day, and what I thought it meant to be a cop and how that had changed instantly in a ten minute conversation. I was quickly learning that civil service was a rose with thorns; a lot of thorns.

Paddy Wagons and Shotguns

GIMME A MINUTE DUPAY

Toward the end of my assignment in the city jail, I was sometimes allowed to make runs in 99 by myself. One night, district car # 28 was having trouble with an arrest near North Vancouver and Hancock and "could you hurry?" they asked me over the radio. I pulled up and saw that one of our black officers was struggling on the front porch of a house with a middle-aged, drunk, black man threatening him with a shotgun. After I jumped out of the wagon, leaving the door open, I ran up the stairs and grabbed the shotgun. I helped the officer get handcuffs on the man and put the weapon in the wagon.

We stuffed the handcuffed prisoner in the back of 99 and the officer hopped inside, telling me to shut the door with him inside. "Gimme a minute, DuPay!" he told me authoritatively. I did as I was told, stepping back and remembering Captain Harms admonition about keeping my mouth shut. As soon as the door closed I heard a lot of crashing and banging going on inside the van. I heard the officer yelling "Don't you *ever* call me a nigger! And don't you *ever* point a shotgun at me again! Do you understand me asshole?!" A few minutes later there was a calm knock from the inside of the van, and I let the officer out. I guess they had reached an understanding. The black officer was not an old timer, but he *was* a veteran officer. Of course he was mad at having to wrestle a guy with a shotgun and so was I, but I was offended when he just presumed I wouldn't question the beating up of a drunk, handcuffed prisoner. To me it felt wrong because I always felt the beating of a cuffed prisoner was not a fair fight. And none of the cops I worked with ever condoned the beating up of drunks or winos, even if they got a little lippy. The truth is, I didn't confront this officer about what he did. I let it happen, because I wanted and needed my probationary year to be up, and I didn't want any more trouble. During my first year, because I needed to keep my job, I let a lot of things slide that I knew were unconstitutional and just plain wrong. I knew where I stood in the bureau. At the bottom. The black officer didn't stay with the Police Bureau long. He became involved in city politics and wound up elected to city council. His name was Dick Bogle.

East Precinct

WE HAVE A JOB TO DO, LAW OR NO LAW!

THE SUMMER OF 1961 PASSED, then fall, then winter, and then the glorious Portland spring of 1962 began, with flowering shrubs and rose bushes blooming everywhere. I was back on graveyard shift again, transferred for training to East Precinct. East seemed to be the favored place to work. The precinct was in an old Water Bureau building located on the near east side at 6th and Alder Street. The visitor's counter was just inside the front door. There was office space in the back for the captain and the lieutenant. The roll-call room was on the 7th Street side of the building and housed a small holding cell. Upstairs was the officer's locker room and lounge, with pool tables and a place to take a shower. The basement held a small firing range which I used often. Next to East Precinct was the Police Club, also known as the Portland Police Athletic Association, (PPAA). It was a watering hole run by officers *for* officers and it was a joke because the only exercise anyone got was lifting their drink to their mouth. It was a place where an officer could drink in a protected environment away from the prying, judgmental eyes of curious citizens.

Once you walked through the doors of the Police Club, you were entering a different world. There were no cops to worry about, who might bust you for drunk. Everyone at the bar was a friend, and a fellow off-duty cop. In the club it wasn't against the law to be drunk and no one said anything when you left, staggering and intoxicated, to drive home, or to go to work on graveyard shift. Years later, I finally understood why the police radio dispatchers, stuck with working New Year's Eve, started to slur their speech after about three a.m. It was funny to hear their slurred speech and mispronounced words. No one ever said anything about their obvious tippling on duty, so nothing ever happened to them. At that time, police dispatchers were all sworn officers and all male. It was at the Police Club that I began to realize that the police fraternity was different somehow. My fellow comrades and I were above the law. Police watch the people, but who watches the police? Nobody I was to find out, at that time, because the cops didn't allow it.

My regular coach at East was one of the old timer officers, Fred Brock. Fred had worked the *Avenue* in the North End area for a long time and was well known by its denizens. The Avenue (Williams Avenue) was a good training ground because it was busy. Roll call was usually informal at East. We all stood in a large, rectangular room with windows looking northerly and easterly, while the sergeant read the current information on local wanted subjects and passed out the hot sheets with lists of stolen cars. Unusual cases were discussed and we were expected to read the wanted teletypes and crime reports from our own districts, as well as others, to find out what was going on. After roll call, we went out to our district and drove around getting the feel of things. My coach/partner Fred and I were assigned district 33. It ran east from the Willamette River to 15th Street and north from Fremont to Killingsworth. Not a large area geographically, but busy for its size, and predominately black.

There were two black, old timer officers on the graveyard shift, named George and Horace Duke. We called them "The Duke brothers." They joined right after WWII, so they had been around a long time. The Duke Brothers were assigned to a predominately white district in Sellwood, district 18, and were well-respected as policemen who went out and arrested people who broke the law, irrespective of what color they might be. They were ex-military, tall, good looking and considered one of us. Although there were only a few black officers on the force, they were usually hidden away on the night shifts as jailers or working the radio dispatch. This was how the bureau preferred to assign black officers at the time. It always seemed to me that the bureau wanted to keep them out of sight. And they did. The Duke Brothers were treated differently, however, from some of the other black officers we had on the force. They were highly respected and were actually allowed to go out, do police work and arrest people.

Invitation Only

WHAT'S THE PASSWORD?

In Portland, in the early 1960s, there were no crack houses but there were after-hours clubs and houses of prostitution that we cops commonly referred to as *whorehouses*. They looked like any typical rundown house, in need of a coat of paint, located in low income areas all through the city. But once you walked in the front door, you'd find fancy over stuffed sofas and chairs, draperies covering the windows and fine lamps on end tables. The operators sometimes sold dope, like heroin, marijuana and pills. After-hours joints were usually located in private residences, and admittance was by invitation only. These places opened as soon as the legal bars closed, usually served drinks and allowed dancing and gambling. Marijuana was generally available in the after-hours clubs, as well as black market prescription drugs like Seconal, Nembutal and Tuinal, also known as reds, yellows and blues. There were several whorehouses that we were aware of and we often stopped and talked to the customers going in or coming out. We did this in order to find out who was operating them, tag the cars they drove, put their names on a FIR card, and hold it against them if we ever needed to in the future. The clientèle was mostly white and Asian. The black pimps told me that black guys didn't pay for pussy which is why they were never customers. According to the pimps, they thought themselves better endowed than other races and better sex was their reward for being black.

I remember Herman J. Canyon, also known as "Candy Canyon," a black pimp living in north Portland, chuckling once, during a brief conversation with me. He shared with me some of his views on race, joking about the "poor white guys," and how the more they "paid for pussy," the more money *he* made. I always admired Candy because he was amusing, honest for a crook, good-looking and an entrepreneur. He operated a thriving business selling coin-operated machines. Machines like juke boxes, cigarette machines and candy machines. In fact, that's how he first started out, selling candy machines and that's how he got his nickname; from the candy vending machine business.

When we found out about a whorehouse or after-hours joint, we turned the information over to the vice squad. That was their job, busting whorehouses. There were several night clubs and bars in the ghetto that were trouble spots and we dealt with them.

The Red Sands at NE Union and Shaver was one of the worst trouble spots in the city. (Union Avenue has since been renamed Martin Luther King Blvd.) The folks at the Red Sands had a bad habit of serving already intoxicated people. We would get calls on fights, drunken melees and the regular unwanted's in the street, staggering around, and blocking traffic. Kings Tavern, on Williams Avenue, was even worse—a real dive. It was dangerous for a policeman to be in that place alone. A police presence tended to interfere with the constant drug dealing and the drug dealers resented that. The Cotton Club, on North Vancouver Avenue was operating at that time also and had its share of violence. It has since been demolished to make room for the I-5 freeway. There was a lot of hostility and competition among the black prostitutes at the Cotton Club, most of whom were very attractive. The traffic was mostly white male customers and the girls would sometimes get into fights, throw drinks at each other, pull their wigs off and generally cause a disturbance. Thankfully it was located in another police district, and I wasn't often called there.

And then there was Van's Olympic Room at 3530 North Vancouver. Van's was different, in that its clientèle was a little more high income, and Van's didn't have the serve all mentality of the Red Sands, which was closed down by the State Liquor Commission sometime in the 1960s. Van's was a popular hot spot and Fred Brock and I would stop by for coffee, nightly. The music was a grand piano, the top of which served as a dancing platform for the exotic dancers or a big box radio that played the classic songs of the day. Then *exotic* meant a G-string and pasties. That was all the customers could see for the price of a drink. The dancers would show more, for the right price, later.

Elwin Van Riper owned Van's. He was a white man, with a slight build and in his middle forties. He had slicked back, black hair and a neatly trimmed mustache. His hair and mustache appeared dyed and the color looked painted on and artificial against his snow white skin. Van usually sat at the end of the bar chain smoking cigarettes and watching the dancers jiggle. He was smart enough to remain on the sidelines and allowed the club to be managed by a black man named LeRoy Clark. You could tell by looking at LeRoy that he had it all together. He was intelligent, a smooth talker, a good dresser and in charge. Women called him "pretty," because of his smooth skin and good looks. LeRoy had an air of mystery about him. Rumor had it that he was involved in the drug trade and so we watched him. Big Jim, a tall, older black man, worked at the club as a cook, dishwasher and bouncer. Big Jim and I became somewhat friendly, over time, or so I thought. I ended up coming within a heartbeat of shooting him when I worked the vice squad. But that's *another* story.

Learning the Rules

IT DON'T MATTER WHAT HE DID!

ONE NIGHT, SHORTLY AFTER LEAVING Van's, Fred and I got a call on a drunk who was disturbing. When we arrived we found an older house in ramshackle condition. A crumbling concrete retaining wall opened to a stairway that led up to an old wooden porch. On the porch was a black man yelling and hollering obscenities. We got out of the police car and stood on the sidewalk trying to talk to the man and calm him down. "Sir, there are people trying to sleep. People have to work tomorrow, you're going to have to calm down," Fred told him patiently.

"Fucking Mudderfuckers! God damn assholes! Mudderfuckers!"

"Keep your voice down!" Fred commanded.

"Dats all you is—you Mudderfuckers!"

After about ten minutes of trying to get him to quit cussing and go inside the house, Fred Brock had had enough. He charged up the concrete stairway and up onto the porch. He grabbed the profane one, putting an arm around his neck in a choke hold and dragged him kicking and screaming down the stairs to the police car. I helped Fred handcuff the man and we put him in the back seat of the patrol car and called for 99. Fred wrote the arrest report and handed me the booking slip. We arrested the man for being "Drunk on the Street." A few minutes later, after 99 left for jail, I asked Fred why we'd arrested the guy for being "Drunk on the Street," when he hadn't come within thirty feet of the street. "Look son," Fred said condescendingly, "It don't matter *what* he did. It only matters what I *tell* the judge he did! And the arrest report says he was drunk on the street! Besides, we're expected to solve problems. That's our job and law or no law, *we* solve the problems!" Why did Fred assume I wouldn't question an illegal arrest or a false police report? But again, I remembered what

Captain Harms had told me. I was beginning to get the picture, so I just smiled and nodded my head philosophically. The police officer *was* the law.

Fred Brock didn't actually make a bed in the back seat of patrol cars and sleep with a pillow and a blanket, like a couple of my first police coach's did. But usually around 5:30 or 6:00 in the morning, he would park the police car on NE Shaver at Union Avenue. There, he would "rest his eyes for a bit," while I watched for cars on Union running the red light. We did have to get those twelve movers a month. How interesting, I remember thinking; traffic tickets were important, but the truth was not. I worked for Fred later on as a detective, and I found him to be essentially the same good cop he'd always been. He might have been creative with the rules from time to time, but he got the job done, and he didn't go out and hurt people. When he wasn't coaching me, Fred had another regular partner, Charlie Mayhew. Coaching rookies like me wasn't a full-time job for Fred. I worked with Mayhew several nights when Coach Brock was off duty. Mayhew worked a full-time day job, as most cops did during that time, and when I was assigned with him, we would make the usual bar checks winding up at about 2:15 a.m. at the BelAire. The BelAire Cafe and lounge was on Union Avenue near Alberta Street and was a respectable establishment with a good restaurant. They catered to a mixed clientèle of both black and white and rarely had any trouble.

Because it was after hours when we arrived, we always helped ourselves to pie and coffee from behind the counter, in the restaurant portion of the establishment, without paying. We would walk behind the counter and snoop, rooting around to see what was available. They usually had apple and cherry and of course their famous lemon meringue pie, (which was my favorite) with the usual stale, old, burnt coffee in the coffee urn. Sometimes, if we were really starving, we'd go in the kitchen and get into the cold cuts and sliced cheese. We were always grateful for the pie and coffee, cold cuts and cheese, and the respite of a short break.

But I was never comfortable, having grown up in the restaurant business, not paying for the food. That part always bothered me, but after a long shift and hardly any time to stop for a meal, I was also grateful for some food to keep me going. Street patrolman are often so busy, going from one call to the next, they can't stop for regular meals and it can be a big problem when you're tired *and* hungry, and trying to wrestle with a resister intent on hurting you.

After closing up the lounge and seeing the barmaid safely to her car, Mayhew would drive down the street to a lumber yard on Union and Shaver. He would park way in the back behind a pile of lumber. Off came the gun belt, out came the blanket and pillow and off he went into the back seat to sleep. God damn it! This bullshit of sleeping on the job really pissed me off. Believe me, I could hardly wait for my one year probation to end. Later as a working officer on graveyard shift, I resented the fact that my closest covering officer could be asleep when I needed him the most. I was starting to hate fuck-off cops. Their attitude that police work didn't make a difference made me angry. That they used the profession as a way to sleep and then get *paid* for it, seemed unconscionable to me.

Police Academy

IF A SHOOTS B

By now I had been working the street for nearly ten months and hadn't yet been to the Police Academy. As new officers came to work, they were assigned directly to street duty with a coach until a large enough number had been hired to form a class. When the academy did start, we attended eight hours a day, five days a week. Having already worked the street helped me a lot, compared to the other less experienced guys. It provided a better understanding of the 320 hours of concentrated study that was the academy. While growing up, I had assumed that police officers had special powers. Powers not given to normal citizens. They don't. John Q. Citizen has the same basic powers of arrest as a cop, with one notable exception; you must *be* a police officer to serve any kind of warrant. In truth, much less is expected of the proactive citizen by the courts than is expected from the police. Most constitutional restrictions on "arrest, search, and seizure," apply only to law enforcement. Officers are expected to know and follow the rules. So, if cops don't have special powers, and in fact deal with special restrictions, what do they have? Specialized *knowledge* and *training* is their only advantage. It was the academy's job to impart that knowledge to me and they were successful in doing that. We learned the finer points of investigating burglary, homicide and other criminal acts, along with traffic accident investigation. We learned about evidence. Here's an example; if "A" shoots "B" in the presence of "C" what "C" then testifies to is direct evidence. If "C" hears a shot and comes into the room to see "A" standing over "B" with a smoking gun, that's circumstantial evidence.

The police studies were easy for me and I enjoyed firearms training. I discovered I was a good natural shot, and I learned that the only round that counted was the first round. "Right between the eyes," I was told by my firearms instructors. As I wanted to come home safely at night, like all cops do, I wanted to be able to defend myself. It's important to remember that as a young recruit, we had six-shooters, not the fifteen round Glocks of today. It was always in my mind to make that first shot count, simply in order to stay alive. Because I knew proficiency with a gun could possibly save my life, I practiced at the firing range often. With an overall score of 93 percent, I graduated number one in my class of nineteen officers. It was at that time that I realized police work was my forte. That and writing. I received a mark of *excellent* on my required notebook, and on my human relations thesis. I was proud of myself when I saw my diploma and discovered I'd graduated number one in the class. It was a great feeling and I couldn't help thinking I'd had a huge advantage, because of working the streets for ten months previous to academy training.

I was in a class of eighteen male and one female officers and they were all white. Interestingly enough, of the nineteen graduating officers, six became detectives including myself. One became the Chief of Police in Hood River, Oregon, one the Chief of Police in Hillsboro Oregon, and the rest never advanced above patrolman. Two soon quit. One didn't like police work and spent his career as a jailer. One tragically suffered a career ending disease. One was arrested for rape and sent to prison. And one blew his brains out with a .357 magnum, but that's another story.

Traffic Division

CAR 390, THIS IS A FATAL

After graduating from the Police Academy March 8, 1962, I'd been a cop for nearly a year. It was around that time, that I was transferred to the Traffic Division and assigned to the three to eleven swing shift. My coach was Officer Paul Peterson. He was an old timer but liked his job and worked hard. Pete kept us busy catching traffic violators and writing citations. The traffic officer's primary job was issuing tickets and writing detailed reports of traffic accidents. I found the work pace in traffic much faster and was beginning to have fun in my profession. Traffic districts were much larger geographic areas than prowl districts. We were free to roam. Roll call was more formal and we stood at attention, with note book in hand, writing down the information provided by our sergeant. We actually studied the stolen car hot sheets, and actively looked for stolen cars. *This* felt more like the kind of career I'd imagined having, while in the back of the Coffey brothers car, when I was a teenager.

After roll call, on my first shift in traffic, we went to the basement parking area and found our assigned cruiser, a black and white '61 Plymouth sedan. Pete and I were barely out of the basement when the radio cracked, "Car 390, take a 12-1, 12-9 code 3 at North Lombard and Greeley."

"390 copies, on the way," I answered. I turned on the red light and switched the electronic siren to the wail position. Pete jammed the accelerator to the floor and we were flying. A 12-1 was a traffic accident, a 12-9 was to check for injuries and code 3, was red lights and siren. It didn't take long to arrive at Lombard and Greeley, in north Portland. One car had run a red light and hit another car broadside, spinning it around multiple times. Fortunately no one was hurt. I told the dispatcher that we were 10-97, (arrived at the scene) and didn't need an ambulance. Neither car was drivable, so Pete ordered a couple of tow trucks. After gathering all the information from both drivers, we measured the skid-marks and sat in the car writing the report and drawing a detailed diagram of the accident scene. We were out of service a total of about 45 minutes. With paper work completed, we told radio we were back in service. I was ready for the next adventure. It didn't take long. Cruising around north Portland, Pete pulled through the parking lot of the Nitehawk.

The Nitehawk is a cafe and lounge still located on Interstate Avenue, which is also Highway 99, and at that time was the only road to Seattle. We'd noticed a little blond boy in the back seat of a parked car, sitting alone and crying uncontrollably. Pete and I got out of our car, walked over and stood next to the vehicle. Looking in through the open window, Pete asked, "Well hello there, fella. Where's your Daddy?"

"I dunno!" the boy wailed.

"How old are you?" Pete asked.

"F-four," he said, sobbing.

"Where's your Mommy then?" Pete persisted.

"In der," the boy said, pointing to the lounge with his chubby, trembling right hand and continuing to sob. "Stay here with the child," Pete told me grimly, "I'll see if I can find this kids *Mother!*" He said the word Mother as if it were a swear word. Pete had a wife and several children of his own and was a good family man. He was hot and indignant as strode into the Nighthawk. While Pete disappeared inside the Nitehawk and was gone about ten minutes, I was left alone to stand next to the vehicle with the distraught child still inside. I wasn't sure what to do, or what to say to comfort him. I tried to think back to my own experiences when I'd been scared as a kid. What had calmed me down? It hadn't been cops. Generally, it had always been my mother. I realized I didn't have the solution for this little boy. He wanted his mother and she wasn't there for him.

When Pete came out, he had a woman in tow. I approached, in case he needed help. The woman appeared to be in her early forties and was slender. She was attractively dressed in a tight, white knit skirt, red pullover Cashmere sweater, and high-heel black pumps. She was also drunk, profane, and very upset at "this asshole who jerked me off the bar stool!" Pete took her criticism in stride and told her she was under arrest for being drunk and disorderly and the fight was on. She was drunk-wild and strong for her size, and she managed to hit both of us a lot. Being new to the job, I wasn't sure what to do. I'd never been hit by a woman before and had been taught by my father, that if I was ever hit by a girl, not to hit back in retaliation. We both tried to get the woman in handcuffs but she managed to get off a high-heeled shoe and attack again with renewed enthusiasm. I learned that a mad, drunk woman with a high-heeled shoe could be damned dangerous. Pete finally decked her with a solid forearm to the jaw. It stunned her and we snapped on the cuffs. After we got the cuffs on her and could catch our breath, I looked over and saw the little boy watching. He was looking out the open car window, as he continued to sob, his little shoulders shaking, his face covered in tears and snot. I felt sad for the boy having to see his mother in handcuffs, after a wild fight with two police officers and then being carted off to jail, but I felt angry at the mother, too. What kind of woman leaves her toddler son defenseless in a parking lot, late at night so she can go into a restaurant and drink? A female officer from the Women's Protective Division arrived and took the child into protective custody. The paddy wagon took the woman to jail and we spent the rest of the shift writing those never-ending reports.

The Probationary Year

TODAY YOU HAVE BECOME A MAN!

THE NEXT FEW WEEKS WENT by fast. I became proficient at traffic accident investigation, learning how to compute vehicle speed from skid-marks with a formula for "co-efficient of friction," and generally gaining confidence. My probationary year was just about up and I was still employed. I hadn't pissed anybody off enough to get the ax, but still, I was nervous. On April 6, 1962, I went to the barber and got a fresh haircut, and went to work early. That morning I dressed in a freshly pressed uniform, shined my shoes, polished my brass buckles with Brasso and stood back looking at myself in the full-length mirror. I still looked sharp and was beginning to feel like I belonged in the uniform. My wife at the time, used to joke, saying I'd been born a cop and born wearing a uniform. Looking back I can see how she might feel that way. I did feel as if I belonged in a police uniform. I walked into the traffic office and took my place in line at roll call. The sergeant read the usual information and passed out the hot sheets. He called my name, "DuPay! Step forward!" I did so and was handed a letter from the Chief of Police. My hands were perspiring as I read it. It was a form letter and began:

Sir,

You will complete your probationary period on April 6, 1962 and become a regularly employed member of the Bureau of Police. I would like to take this opportunity to congratulate you on your achievement and call your attention to the fact that your career as a police officer has just begun.

I sincerely hope that you will strive to improve yourself and conduct yourself in a manner which will qualify you for future promotion, when you become eligible.

Yours truly,
David H. Johnson
Chief of Police

The sergeant shook my hand and said, "Congratulations, son! Today you have become a man!" I was thrilled, proud of myself, and couldn't help but smile broadly as I shook his hand. I almost swaggered as I picked up the keys to the cruiser. I pulled out of the basement parking area, picked up the microphone and said, "Traffic car 380 is 10-8." I drove out to my district and drove around for a while getting the feel of being a real cop, alone, with no coach. It felt great! I was just 26-years-old. Soon a motorist ran a red light in front of me. I pulled him over, remembering what I'd been taught, and issued a citation. That went okay I thought, as I pulled away. Soon the radio cracked, "380, can you take a 12-1 at 33rd and Alberta Street?"

"10-4, 33rd and Alberta," I said. I began to drive and soon saw the accident up ahead. I felt a twang of apprehension flash through my guts. Could I handle an accident by myself? It was a rear-ender, and I told radio I was 10-97. I put my apprehension aside, took a deep breath, got out of the car and found myself operating on "auto pilot." I wasn't Don DuPay at this accident. I was *Officer DuPay* at this accident, and Officer DuPay knew exactly what to do. There were no injuries, so I called for a tow truck for one car, obtained the necessary information from the drivers and sat in the cruiser writing the report. I felt indestructible. What had I been worrying about? I drove to a coffee shop, paid for a cup of coffee and savored the moment.

Partners and Friends

AND EQUIPMENT UPGRADES

My first real partner was Officer Frank Jozaitis. We had become friends while in the police academy of 1961, and we both enjoyed firearms training. Frank had been around guns all his life and liked the big caliber weapons, the heavy hitters. He was as I called him, a "gun-nut." Frank always carried a .357 magnum and was a good natural shot, qualifying as an expert marksman during the academy. His basement was stocked with all the equipment to make lead bullets and hand-load them. We came to spend a lot of time in the loading room, doing just that. My gun was a Smith and Wesson .38 special, the kind of hand gun you see in old gangster movies. It was passed down to me by a man named George, who was my first wife's grandfather. George had carried the weapon for about thirty years as a special merchant policeman on his beat in skid-row, also in Portland Oregon, during the 1940s and 1950s. The gun was owned even before that, originally purchased by a Detective Abbott, who carried the gun in the 1920s while working with PPB. Abbott had scratched his name on the butt of the gun. I felt the gun had been passed down to the right person and I was proud to carry it and enjoyed knowing its odd and interesting history.

Police Bureau policy forbade officers to use automatic pistols or carry any rounds except a standard, factory loaded, round nosed, lead bullet. The problem was that these rounds weren't very effective. True, it would go through flesh and bone, but it would bounce off a tire and more often than not, stop halfway through a car door. More interested in surviving on the streets than adhering to the chief's bullshit policy, Frank and I decided to correct the problem by loading up some hot .357 magnum rounds for his gun. We kept increasing the powder load until we both felt it was about all the gun could handle. We did the same for my gun and readied up some test rounds. I fired one into the front end of an old junker car we were using for target practice, over in SE Portland, near Woodstock. The new and improved round went right through the grill, through the radiator, through the firewall and stopped in the upholstery of the seat back. I fired another round into an inflated truck tire. BAM! Flat tire! No problem. I felt better. Then Frank fired his hot loads. They went off like a cannon and the rounds went through the entire car the long way, and cut a two inch sapling in half behind it.

We both felt better and a lot *safer*. We felt that now, we might live through our shifts. Please understand. This was *not* done out of a desire for blood or a power trip, but just to be as well armed as the criminals on the streets, who were very well armed. There were lots of officers' hand loading at that time and it was quite common. I remember one sergeant friend of mine, Gary Snowden. He was a hand-loader himself, who once said, "Philosophically, if I have a legal right to kill a man, it doesn't matter if I use a little bullet, a big bullet, or run over him with a truck!" Bluntly put, I thought, but true.

Ironically, today's officer can carry high powered .45 and 9 mm. semi-automatic pistols that hold over fifteen rounds. Nothing has changed on the streets, however. Citizens, both good and bad have always been armed, and at that time, they were better armed than many of the police. A citizen could go out and buy a .45 automatic, but a police officer was not allowed to use one. This is why Frank and I hand loaded; we wanted to be safe and live through our shifts, just like our fellow officers did. The officers always protected themselves during that time, by hand loading. Command never seemed to know what kind of ammo the officers were using back then, and when they suspected we were hand-loading, they never said anything about it. They didn't *want* to know.

Frank and I were normally assigned traffic district 390, which covered the entire north section of Portland. After roll call we would cruise around the north and northeast section looking for traffic violators. We would volunteer to cover or assist other officers and look for problems. We loved to cover hot calls, which were any crimes in progress. One popular traffic crime was street racing. North Lombard Street was narrow, too narrow for the amount of traffic it carried, but in spite of that, it seemed to be a street where the younger kids would race each other, particularly after school let out.

One afternoon, we were parked at the curb about a block away from a McDonald's restaurant. I was sitting behind the wheel, and Frank was handing a young boy a pedestrian ticket for running out in the street in front of traffic, when I saw a bright red Corvette convertible fly off the McDonald's parking lot, tires smoking. The Corvette took off up Lombard, humming through the gears and screeching the tires. I couldn't believe the driver didn't see us in the black and white. I tore off after him. We already had one charge on the driver, "failing to stop when exiting private property," or as we cops used to call it, "no-stop-private-prop." I soon had him clocked at 65 mph in a 35 mph zone. I pulled in close behind, after turning on the red light and siren. Instead of pulling over, the 'Vette found another gear and accelerated up to about 85 mph, and the chase was on. He'd just racked up another charge of "attempting to elude a police officer," with "reckless driving," thrown in there for good measure.

I was busy driving and Frank was on the radio giving our situation and location. "390, we've got one running from us. It's a red Corvette east on Lombard from McDonald's. He just hit 85!" Frank said, excited and leaning forward in his seat. The driver of the 'Vette, realizing he couldn't shake us, slowed and four wheel skidded around the next available corner. He had to slow down to make the corner. He was running at 55 and 60 mph through uncontrolled intersections. We stayed behind him. We couldn't overtake him, but he couldn't shake us either. He turned left, he turned right, and was getting more careless with every turn. Although Frank was giving radio a play-by-play, no other officers could seem to find us. The truth was, we were going too fast. The kid in the 'Vette grabbed the next left and drove into an unimproved, unpaved road with dirt, grass, and deep pot holes. The road was so bad, the kid bounced up and came within a hair of flying out of the open-topped vehicle. He soon lost control of the car and finally it bounced to a crunching halt in the dirt and rocks.

We were bouncing around too, but were buckled in, and right on his ass. As soon as both cars stopped moving, we jumped out and arrested him. The boy was a juvenile driving his dad's car. "390, send us wagon 99 and a tow truck," Frank said. As we both sat down in the car, to catch our breath, I noticed our oil level indicator light on the dashboard was showing red. I got out and looked under the police car. There was a hole in the oil pan the size of a fist and oil was spewing everywhere. "Frank, we hit a rock! Dammit! There's oil everywhere! Now we're gonna have to be towed and get a ride too! Shit!" We were both disappointed. It meant we'd have to wait for over an hour before we could get back to work. "390," Frank said. "Go ahead, 390," said the dispatcher. "Make that *two* tow trucks and send another car by. We need a ride back to Traffic," he said forlornly. "10-4 390, on the way."

Cops will tell you that partners form a bond not understood by non-officers. And it's true. When you sit forty plus hours a week in the same police car with a guy, pretty soon you know him better than his wife. You become dependent on the guy for your life. Some guys are born to the job, and are natural policemen. Sure, they have to learn the mechanics, but they have an *instinct* for the work. Frank Jozaitis was that kind of guy. I always felt that I was too. Over the years, there were others I worked with that I could trust with my life too. But not many. When you had a good partner, you knew what the other guy was going to do. You knew what he was thinking and where he would be at all times. Frank and I communicated with our eyes, or an imperceptible nod of the head and it could be nearly telepathic. When I had to work with someone I didn't know or had to work with an officer I had no faith in, I operated on auto-pilot and conducted myself as if I were working alone, taking the lead and making it clear that I was the one in charge.

Bus's Kill

GOD, I HATED FATALS

THE TRAFFIC DIVISION DIDN'T HAVE a ticket quota like prowl, but traffic enforcement was our job. Police tasks tend to be quite specialized and complex, more so than most people realize. One afternoon, Frank had taken an extra day off and I was assigned the downtown northwest traffic district near NW Couch Street. I would be working with an officer I had never worked with before, which I was not looking forward to. After roll call, *Jerry* and I cruised skid-row and wrote a few citations. The radio cracked, "Car 340, take an accident involving a city bus and a pedestrian. Make a 12-9 code 3 at 5th and Everett." I had a bad feeling about this call. "340 copies. On the way," I answered. I always drove when I wasn't working with Frank. I didn't trust another cop I hadn't yet worked with. We hit the red light and siren and were 10-97 shortly. The bus had run over a pedestrian. The deceased was a wino and had passed out at the bus stop and ultimately rolled down into the gutter. The bus driver didn't see the poor man and crushed him like a bug. The upside is that the wino didn't know what hit him, having been unconscious at the time of impact. When we worked skid-row, we always carried little glass ampules of smelling salts. This was a common way to wake up a dead drunk, but this guy was truly dead and the smelling salts in my pocket would be of no help to him now.

"Car 340," I said into the mic,"

"Go ahead 340," said the dispatcher."

"I need the coroner out here with the meat wagon to pick up the body."

Jerry was doing all the paper work on *this* one, I decided. There were a lot of people on the bus and they all had to be interviewed. Meanwhile, I had a look at the body, which was gruesome. God, I hated fatal accidents. There was always so much blood. The thought flashed through my mind—*this is the second dead body I've seen*. There would be more, I knew. I heard the radio crack, "Coroner's office has been notified, 340," said the dispatcher. "340 copies" I said. After the body had been removed and a new bus driver provided for the bus, we went back to the office so my partner could finish the written reports. Fatal accident reports had to be done right. You were always pretty sure the report would be used in some kind of a lawsuit. They had to be completed correctly.

An hour later we were back in the car. "Car 340 is 10-8 from the fatal," I said into the mic, which meant we were done. "Good 340. I don't have a prowl car available. Take a fight, some kind of knife involved, upstairs at the Tropic Hotel."

"340 copies" I said. I turned on the red light and we took off. I pulled up right in front of the hotel door and quickly angle parked. "340's 10-97" I said into the mic, and jumped out of the car leaving the keys in the ignition, and the driver's door open. I hit the front door of the flea-bag hotel and saw two men scuffling at the top of the first floor stairs. I ran to the top of the stairs and grabbed one of the winos by the back of the shirt and threw him down on the landing. The other wino had the knife and both were drunk, dirty and sweaty. Trying to keep one guy down and get him cuffed was keeping me busy and the other guy with the knife was threatening me. Standing across from me, with a small, bloody pocket knife, the wino seemed determined but extremely drunk. He was swaying and struggling to stand upright.

I looked around for help from my temporary partner, Jerry, and when I glanced down the stairs at the street, the dipshit was still in the police car looking for his flashlight and pulling the keys out of the ignition. "Goddamn it Jerry! Get up here and help me!" I yelled. "FORGET the fucking flashlight!" I bellowed angrily. As I straddled wino number one, I was breathing hard and sweating. I looked up at wino number two and our eyes locked. The knife wavered in his hands, as the other wino struggled beneath me. "Drop the knife or I'll fuckin' shoot you!" I told him flatly, as I glowered at him, big-eyed with anger. Officer Dip finally ambled up the stairs, huffing and puffing from the effort. Though he was only in his late 20's, he was overweight and didn't seem strong or able bodied enough to be a good street cop. As I continued to struggle with the wino under me, I looked into the knife-wielding wino's eyes and saw the decision to back off. He dropped the knife as the Dip approached, lifting up his hands in a weak surrender. I looked in the Dip's eyes and saw fear.

After both wino's were arrested, and cuffed, I got on the radio, "Car 340, send the paddy wagon for two."

"99 is on the way 340."

I ignored Jerry for the rest of the shift and took the lead. He knew he'd fucked up. Later that day I had a discussion with the sergeant about Officer Dip. I told the Sergeant that the guy was going to get some policeman hurt one day, but it wouldn't be me. I made it clear I would not work with him ever again. Eventually, he was assigned to work radar. Alone. That kept him busy and productive and he wasn't likely to get a policeman hurt. Not everyone is able to work the streets, but the ones who do well there, have to be able to fight and *win*. After work that night, I drove over to Frank's house and we had some beers and talked for a while. His wife Emma was home and she made some coffee for herself and joined us. Their four kids were asleep. "Thanks a lot Frank! Thanks for taking the day off! I had a fatal accident, two drunks with a knife to arrest and no backup!" Frank handed me an ice cold beer, laughing. "Have another beer, Don!"

The Stinker

CHUGGING AGAINST THE HEDGE

IT WAS A WARM AFTERNOON and Frank and I were cruising the area of Pier Park, deep in the St. Johns district. We noticed an old beat-up, rattle-trap Chevy, driving slowly on North St. Louis Street. The guy was driving westbound in the eastbound lane, doing about 10 mph, and trying his best to avoid the oncoming traffic. We watched him drive for two or three blocks and followed him with our red light on. Frank was driving and motioned for the guy to pull over. The man didn't pull over, he just passed out at the wheel, jumping the curb and coming to rest against a tall hedge. We jumped out of the cruiser and ran up to the car. I opened the driver's door. The smell of booze and piss just about knocked me over. The engine was still running and the car was in gear, chugging against the hedge. I turned off the ignition and set the handbrake. Meanwhile, Frank grabbed the guy, pulled him out of the car and propped him up against the fender, asking him just what the hell he thought he was doing. The guy couldn't stand and could barely talk.

The inside of his car looked like he'd been living in it. There were two or three empty cases of beer cans and several empty whiskey bottles. He mumbled that he had been on a binge for about ten days. The guy was as big a mess as the inside of his car. He had pissed his pants and stunk to high heaven. We arrested him for drunk driving, and called for the wagon and a tow. We sat him on the curb to wait. No way were we going to put the stinker in our police car! Later in the traffic office, we talked the guy into taking a blood alcohol test. Police didn't use Breathalyzers then. Instead, there was a jail nurse who took blood samples to test for alcohol. She stuck a needle in his arm and took some blood. It was sent to the lab for analysis and Frank and I helped the jailers lock him in a cell. When we got to work the next day, we found the blood analysis report in Frank's in-box. Frank took one look and whistled, then laughed.

"Hey Don, look at this!"

"What ya got?"

I took the sheet of paper from him and scanned the page. It came up at .45 alcohol, which is about 80 proof. Today, .08 is legally drunk, so the amount of alcohol in this guy's blood *could* have been fatal. "We probably got drunk just sitting next to him," I said to Frank with a laugh. "If we'd put him in the car, we could have been arrested for driving with an open container," Frank responded with a chuckle. At that point, the jail nurse went up to his cell to see if he was still alive. He was. It was the highest blood alcohol level any of us officers had ever seen. I heard there were some heavy drinkers in St. Johns, some apparently binge drink.

Officer Gump

IGNORING POLICE CALLS

After roll-call, Frank and I picked up an unmarked car in the basement. It was fun to use an unmarked car for a change. It provided the officer with a way to watch civilians without them knowing the car was a police car, though we were still in our uniforms. This one was a blue 1957 Ford two-door. The red light sat in a magnetic holder on the floor and plugged into the cigarette lighter. There was another magnetic stand on the dashboard for the red light when it was needed. Someone had put black electrical tape on the backside of the red-light to keep it from flashing in the drivers' eyes. The siren was an old electric wind-up and could be activated by a push button on the dashboard and another push button on the floor near the headlight dimmer switch. As long as your finger was on the button, the siren would wind up. When you removed your finger, the siren would wind down. If you were working alone, this car would keep you busy driving, pushing the siren button, positioning the red light on its stand, and talking on the radio all at once.

As it turned out, we wrecked the car that day. We had been cruising in the ghetto area of Union and Prescott and stopped to write a traffic citation. We noticed that the district car, the regularly assigned prowl officer was parked at the curb about two blocks down. I called this guy "Officer Gump," because he reminded me of the cartoon character Andy Gump. His first name was Saul and he didn't have much of a chin. It disappeared into his neck fat, and then migrated downward toward his flabby belly. Particularly noticeable about Gump was his less than impressive height. He stood about five feet eight inches, had stooped shoulders, (which made him look even shorter), and a defeated, sulky demeanor. He didn't look like he was *able* to be a policeman. Any physical tests he had passed, he'd done years ago. Gump was physically unim-

the blood analysis report in Frank's in-box. Frank took one look and whistled, then laughed.

"Hey Don, look at this!"

"What ya got?"

I took the sheet of paper from him and scanned the page. It came up at .45 alcohol, which is about 80 proof. Today, .08 is legally drunk, so the amount of alcohol in this guy's blood *could* have been fatal. "We probably got drunk just sitting next to him," I said to Frank with a laugh. "If we'd put him in the car, we could have been arrested for driving with an open container," Frank responded with a chuckle. At that point, the jail nurse went up to his cell to see if he was still alive. He was. It was the highest blood alcohol level any of us officers had ever seen. I heard there were some heavy drinkers in St. Johns, some apparently binge drink.

Officer Gump

IGNORING POLICE CALLS

After roll-call, Frank and I picked up an unmarked car in the basement. It was fun to use an unmarked car for a change. It provided the officer with a way to watch civilians without them knowing the car was a police car, though we were still in our uniforms. This one was a blue 1957 Ford two-door. The red light sat in a magnetic holder on the floor and plugged into the cigarette lighter. There was another magnetic stand on the dashboard for the red light when it was needed. Someone had put black electrical tape on the backside of the red-light to keep it from flashing in the drivers' eyes. The siren was an old electric wind-up and could be activated by a push button on the dashboard and another push button on the floor near the headlight dimmer switch. As long as your finger was on the button, the siren would wind up. When you removed your finger, the siren would wind down. If you were working alone, this car would keep you busy driving, pushing the siren button, positioning the red light on its stand, and talking on the radio all at once.

As it turned out, we wrecked the car that day. We had been cruising in the ghetto area of Union and Prescott and stopped to write a traffic citation. We noticed that the district car, the regularly assigned prowl officer was parked at the curb about two blocks down. I called this guy "Officer Gump," because he reminded me of the cartoon character Andy Gump. His first name was Saul and he didn't have much of a chin. It disappeared into his neck fat, and then migrated downward toward his flabby belly. Particularly noticeable about Gump was his less than impressive height. He stood about five feet eight inches, had stooped shoulders, (which made him look even shorter), and a defeated, sulky demeanor. He didn't look like he was *able* to be a policeman. Any physical tests he had passed, he'd done years ago. Gump was physically unimpressive and lacked the natural aggression of a good police officer. I wondered if that was the reason he never answered his calls. If he was fearful, all he had to do was wait. Frank and I, or another able bodied officer would show up and solve his problem for him.

On that day, Gump was talking to a semi-attractive woman who was sitting in the front seat with him. I noticed her as we finished writing a citation to a speeding motorist, and drove passed. As we passed his car, I recognized the lady as one he met and talked to often. Having a female civilian in a patrol car was against policy, unless she was a crime victim or an informant. We knew *this* girl was neither. We thought no more about it. Then twenty minutes later the radio cracked, "Car 33, you have a hold-up in progress at the convenience store at 10th and Alberta." Car 33 was Officer Gump's car. Frank and I waited, listening, but Gump didn't answer. Again the radio dispatch called, "Car 33, can you take a hold-up?" No answer. Finally, Frank grabbed the microphone. "390, we're a ways away but we'll cover!" By now we were about three miles away, near Broadway Street. "Check. 390 will cover," said the dispatcher, and then again dispatch asked "Car 33 can you take this hold-up?"

Finally, car 33 answered, *after* we had already volunteered to cover the call. Gump must have decided it would be safe enough for him to show up at that point. I used the red light and siren until we got within hearing distance and then let the old growler wind down. I noticed that the brakes were getting worse each time I hit them. High speed stop and goes are hard on brakes. Jamming the gas pedal to the floor, and hitting the brakes hard to slow down for the next intersection can really damage a police car. When you bust a red light you don't want to hit a civilian. This was something I always considered when I had my siren going. However, by the time we got to the hold-up scene, there were no brakes left in the car, and I hit a concrete retaining wall, located near the store, in order to stop.

We lost both headlights, the grill and the radiator. No damage to the wall. There was a lot of confusion with the crash, after we'd hit the wall, which was right near the front entrance of the store. The car radiator was steaming profusely, and the red light was flashing as Frank and I jumped out, guns drawn, and overtook and handcuffed the surprised hold-up man as he came out the front door and tried to escape. The man didn't know what hit him, because it all happened so fast. Finally car 33 rolled up and we turned the prisoner over to Gump, who was clearly pissed off that two traffic cops had gotten there first, and done his job for him. As he led the prisoner to his car, Gump seemed sullen. He mumbled something unintelligible under his breath, and scowled in our direction. As Frank and I watched him walk away, we both chuckled and made no attempt to hide our amusement.

"Car 390," said Frank, send us a tow. There is some damage to the police car."

"Tow on the way, 390."

Back in the traffic office, Frank and I had to write a lot of reports. When you damage a police car, the worst part about it is all the report writing. Copies to everybody. Our sergeant looked at the damaged unmarked car and then read the arrest report on the hold-up man. "Good work on the arrest!" he said. He wasn't too happy about the car. Hey, what can I say? It wouldn't have been the first car I wrecked in the line of duty. I would end up wrecking a total of four police cars doing dangerous pursuits, but more on that later.

Upturned Cars and Onlookers

MAINTAINING ORDER AT THE SCENE

Accidents are scenes of serious emotional and physical trauma. There is a lot of confusion for the investigating officer to deal with. He must immediately take control. Are people injured? Who? How many? How bad? Is an ambulance needed? Or more than one ambulance? Is there danger of fire? Is someone drunk? Is someone dead? Is someone to be taken into custody? How does the officer keep others from crashing into the scene? How can he handle the crowd of curious onlookers who generally begin to assemble and often get in the way? It is a kind of pressure all its own. Frank and I thrived on it. "Car 390," said the dispatcher. "390, go ahead," said Frank.

"Take a 12-2 (injury/accident) at North Van Houten and Fessenden. One car's upside down and an ambulance is already on the way."

"10-4, 390's on the way," Frank said.

We could see it was a good one alright, as we pulled up. Frank said "10-97" to radio, telling them we had arrived at the scene. A 1953 Ford was turned upside down in the middle of the street and an old pickup truck was on the sidewalk on its side. The ambulance pulled up behind us. The driver of the Ford had some serious head injuries and would require surgery right away. The passenger had some cuts, but would be okay. The unoccupied pickup truck had been parked at the curb. Two young men had been speeding on North Fessenden Street. They lost control of the Ford while passing a car and hit the parked pickup. It was a spectacular accident scene with two vehicles up-ended and we noticed a newspaper photographer taking pictures. We hung around but there wasn't much more to do. The tow trucks were able to right both vehicles, the debris was swept up, the photographers packed up their cameras and other gear and the street was cleared. Our job was done. A big photo of the accident scene appeared in the next day's newspaper.

Our time out of service was less than an hour. The next couple of hours were boring. We tried sitting at two or three intersections waiting for someone to blow a red light. While waiting for someone to run a red light, we noticed a district car parked at Lombard and Woolsey streets. The officer was an old timer, fat, paunchy and in his fifties. He appeared to be watching for someone to run the red light too, but was reading comic books in the meantime. He was a prowl officer but hanging around the intersection, hoping to get one of the twelve movers he'd need for the quota. It was after all near the end of the month. Frank and I looked over at him, and shook our heads, chuckling.

Movers and Violators

AND THE A & W

FRANK AND I AVERAGED FOUR to six movers a piece each shift, even when handicapped with a marked car. Some shifts we would investigate two or three accidents, besides. We were always looking for problems and listening for something to cover on the radio. Work was fun with Frank, and we gave eight hours work for eight hours pay. One night, we were catching up on our paper work from the shift and drinking coffee at the A&W, located on 12th and Columbia Blvd. It was almost ten at night, and we got off at eleven. I told Frank I'd buy him a beer at the Police Club, maybe two. After taking off, we pulled over, a few blocks away, to a pay phone, and Frank called Emma to tell her we would be stopping by "the club," after work and not to worry if he was late. Frank left the phone booth and we cruised down Lombard Street. We passed a service station with both front doors open. There was a car in the gas bay, and something didn't look right. There was a tall guy inside the office at the cash register. It wasn't the regular attendant that we knew.

We knew what the regular attendant looked like because we often used the restroom and phone there. I pulled on by and circled around, positioning for a better view. We could now see the other guy with the attendant back in the service bay. The guy was pointing to a bunch of fan belts high on the wall. Meanwhile, the tall guy was taking money out of the till. We were watching a "till-tap," in progress. One guy keeps the attendant busy and the other empties the cash register. "Bullshit goin' down!" Frank said grimly, "Hit it!" I hit the gas, turned on the red light and siren and screamed across the street skidding to a halt and blocking their car. We surprised them.

The suspect in the service bay tried to run down the street. He got about a half a block before Frank tackled him. The suspect at the cash register came out the door with his head down, like he was doing a nose tackle. I was between him and his car and he was coming full speed. I side stepped his charge and hit him on the head, as hard as I could with the only thing I had in my hand, my five-cell flashlight. The flashlight bent and broke, bulb and reflector flying one way and the five D cell batteries spewing in the other direction. "Piece-a-shit!" I cursed. Frank had secured his prisoner and then helped me with mine, calling dispatch as usual to report on the situation. It was a normal call: tow truck, paddy wagon 99 and "two thieves in custody 10-8 and out." I picked up the broken five cell flashlight and walked around the parking lot hunting for my five batteries. After 99 and the tow truck left, Frank and I looked at the destroyed flashlight. We were both surprised it had fallen apart so easily. There were no heavy duty flashlights made for law enforcement at that time and we did the best we could with what we had, but it wasn't good enough.

We worked a lot at night and usually had the five-cell in hand. It *had* to hold up better than this. It was time to go back to Frank's basement for another *equipment upgrade.* I kept my promise on the beer and stopped and bought a six-pack, meeting Frank at his house. Frank took his five-cell and opened two packages of hack saw blades. We fit the small narrow blades into the grooves of the barrel, taping them in place with black electrical tape. We added two more layers of reinforcing blades and wrapped them around and around, with more electrical tape, to secure them in place. When we were done it felt pretty solid and was *a lot* heavier. "Honey," Frank yelled up the stairs to Emma. "Did the kids eat that cantaloupe we bought yesterday?"

"No?" she said. "Why?" I ran upstairs and got each of us another beer and the cantaloupe out of the fridge, smiling over at Emma as she stood cooking at the kitchen stove. When I was back in the basement, Frank put the cantaloupe on top of a wooden crate. He reared back and hit the melon as hard as he could. SPLAT! Seeds and melon slime went flying everywhere. "Not bad," I said. "But we need something harder than a melon." Frank went upstairs and rummaged around in the kitchen looking for a more suitable target. He came back down with a big acorn squash. Now it was my turn, I reared back and hit the squash a good one. It smashed into pieces, with fragments thudding against the cement walls. Emma came down the stairs at that point with her cup of coffee, ready to join us as she usually did. This time she stopped, though, as bits of squash went flying past her, to splatter against the wall. She eyed the squash, saw the remains of the cantaloupe, glanced at the beer bottles, put the obvious two-and-two together in her mind, and offered us a friendly, "What's up?" as a chance for us to explain ourselves. "Equipment improvement," I said, laughing, while Frank brandished the new and improved club-flashlight like a trophy. We both felt better. Emma just shook her head and laughed.

Street Racing

SOME THINGS NEVER CHANGE

SOME THINGS CHANGE AND SOME things never change. When I was at Grant High school in the early 1950s, we kids had a couple of prime cruising areas. We cruised our cars in downtown Portland, up SW Broadway and back down SW Sixth Avenue, round and round the circuit, rapping our pipes and looking for girls. The only drug around was alcohol. Our downtown "Broadway Gang," was the only gang in town and about all they did was slick back their long duck-tail hair, cruise the scene, and drink beer. When we got tired of downtown, we cruised NE Sandy from the Hollywood district to Jim Dandy's drive-in at Ninety Sixth Avenue. People complained about the noise, the congestion, and the rowdy kids in fast cars endangering everyone. In truth teenagers back then *did* drag race, speed, and drink beer. They didn't care. They were teenagers and they were bored. They used beer and fast cars to entertain themselves. They still do. As a traffic cop, however, it was my job to stop drag racing, speeding and beer drinking. Let's face it, two cars waiting for the traffic signal to turn green, jamming the pedal to the metal, and racing in heavy traffic is a damned serious danger.

It's also hard to overtake, stop, and control two speeding cars at once. But Frank and I had a lot of success at it. The racers were often so engrossed in watching each other, that they didn't even see the marked police car right behind them. We would accelerate right with them and punch the speed clock locking-in their top speed. If there was no traffic in the oncoming lanes, we would accelerate in that lane with the red light and siren on, to try to force both cars to the right hand curb. Once stopped, Frank would jump out and control one driver, issuing a speeding ticket, and I would cite the other. With practice, we became good at this technique. If one of the speeding cars turned off into a side street and tried to slink away, we always took *that* car and let the other one get away. But six times out of ten, a two-man car could get both speeders.

One evening, we were behind a car and a motorcycle that had been drag racing on North Lombard, traffic signal to traffic signal. As they took off at the next green light, the bike won the race. Frank was driving and punched the speed clock at the bike's highest speed of 78 mph. The legal speed limit was 35 mph. We turned on the light and siren, and the car pulled over to the curb. The motorcycle slowed down as if to stop, but pulled into a driveway and up on the sidewalk out of traffic. As we started to get out of the police car, the youth on the motorcycle turned around and gave us the finger. He gunned the cycle into a wheelie and roared off down the sidewalk narrowly missing a curious pedestrian. We excused the car driver and took off after *the finger.*

Now, in a car and motorcycle chase, the advantage is not always with the cyclist. True, the cycle can get into locations a car cannot and that can be a problem, but a two wheeled motorcycle cannot corner as well as a four-wheeled police car with good suspension. Then, there is the psychology of the high speed chase, the mental battle between pursuer and pursued. If a cop is unable to overtake and stop an eluder in the first few minutes of the chase, he is wise to just sit back and let the mental war take over for him. Stay behind the eluder, but keep him in sight and keep pushing him. The police car has the flashing lights, the siren, and the radio, and they're all working in the cop's favor. The eluder, after the initial thrill has worn off, realizes he may be in big trouble as he continues to hear the siren and see the pursuing car and the flashing lights. Unable to shake the cop behind him, he takes more and more chances, until he is driving way beyond his abilities. That's why most high speed chases end with the eluder crashing. It's a dangerous business for eluder, officer and innocent citizen.

"390, we have a motorcycle running from us, North on Woolsey from Lombard," I said into the mic. Frank was doing a good job of keeping the cycle in sight. "We're approaching Columbia Villa housing area," I said. I gave radio the license plate number of the cycle, just before it jumped another curb and went through a yard and caught the next street over. We didn't follow him through, though. Frank gunned it passed the yard, sticking to the street. "We'll catch him on Fessenden," Frank said, running a red light. Two blocks later, we screamed into the road only a few feet behind the motorcycle.

"He's west on Fessenden street doing over 80!" I yelled into the mic, glancing at the speed clock.

"It looks like he's heading for Pier Park!" Frank said.

"Shit! If he gets into the park we'll lose em!"

The biker knew it, and flashed us the bird again, thinking he would be able to escape. He took his right hand off the handle bar for a second. It was a mistake. He hit the park doing about 60 mph, and couldn't turn fast enough. The bike disappeared into a grove of trees and crashed. We had him now. *Maybe.* We bounced into the park and slowed down, pulling up near the grove of trees. The cycle was on its side. The front wheel was bent and the handle bars broken, but the rider was nowhere to be found. He must have hotfooted it out of the park. Radio had obtained the registration address on the cycle, though, and as soon as the tow arrived, we headed over to the listed house. It was about a mile and a half from where the driver crashed the cycle. Frank positioned the police car out of sight, about a block and a half from his front door, and we sat waiting.

About twenty minutes later, we saw the boy. He was bleeding from scratches on his head and arms, limping, with torn pants and looking over his shoulder fearfully, but headed for home. We exited the car, and approached him quickly, not too concerned that he would run. He was tired, and beat-up and we arrested him without incident, for speeding, attempting to elude a police officer, damage to park property, and leaving the scene of an accident. Frank relished this arrest, and couldn't help but gloat a little. "Next time you give a cop the finger, son, you better make sure you can get away," Frank told him, smirking and smiling over at me, as he snapped on the cuffs. I stood with my arms crossed over my chest, and smiled. The boy remained silent, his head hung in defeat. Dispatch came over the radio as we got in the car: "You got him?" the dispatcher asked. "Yep, we got him." It took the psychology of the high speed chase and a little luck to catch the kid. But then, we usually won.

Frank sometimes got tired of driving and we often switched positions halfway through a shift. After the kid was arrested, Frank told me he'd done his high speed chase for the evening and handed me the keys. "It's your turn buddy!" he said. We both figured we'd had enough of St John's and Pier Park for a while and so I drove around the ghetto part of our district, which was almost the entire North End. It was starting to get dark, a prime time for trouble. And sure enough... "Car 33," the radio cracked. There was no answer. "Car 33, are you on the air?" No answer. Frank and I wondered where Gump was *this* time. Maybe this fuck-off cop was chit-chatting with his girlfriend again. We hadn't run across him yet this shift, but we were about to.

"Any car close that can take a burglary in progress at the drugstore at 15th and Fremont?" asked the dispatcher. "390 is at Vancouver and Fremont near Van's Olympic Room," said Frank. "We'll cover for you." We were already on the same street and only about a half mile away from the drug store. We turned on the red light and I kept the gas pedal to the floor. We caught the next two traffic signals on green and didn't have to slow down much. As we got to the call, I slowed to a stop about a half a block from the store and killed the lights. Frank told radio we were 10-97 and we jumped out of the car running. All the windows were intact at the drug store. Frank took the front and I took the back. The back door in the garbage breeze-way was ajar and in splinters from being pried open. Frank shined his flashlight in the front window and banged on the glass. "Police Officers!" I could hear him say loudly. There was crashing and banging going on inside the store and I crouched low, hiding in the darkness.

Here he comes, I thought. The splintered back door opened wide and out he came. It was clear, he presumed there was only one cop banging on the front door and he'd sneak out the back. He didn't see me down low and when I raised up, the leverage caught him just right. He went ass over tea kettle, sailing over my right shoulder and crumpling to the ground in a heap. After I jumped on him, I pulled him up and then handcuffed him to a garbage dumpster. His pockets were stuffed with money, pills and a cheap bottle of red wine. Frank watched him while I walked the half block back to our car. I waved at Officer Gump, who was just pulling up. "What's going on?" he asked sullenly. "Frank's got the burglar handcuffed to the dumpster. He's out behind the drugstore and he's got some loot on him." I said matter-of-fact.

"Nice of you to drop by," I added sarcastically, as an afterthought.

"Fuck you DuPay!"

A couple of days later, our Sergeant asked Frank and I to stop by his office after roll call. The sergeant had a letter from Gump, which he read to us. Gump accused Frank and I of "ambulance chasing," his calls and suggested that "traffic cops," should work traffic and leave the "real police work," to older "more experienced prowl officers," like himself.

"That's bullshit! There's a hold-up man and a burglar in jail! Now! Today! Because Frank and I caught em' red handed! That's what I thought we got paid for! Maybe he should pull his girl-friend's finger out of his ear so he can hear his calls!"

"Okay, take it easy Don."

"Fuck him, I don't care *what* he thinks!"

I was so angry I was shouting. I had to step back and take a deep breath to gather my composure, while Frank stood next to me silently. He was leaning back on his heels, hands folded behind his back, chin high and a grim look on his face. The sergeant was a laid-back old timer, and had seen it all. He'd *had* to read the letter to us, per protocol. But it was clear, he was no more impressed with Gump and his abilities as a police officer than we were. He laughed good naturedly as he tossed the letter down on his desk. Looking up at us standing there, he smiled and said, "Don't worry about it, guys, just keep up the good work!" I hated lazy, fuck-off cops like Gump. They made my blood boil, not only because they were disengaged and didn't give a damn about doing good police work, but because their indifference made them dangerous to other cops *and* to civilians and the whole idea of public safety. Nothing more was ever said about the matter, but the command structure must have admired crybaby Gump's superior police abilities. They eventually promoted Gump all the way to Captain, which really frosted me because I knew what an incompetent police officer he'd always been back when we were patrolman. I always felt that guys who were never good cops were often good at taking promotional exams, and Gump was an unfortunate example of that time honored tradition. The good test takers were rarely ever the good, hardworking cops.

The Low Speed Chase

GO BIG OR GO HOME

In the middle 1960s Portland cops began seeing small, red and white, Honda 50, motor-scooters everywhere. The scooters became a fad and every kid seemed to own one or have access to their older brother's machine. This was my recollection, working traffic enforcement in the North End. The St. Johns Honda dealer on North Lombard Street had a row of about thirty, lined up like little tin soldiers in their show room window, with signs advertising how easy they were to ride. "You meet the nicest people on a Honda," was their popular advertising slogan. They were cheap to buy and two dollars' worth of gas could last a whole day, due to their small motor, (fifty cubic centimeters) something akin to a lawnmower engine. Precisely because they were small and agile machines, it was easy for kids to forget they were in fact, a motor vehicle. The kinds of kids who would *forget* this were the kinds of kids who were used to running red lights, blowing stop signs and sidewalk hopping on their bikes. Because the scooters had a "putt-putt" motor, they were legally a motor vehicle and the rider had to have a valid driver's license, to drive one, a fact that seemed to escape many who used them or loaned them out.

One afternoon, as rush hour traffic saturated both east and west lanes of busy North Lombard Street, I observed a young boy, who appeared to be no more than fourteen, on his Honda 50, slithering in and out of traffic, like a snake on a mission. He was hunched down over the handle bars, head low and staring straight ahead, glancing over his shoulder now and then, to make sure he could avoid another near collision. The boy was dangerously weaving right and left, passing cars on both sides, cutting them off, and causing then to jam on their brakes to avoid hitting him. At one point the boy jumped a curb and rode on the sidewalk for a block, passing several slow moving cars stuck in heavy traffic, and scaring shocked pedestrians carrying bags of groceries.

I knew I had to pull him over to keep him from killing himself, or anyone else, and so I maneuvered my police car right in behind him. Seeing me so close startled him and he turned right at the next intersection to avoid me, north on Ida Street. I hadn't turned on my red light or touched the siren, as I rolled down my window and motioned for him to pull over. The boy glanced over at me briefly, and then quickly turned back to the road, lifting his haunches up as if he were in a motor cross race, trying to make the scooter go faster. My speed clock showed we were going exactly 35 mph. Even by hoisting up his body, in an effort to increase speed, he still couldn't outrun me. At 35 mph, the machine was going at its maximum speed. It was both amusing to me, and irritating that this frightened kid thought he could outrun a police car doing thirty-five on a scooter, against a car that could do 110 mph if necessary.

At first the boy tried turning at every intersection that came up, but he'd have to slow down to make it around the corner, then go back up to top speed again. After about five minutes of pursuing him, I turned on my red light and hit the siren while right behind him, but all he did was turn and stare at me, then look back to the road. At one point, it looked like he was shouting "Go away!" The boy eventually found himself on a dirt road near the Portland city dump, in St. Johns. Still, he ignored the red light and my intermittent short bursts of the siren. The dirt road widened and I pulled directly alongside the scooter, yelling at the boy from the car window, "Pull it over! Turn it off! Pull over damn it!" He turned his head sharply and stared right at me, then straight ahead, looking even more determined to elude. I looked at the speed clock again. Once again, only thirty-five.

As we were on the dirt road with no other traffic I decided how to end this low speed and very dangerous chase. No matter what happened now, the boy on the scooter would probably be injured but I couldn't let him injure anyone else with his foolishness. So, again I pulled directly alongside and yelled out the window, "Pull over and stop!" He ignored me, waving me off, and cranking on the throttle to coax more speed out of the little motor that would never go past 35. Finally, when I thought I could run him into some brambles alongside the road, I opened the car door and slammed the rear of the scooter twice with the end of the door. This caused the scooter to go into a wobble, which it couldn't recover from.

I watched as the boy flew off head first, sailing over the handlebars, and landing in the brambles like he was sliding into first base. The scooter stopped with one final putt-putt before skidding on its side, to a halt. The boy wound up in some roadside blackberry bushes a few feet ahead, scratched but not seriously injured. Shaking my head, I stopped the police car, slowly got out, leaving my door open, and picked my way through the brambles to find a scratched, angry, unrepentant, and crying teenage boy. I bent over him, as he lay on his side moaning, and helped him to his feet. After I handcuffed the boy, I held his elbow and directed him back to the road, where I shoved him in the back of my car. He sat in the back seat, with his head down, looking both dejected and angry. I leaned into the window.

"Why didn't you stop?"

"I dunno, I didn't wanna I guess," he responded.

"You coulda killed yourself and someone else too. Do you know that?" The boy was still crying and sniffling, as he sat in the back seat, glaring at me as if the whole thing were *my* fault.

"Why didn't you just go away?" he sobbed.

"Sorry, but that's not the way it works. I'm a policeman. We don't have that option."

"I coulda got home okay, if you hadn't a been chasin' me."

"How old are you anyway, son?" I asked wearily, and trying to regain my composure. "Thirteen. Well, I'm almost fourteen. In a couple weeks..." He sucked in his breath raggedly, trying to get control of his emotions, and not seem like a little boy. In the process, he did a little snort and looked down, embarrassed. I had to keep from laughing a little, so I looked away and tried hard not to smile. He seemed for all the world like a little six-year-old trying to be brave and not a teen boy at all.

"Do you have any idea what you did *wrong?*" I asked, trying to be stern.

"I wasn't doin' nuthin' wrong!" he said.

"Is that right?"

"I was just ridin home from my girlfriend's house."

"You have a girlfriend huh?" I asked doubtfully, looking at him with raised eyebrows. I paused, for effect and made him wait. "Well, let's see, as I remember, you ran *two* red lights, one at Greeley Street and one at Chautauqua Street. You cut several cars off passing improperly on the left. You passed more cars illegally on the right. You drove a motor vehicle on the sidewalk endangering pedestrian's lives and finally you attempted to *elude* a police officer! Besides, you don't even have a driver's license, *do* you?" By now the boy was beginning to realize the seriousness of the trouble he was in and had stopped crying. The scratches on his face and arms had stopped bleeding and he was trying to look out the back window to see what had happened to the scooter. It had some scratches on the paint, and a broken headlight but was otherwise intact. The boy had some cuts and scrapes and a fractured ego and was also intact.

"You shudda just stopped chasin' me," he said again. "I'd a been okay. Now my dad's gonna kill me. His scooter's all messed up. Can't you jus take me home?" he pleaded. "Nope. You're going downtown to the Juvenile Division where they'll have a nurse look you over and then they'll take you over to Juvenile Detention Hall. The scooter will be towed to the police impound."

"Look son," I said with as much sympathy as I could muster, "You're damned lucky. You're lucky you didn't kill yourself. You're lucky you didn't hurt anyone else, and because you're a minor, your dad will have to pay for everything you've damaged. Your scratches will heal, you can get a new headlight for the scooter, and hopefully, your father won't be all that mad at you."

"Awww, man, you don't know my dad! Now, I'm fucked!"

"You made some bad choices today, son, but you're grown

up enough to deal with the consequences." I said, growing more disgusted by the minute.

"That's all I can say, right now," I concluded.

"Am I really in trouble?" he asked.

Again, I just shook my head, realizing that the boy *still* hadn't grasped the danger he'd caused, or the crimes he'd committed. "The juvenile court will decide what to do about all these citations you've racked up," I said. "It will be a few years before you can drive again for sure," I told him philosophically, like I was simply discussing bad weather with him. "And your right to apply for a license *will* be suspended even when you *do* turn sixteen, but that's what happens when you break the law son, you have to pay up." I still didn't get the feeling the boy grasped the depth of his offenses. Had he been an adult I would be taking him straight to jail, and he would be looking at thousands in bail and a long jail sentence. So, I decided to punish the kid a little more. I waited for the tow truck to arrive, so the boy had a full view of the crashed scooter. The tow truck driver wrapped towing straps around the body of the little red and white scooter and hoisted it up. It now dangled from the end of the tow cable like a fish on the end of a fishing pole, swinging back and forth forlornly. The boy groaned an involuntary sob and broke into tears again as he watched the precious scooter dangle comically in the air, and then disappear into the distance.

It was after that, that I drove the boy downtown to the juvenile division. There was no further conversation, and every now and again, I heard the occasional choked sob from the back seat, as he no doubt began to think about how much trouble he had caused for himself and for his parents. I turned him over to the juvenile cops downtown and I remember thinking how glad I was that he hadn't hurt himself or anyone else, because he could have, given his reckless behavior. I never followed up on what happened to the kid, though I often thought about him in the months that followed the low speed chase. The hectic business of police work doesn't allow most officers the time to do much follow-up. After

I got back in the car, I turned on the ignition, and the radio came to life again. "Car 390, can you take a 12-9 code three at Union and Alberta? Car into a pole."

Columbus Day Storm

GLASS AND METAL FLYING

COLUMBUS DAY, OCTOBER 12, 1962, started out like any other work day for me. Ray Freauff, a longtime non-cop friend and I had been building a patio roof-cover in my back yard. We quit for the day about two o'clock in the afternoon, as it was nearing time for me to go to work. I showered, picked a clean uniform from the closet, and got dressed for work. My wife was getting dressed for work too, as she worked as a waitress at Elmer's Pancake House on 82nd Avenue. We were drinking coffee together at the kitchen table, while she put on her make-up, both of us waiting for our teenage babysitter to arrive. The babysitter normally came at two o'clock, to watch our nine-year old son while we worked. It took two jobs to eat, make our $47 per month car payment and $85 per month house payment. Those were the days. Though it wasn't easy, as I made only $105 a week.

Soon, Frank came by to pick me up. I usually rode to work with him while my wife had our car for the day. After roll call, Frank and I picked up our regular cruiser, a black and white 1961 Plymouth in the basement parking area of police headquarters and drove out to our normal North End traffic district. Not knowing that after today, nothing would be normal in Portland for a long time. It was a cloudy day and the air had a strange metallic smell. It was heavy, almost like you could cut it with a knife. A strong breeze came up and radio began to get busy with calls on power outages, occurring primarily in the center of the city. The breeze grew stronger, becoming stormy. Traffic signals began to blow back and forth on their retaining cables, and we saw small tree branches coming down all around us. "Jesus" I told Frank, "I sure hope this wind dies down." But the wind didn't die down, it grew much stronger. Frank nodded his head slowly, in agreement, as he looked out the car window. "Car 390, can you check a downed power line at Denver and Ainsworth?" the radio cracked.

"We'll get it," said Frank.

We found the downed line in the street, with sparks erupting from the power pole. Power poles usually have a metal tag with the pole number and the map number so the electric utility company knows their exact location. We got the number off the tag and gave it to radio, speaking loudly into the mic, to be heard over the wind, which had picked up even more. Radio was starting to keep two lists; one detailing problems for the power company and another list of problems for the city department of Public Works. We had barely put down the microphone when we heard a loud crash. Looking behind us, we could see sparks showering not far from the car. Two more power lines had come crashing down, and we watched them, arcing and spitting behind us. It was starting to get dark, and the wind was still getting stronger. The electric companies would have their work cut out for them.

We drove a short way up Denver Avenue and saw an old lady out in her front yard. She was picking up walnuts that were blowing down from her walnut tree and using her pink and brown calico house dress for a basket. Just as we pulled up, a large limb broke off and crashed near the old woman. She didn't seem to notice and was oblivious to everything except the walnuts. By now it was almost impossible to stand up against the wind. Frank jumped out of the police car, leaving the passenger door open and told the old lady "Please go inside the house, now!" Even though the power lines were down, and a tree branch fell and almost hit her, it was hard to convince her she was in any real danger.

There was nothing else on the old woman's mind except walnuts. Frank and I exchanged a look of frustration, shaking our heads in disapproval. He took the old woman by the arm, and assisted her to the front door and closed it, all the while listening to her entreaties, as she told him, "It's not a bad storm. I just wanna get some more nuts, that's all!" In truth, Frank had to push this old lady, with his hands firmly on her shoulders, into her house and admonish her to "Stay in the house, okay?!" Turning, Frank struggled against the wind back to the police car. He pulled himself into the front seat and grabbed the car door to pull it closed. The wind was blowing so hard against the door that it wouldn't budge. I had to get out of the car and it took both of us pushing as hard as we could against the door to finally get it shut. This was getting to be a mess. By now all hell had broken loose. Power poles were coming down all over town and transformers were exploding, lighting up the night sky with brilliant flashes of light.

A huge old oak tree, on North Vancouver, came crashing down in a yard, crushing a car at the curb. The car horn started blaring, adding to the noise of the storm. Bill boards and other signs were blowing down the street, along with flying glass from storefront windows, and shingles and branches were flying everywhere in the tumult. The air was full of dangerous, sharp objects, and it seemed every time Frank and I got out of the car, we risked getting impaled by something. Hospitals were now on emergency power and were starting to get injured people coming in for treatment. Battery operated burglar alarms were ringing constantly from dozens of store fronts without plate glass windows and of course, people were starting to steal. Anything that was not bolted down or already blown away was being stolen from local businesses in groups of twos and threes, mainly men but also women. We saw people walking off with TVs, stereos, radios and vacuum cleaners. We even saw two people lugging a love-seat to their waiting car. The looters were sporadic, and really only endangering themselves by being out in the storm, and though we would have liked to arrest them, we were on other calls and there were too many, over too large an area to control at any one time. All we could do was yell out our patrol car window, "Get off the street! Get off the street!" Mostly, we were ignored by the looters.

Fire trucks, ambulances, and police cars were now having trouble moving around, as many main streets were blocked by fallen trees, utility poles, and crushed cars and trucks. Public Works was using chain saws and snow plow dump trucks to push trees aside for emergency access to hospitals. All the tow trucks in the city were out working. On-duty officers were ordered to refill their gas tanks at Stanton Yard, which was not usual procedure. Stanton Yard, on Stanton and Mississippi Avenue, was a Public Works Depot for dump trunks, paving trunks, street sweepers, and snow plows. All off duty officers were ordered to duty, whether it was their day off or not. This was a bona fide emergency and we police had to do our part. The public works equipment depot at Stanton Yard was preparing emergency gasoline and power generators for fire trucks, police cars and ambulances. With all police officers coming on duty, there were not enough cars to go around. The officers were beginning to ride three and four to a car. Vice officers and detectives were ordered to patrol in unmarked cars, and had their badges pinned to their suit lapels and jackets.

Except for car headlights and flashes of light from exploding transformers and burning power poles, the city was completely dark. No traffic signals were operating and there were not enough police officers to direct traffic at major intersections. Public Works began putting out portable stop signs but there were not enough of those either. Portland had never been hit by such a violent storm before. We were not prepared. Though we thought it was a tornado, we later learned it was actually called an *Extra Tropical Cyclone*.

Tragedy brings out the best and the worst in people. Some citizens were starting to direct traffic on their own using emergency road flares, while many other citizens were looting and committing other crimes. Frank and I picked up two cases of flares at Stanton yard and were giving them to citizens directing traffic, replenishing their supply. Restaurants had no power either but many Portland restaurants were fixing cold sandwiches and making coffee on Coleman stoves for the public and for the rescue personnel who needed them most. Red Cross emergency services had kicked in and they were setting up emergency shelters and also providing sandwiches and hot coffee. We cops were all doing our best to take care of the citizens, and attend to their assortment of needs. But Frank and I were worried about our own families.

I tried to call home and check on my older son, but the phones weren't working.

I couldn't reach my wife at work or anybody I knew. Frank couldn't either. While we worked the shift, we could only hope our families were safe and our houses relatively intact. Gradually the wind died down leaving the rubble strewn aftermath. Not one store on the entire length of Union Avenue had a single plate glass window left intact. The streets and sidewalks were layered with broken shards of glass, of every conceivable size and shape. Burglar alarms were clanging more slowly now as back up batteries were beginning to run down. Every power and telephone pole on a four mile section of North Columbia Boulevard was down. I remember thinking, it looked just like a big giant had pushed them down all in a row. It represented the eeriest sight for me, looking down that long stretch of land and seeing the symmetrical sight of all those downed lines. It was the awesome power of nature wreaking havoc on our little town.

All night long and into the next day we patrolled the main streets to keep people from looting. There wasn't much the police could do to prevent the rampant theft. Just imagine every store front on Union Avenue being wide open, and citizens pulling up in cars, climbing in and out of broken windows, driving over shards of broken glass, trying to circumvent tree limbs, all so they could fill up the backs of their family cars and station wagons with merchandise that didn't belong to them. All we could do was drive by and yell out the patrol car window, "Get off the street! Go home! Get off the street." Finally, the Oregon National Guard had to be called out to assist the police in keeping order, because there was so much bedlam from the looting. Frank and I were called off the street at noon. Our shift had lasted twenty one hours straight, and we were thoroughly exhausted and in desperate need of food.

We had not made one arrest or even issued one citation, but we did have a hefty stack of incident reports documenting downed telephone poles, crushed cars, and missing traffic signals.

It was a surprise pulling into the basement parking area, at police headquarters on Pine Street. We had never seen it entirely empty of cars before. Most of the other officers were still on duty, and Frank and I were alone for a brief moment, after pulling the keys out of the ignition. Though we were exhausted, we didn't linger. We were both preoccupied with thoughts of our own families. "I hope everything is okay back at home," Frank offered. "Yeah, you too," I said as I pulled my tired body out of the car and slammed the door shut. We walked the two blocks to Frank's parked vehicle and he gave me a lift home. During the drive we talked intermittently about how we hoped there weren't too many downed trees or power lines over in Lents, near where we both lived. We were worried that if there were, we might not be able to get home. When I did get home, I found my back yard fence had been flattened, the shingles had blown off the roof of the house, and my new patio-cover was destroyed. There was no power, no phone and no family. Christ, I thought, where's my family? The house was vacant and cold, but there was a hastily scribbled note taped to the refrigerator door from my wife. She and our son were with friends.

One is fortunate in life to have friends as nice as Ethel and Ray Freauff were. Although they were also without power, they had rescued my little family from the storm, letting them spend the night warmed around their small fireplace, in sleeping bags and drinking hot cocoa. Their lovely home was located in the Mt. Scott neighborhood about a mile away. I heaved a sigh of relief, as I read the note. Later, my wife told me the news about our small, yellow, import Fiat. It had been blown across the Elmer's restaurant parking lot and smashed into the owner, Walt Elmer's luxury sedan. She worried that the car was totaled and that Mr. Elmer, her boss would be angry, or that she'd have a hard time with the insurance company. In the end, he was very understanding about the entire event and the insurance eventually came through.

The media called this cyclone the "Columbus Day Storm." As Frank and I had gotten off shift at noon, the day after the storm, and had to go back on shift at 4 p.m. that afternoon, we got very little sleep. The city was still very much in a state of chaos, and I'll never forget the sight of soldiers patrolling the streets with their bayonet rifles, and how threatening and ugly those bayonets looked to me. The only purpose of a bayonet is to kill. The city looked every bit like a war zone, and we later learned forty-six people living in the Pacific Northwest lost their lives as a result of the storm. It took several days for all the power to be restored and weeks for the city to recover. I had to rebuild thirty feet of my fence, start over with my patio-cover, and fix the dents in my car. I have often reflected on how fortunate I was, though. I could have lost a loved one or a family member but didn't. Frank and I were very lucky that day.

Losing a Friend to Vice

FRANK'S TRANSFER OUT

Frank was getting tired of working traffic and particularly tired of the detailed diagrams and reports on traffic accidents, which he considered tedious and boring. He felt it was time to do other things in the Police Bureau. He'd spent several months talking about what he wanted to do next, which meant a transfer. We were both philosophical about our partnership. It had been fun and we had enjoyed it but there was always something new to pursue in law enforcement. There was always something around the next corner. Frank wanted to transfer out of traffic and for myself, I was thinking about working alone at night. In early 1963, Frank put in a transfer request. He wound up in the vice squad, as they were always looking for new faces. But the vice squad may have been Frank's undoing.

If Frank had any problems to deal with in life, they were a tendency to drink too much and an eye for the ladies. Vice is the wrong place for a person like that, because it feeds the problem. Much of the vice officers job is to hang around bars and nightclubs and arrest prostitutes, hustlers, pimps, and drug dealers. For Frank, it may have been a little like the fox watching the hen house. The temptations would have been everywhere. Although we weren't partners anymore, I still considered him a friend. He would stop by my house and we would sip a beer and talk. Gradually Frank stopped talking to me about his cases altogether, and eventually he stopped calling and coming around. Partly, this was because we were working different shifts, and we were both family men with wives and children. I could tell Frank wasn't happy working vice, but I didn't know what was wrong. He wouldn't tell me, and I would never have pressed him for details.

Decades later, I learned through a family member (not related by blood) that Frank had had a sexual affair with my first wife, behind my back. My former wife had apparently bragged to this individual, who then told me. Though I never knew how long the relationship lasted, or how serious it was, this betrayal *had* to have bothered Frank. He had always been a good, moral guy and we had been friends and partners for a long time. I never resented Frank for this, after learning the truth. My first wife had been chronically disloyal to me (and many others) and eventually we divorced due to her faithlessness and general lack of regard for me or my personal happiness. By the time Frank had had relations with her, she had already cheated on me numerous times with other men. She had been a former ballet student, thin, lithe and pretty. She was also a textbook sociopath, a chronic manipulator and a pathological liar. She had been unfaithful so many times and with so many men that I couldn't blame Frank for weakening in the face of an easy temptation.

Saturday night, March 13, 1965, Frank took a one time, two hour security gig as a uniformed officer at a private dance in downtown Portland at the Neighbors of Woodcraft Hall, located at SW 14th and Morrison. He earned a check of $12 for his efforts. On his way home from the dance job, Frank stopped at the Portland Police Athletic Association, (PPAA) on SW Alder street for a few drinks, and while there became very drunk. While he was drinking at the police club, he commiserated with a fellow officer about the recent death of another officer. Officer Robert "Bobby" Ferron Jr had died less than a year before. Ferron had been Frank's partner in vice.

While working vice, Bobby Ferron was killed May 23, 1964 when he lost control of his unmarked car, running off the road at high speeds on the Terwilliger curves. The car went end over end and Ferron was ejected from the vehicle, dying four hours later at a local Portland hospital. Ferron was handsome, dark skinned, with even features and a full member of the Sioux tribe. He was one of the few Native Americans ever hired by the bureau that I can recall. With only three years on the job, he was only 25-years-old at the time of his death. After the accident, police recovered

Ferron's body and the car but Ferron's gun was not in the car and never recovered, which upon reflection, I consider sloppy police work. Why would a loaded policeman's gun just be left somewhere in the bushes for anyone to find and possibly use? Ultimately, Ferron had been ejected from the vehicle because he had not been wearing a seat belt, which was common at that time. Very few people went to the trouble to buckle up.

Frank had been rumored to have been extremely depressed about Bobby Ferron's death, often mentioning to friends the memory of Ferron's funeral, in which he had been one of several pall bearers. Frank had talked about Ferron's death repeatedly with numerous officers over a period of several months. Hours before, as he sat drinking in the police club, he was reported to have been reflecting on Ferron's death, saying "that had he been working on that night, this might not have happened." (Official investigative police report, 1965). Frank seemed to blame himself exclusively for Bobby Ferron's death. After drinking from about midnight till 2:15 a.m. on Sunday morning, March 14, 1965, Frank got in his car, like so many others before him, dead-drunk, half-asleep and tried to drive home. He almost made it. He ended up eastbound on Foster road, "Swaying from one side of the road to the other." (Witness report, Paul, 1965).

At 92nd Avenue Frank attempted to make a right hand turn. In so doing, he ran into a car stopped at the traffic light which was headed northbound. He backed up and ran into the car a second time, in his effort to make the turn and then continued south on 92nd, "turning and scraping along the side of my car." (Victim report, Dennis, 1965). The man he'd hit, Dennis, followed Frank and the other male witness, Paul, also followed in his vehicle. Frank finally came to a stop and got out of his car in front of the Round House Tavern on 92nd and Woodstock. The two men approached Frank, after he got out of his vehicle and both could ascertain immediately that Frank was very drunk, and a policeman, and in uniform. When they asked him for his license information, Frank provided it and was cooperative and subdued.

The witness, Paul, then began to walk a block away to a corner pay-phone, to call the police to come to investigate the accident. After Frank spoke with the man Dennis, (whose car had been hit) and after exchanging driver's license information, Dennis began to walk away to wait for the police to arrive. The witness, Paul, was still walking down the street to use the pay phone. Dennis presumed, (in his handwritten witness report) that when Frank began to fumble near his belt line he was merely going "to take a leak," somewhere in the parking lot. As Dennis turned the corner, Frank continued walking into the dark shadows. Dennis then heard a single gunshot and yelled to the other man, Paul, who was nearby but out of sight, "He shot himself!" Both men ran back to find Frank curled up in the fetal position, and deceased on the asphalt.

Somewhere behind The Copper Penny night club, near 92nd and Woodstock, Frank walked in a dark alley to end his life. He probably could have seen his house just a block and a half away, on 94th Avenue, where his four children and wife would have been sleeping.

For reasons I never knew, (at the time) Frank put his .357 magnum to his head and blew his brains out at 3:00 a.m. He was 31-years old and had been a cop for only four years. He left behind a wonderful wife, Emma, and four happy, active children, Anna, Adam, Susan and Frank Junior. Frank had always been an affectionate and loving father, who seemed to genuinely enjoy his children. Whenever I was at their family home, Frank was always glad to see his kids. He would pick them up, hold them, hug them, smile and laugh. When we were in his basement, hand-loading, the kids often wanted to come down to see what we were up to. He'd never let them come down but he would allow them to peek down from the staircase. We would see their little faces peeking down sideways, and Frank would laugh. He seemed like the best kind of father, fun loving and patient.

From looking at the investigative report into Frank's suicide, I know that he had a .23 blood alcohol level. This had to have impaired his judgment to the point that he didn't know what he was doing. And I am certain he was panicked at the thought of getting into trouble for the minor car accidents and for being drunk while in uniform. If he had been thinking more clearly, I don't believe Frank would have killed himself. He would have considered his children. He would have made a different decision. I believe this firmly.

But was it that drove Frank to such self-loathing? I often wondered but never knew. Not until recently, when I was able to examine the full investigative police records related to his suicide did I learn some of the details regarding a motive. What I do suspect though, is that something happened to Frank while he was working vice and he wasn't able to recover. He began drinking more and more, I knew that. I know now that he was extremely depressed about Bobby Ferron's death and had been for several months since Ferron was killed on the freeway in 1964. Frank was also probably scared because of the two minor traffic accidents. It's likely he was afraid he'd be suspended from duty, and perhaps even fired. But why did he have to end his life like that?

As a pallbearer at his funeral, March 17, 1965, at the Zeller Chapel of Roses Funeral Home, I helped carry my friend to his grave. Don Coffey, the older of the Coffey brothers, was also a pall bearer at Frank's funeral. As an idealistic teenager in the early 1950s, Don Coffey had been one of the reasons I'd wanted to become a cop in the first place. He was someone I'd always admired and looked up to. Don stood with me and a couple of the other pall bearers after the services. He wrapped his arm around me. "I know you guys were close, buddy," he said simply. I felt bereft and could only nod my head a little, as I fought back tears. We all talked quietly, trying to understand it. One thing we could agree on, not one of us knew, at the time, why Frank did it. We were confused about why he'd killed himself and very concerned about Emma and their four children. Damn it, I remember thinking, another dead cop and for what?

In an article, by the Oregonian newspaper, a few days after

Frank's suicide, one of the investigating officers said there was no evidence that Frank had been "despondent," before his suicide. I found the statement in that article ludicrous. I always felt there had to have been a valid reason. The mystery of a motive wore heavily on all of us. We just didn't know and no one shared any information with us, about Frank's depression over the death of Bobby Ferron, even when they *could* have. I spent over fifty years wondering why Frank killed himself, and feeling as if I would be forever in the dark. Reading the entire investigative report of Frank's suicide was like a punch in the gut to me. I'd never known why, and it sure would have been good to know those simple facts in the beginning, instead of wondering and being in the dark all those years. Frank was the kind of officer you could rely on, knowing that he would always have your back. He was so professional and calm under stress that while Frank had been working traffic, a Portland citizen wrote a letter of commendation to his supervisor in the Traffic Division.

"JUST A COMMENT:

No doubt you have a lot of officers on your staff that deserve compliments, but seldom get them. The officer that issued my Citation, certainly used his authority, but in a very diplomatic manner, yet definitely was not rude, or arrogant, as in some cases. This man is an excellent officer to represent the city police Force. Please compliment him for me.

Ultimately, Frank's suicide made me heartsick for his family and I genuinely missed him. I missed the rapport we'd had as patrolmen and how we always knew what the other was thinking or would do. I could rely on Frank and Frank could rely on me. We had that rare kind of telepathic chemistry that makes police officers productive and safe while working the streets. When Frank left traffic to work in vice, in 1963, I transferred to an opening on the graveyard shift, also in traffic. Traffic officers worked alone on this shift and that was just fine with me. I didn't want to work with anyone else. After losing Frank in 1965, I felt no one could *ever* replace him. There were other advantages too. A good, hot, unmarked car that was fast, and one good boss. Sergeant Bud

Rowley was the shift supervisor; he was tall, thin and grey haired, with nearly twenty-five years with the department and had seen it all. He had a lot of common sense and didn't bother me or try to micro-manage me while I was out working. Rowley divided the city into four large areas and assigned the SE district to me. It was great. No new green partner to mess with, lots of area to roam and a feeling that I was one of the new owners of the SE district.

Finding a New Partner

OF THE RIGHT CALIBER

NIGHT PEOPLE AND DAY PEOPLE are as different as night and day. The night people I came to encounter, in my over fifty acres of district, were a different breed. At night, the Portland drinkers and party-time people came out. The drug and underworld people came out. The predators came out. Many burglars liked the quiet, peaceful time between three and four in the morning. Newspaper boys, taxi drivers, and owl bus drivers, they were all out at night. Although I was always careful, working alone as I did, I realized that over the long haul, the law of averages would be working against me. I was afraid of being overpowered or surprised by a criminal and maybe losing my one gun. I had been thinking about these issues for a long time, so, I went shopping for a new partner; a silent partner. A chrome plated .25 automatic pistol eventually caught my eye. It was small and easily fit in my right hand pants pocket. It held a total of seven rounds.

Even though it was a small caliber gun, I figured I could, if necessary put five or six rounds in somebodies face and maybe turn a surprise in my favor, if I needed to. The cop mentality is *survival*. It has to be. And no one understands this better than another cop. No police officer wants to kill another human being but if faced with a criminal or civilian who *wants* to kill them, the officer will and should defend their lives. The police officer has the *same* right to survive as any other human being, when facing off with a person intent on killing them. And sometimes this means a civilian will be killed. To protect myself against these dangers, I reworked my traffic ticket clipboard, drilling a hole big enough for my trigger finger to go through. I fixed the board so I could hold it, and fire the concealed automatic at the same time, if needed. Now, when I stopped a motorist at night, I always had a gun pointed right at him during the entire traffic stop. The clipboard acted as a shield.

I felt I was safer because I was in charge and it put the element of surprise in *my* hands. Because I often worried about *back-up* sleeping during the graveyard shift, I felt *my* back-up wasn't on the radio, my back-up was in my pocket.

This may sound extreme, but that is because you are most likely a reader who has never intended to inflict deadly harm upon a police officer just trying to do his job. But the dark streets of the night see it all. Everyone uses those streets, some of these inhabitants are drunk, some of them are angry, and many of them are armed, with a chip on their shoulders and a desire for revenge. I understood this as an experienced street cop. I also understood there were those who *hated* what I represented; authority and law and order. The clipboard acted as a shield against that hatred.

The old timer officers' working this crew wrote about fifty five moving violations per man, per month. They would write citations until about three a.m. when the traffic died down, and then, as I've mentioned before, find a nice quiet place to sleep. If you looked, you could usually find a police car or two parked up by the water reservoir, near the Vista Bridge, in SW Portland, also known locally, as "The Suicide Bridge." They were always there. And inevitably, there was a tired cop sleeping in the back seat. After all, they had day jobs, and there wasn't much traffic out in the wee hours. With only four or five guys on the shift, roll call was informal, and on Sergeant Rowley's two days off we had no supervisor. There was a lot of freedom.

Back in those days, every officer had to work a part time job, if he had a family, because officers were not well paid, and that's putting it mildly. We were not even paid a living wage. The officers on the graveyard shift were all old timers who had enough seniority to work days. But working days meant they could not work a part time job. Working at night meant they could keep their day job, get paid for being night owl cops and sleep their shift away in their patrol car.

My new unmarked car was a screamer. It could do zero to 60 in eight seconds flat. It was an off white 1962 Plymouth with a push-button automatic transmission. The electronic siren was mounted under the hood and two red lights were concealed behind the grill. An additional red light plugged into the cigarette lighter. All it needed was a roll bar. I came to find out that people didn't *make* the car too easily as a police car, and that worked to my advantage. It was the best police car I ever had.

One of the drive-in restaurants, popular with the kids in SE, was called The Speck. It was located at 52nd and Foster, off Powell. These three major streets, 52nd Avenue, Foster Road and Powell, all converged to form a natural "hub" for traffic. It was a landmark. Kids loved The Speck and would often say, "I'll meet ya at The Speck!" The cruising area that used to be downtown on Broadway, had now moved to 82nd Avenue. Kids would race northbound, then come back southbound on 82nd. The result was loud cars, rowdy kids, beer drinking and lots of citizen complaints. Have we all heard this before? I arrested hundreds of kids speeding and causing other problems. Poured out beer bottle after beer bottle and gave the problem a lot of effort. *It didn't make a dent.*

Some things can be solved by police work, and some things cannot. Unfortunately, citizens often don't understand this. Pressuring the police to solve problems that do *not* have a police solution may cause officers to step over the line. I remembered my coach at East Precinct, Fred Brock, saying, "Law or no law, our job is to solve problems!" I found lots of traffic violators out at night, but then I was awake and working. It caused a lot of angst with some of the old timers on the shift. They had been cruising along, writing a few tickets here and there, and then I came along, a fresh-faced kid, eager to work, and ended up upsetting the apple cart by being aggressive and doing good police work. I wrote 96 moving violations my first month on graveyard, mostly speeding tickets.

Where was I finding all these people in the middle of the night, they wondered? "Jesus, DuPay, you're fuckin' things up on this shift!" one old timer muttered bitterly, as he left the traffic office to go home, scowling at me as he walked out the door. I ignored him, as I tossed my reports in the sergeant's in-box.

I didn't care what the lazy bastard thought or what any of them thought, and my sergeant supported me. Sergeant, Bud Rowley, told me to do my job and let the chips fall where they may. In time, I received a commendation from Lieutenant Bill Taylor, a traffic division supervisor, for "making the good arrests." I remember how proud that made me feel. I knew I was doing good work and maybe even making a difference.

One night, I was driving slowly down Powell Street at SE 17th. It was about three in the morning and there wasn't much traffic. Suddenly, a car blew through the red light in front of me. I pulled in behind and followed. He was speeding at 55 mph and crossing over the yellow center line. Reaching down, I picked up the red light and put it up on the dash board. I turned on the siren and hit the lights. His car sped up and crossed over the center line again. He was using both lanes and was 30 mph over the speed limit. "Car 350," I said into the mic, "I've got one running from me south on Milwaukie Street approaching Holgate." I could see that the car was going to run the red light at Holgate. I clocked him through it at over 90 mph. Then the car slowed and skidded into a residential side street and turned off his lights. He was "running in the dark," trying to get away from me. Headlights or not, every time he slowed down, his brake lights would come on and I could see where he was headed. He was trying hard, but he couldn't shake me. "350, I think he's trying to get over to Highway 99," I said to radio. "10-4, 350, I'll see if I can get you some cover," said dispatch. The eluder was now starting to *lose* the mental battle, between pursuer and pursued.

He had almost crashed trying to get to the highway. Soon his car skidded to a halt, and I skidded right in behind him. He had fucked up and driven into a dead end street. How nice, I thought to myself, relishing the moment. I gave radio my location and jumped out of the car, leaving the door open. After running to his car, I pulled the driver out of the vehicle, and slammed him up against the side of the car by the front of his shirt and suit jacket. It was Detective Sergeant George Hempe of the Portland Police!

Jesus Christ! Why me lord? Why me? I thought frantically. Hempe was a middle aged, paunchy, longtime detective. He had thinning dark hair, and was fairly tall. Being a detective sergeant, I'd never encountered him or even worked with him before, but he was a detective, a sergeant and with the Portland Police Bureau *and* he was drunk. This was bad.

I searched Hempe for a weapon, and without cuffing him, pushed him over to my car and shoved him in the back seat. I was furious. "Stay there!" I ordered. He leaned forward and began to wipe his face with his hands, saying nothing. I returned to my car and got on the radio. "Car 350, get my sergeant out here right away! Sergeant Rowley! I've got a problem!" I told dispatch. A few minutes later, two prowl cars found me, and arrived to provide cover. As the four men got out of their cars, and walked over, they all recognized the detective sergeant in the back seat. They began talking among themselves about it, smirking and laughing quietly. Ultimately, they didn't want to be a part of this mess, and began to walk away, hanging back several feet, as I stood with my arms crossed over my chest, still angry. When Sergeant Rowley finally arrived and saw that it was Detective Sergeant, George Hempe in custody, he was flabbergasted. He walked over to the car, bent down to look in, and with his mouth hanging open, he just stood there for a minute, taking in the situation. Then he got angry. He straightened up, his face turned red and in one violent gesture, he grabbed his police cap and threw it down on the pavement, in disgust. After a moment, he calmly picked up his police cap, and put it back on. Rowley then turned back to the car, opened the door and pulled Hempe out. He had to hold him up, as Hempe was so drunk, he could barely stand.

Rowley was very professional as he placed Hempe in the back of his car. He walked back to me and mumbled grimly, "Don't worry about this, DuPay. I think he just came from the police club. I'll take care of it." I nodded and said nothing. After Rowley drove away, I got in my car and drove to the Pancake House on Powell Boulevard and wrote a brief report on the incident. As I sat in the booth, drinking hot coffee and slowly eating scrambled eggs, buttered toast and strips of bacon, I knew what would happen in the long run. I knew for example, that Hempe's conduct and crimes would be swept under the proverbial rug. Internal affairs handled things like that, when one of their own broke the law. Ultimately, I was never allowed to speak to them about it, which really irritated me, because I was the one to chase and apprehend Hempe and I should have at least been able to tell my side of the story. The final outcome was that Sergeant Hempe was suspended from duty for thirty days and kicked out of the Detective Division. He was re-assigned to Central Precinct as a uniformed sergeant. Any citizen doing the same thing, would have gone to jail and lost their driver's license, but that was the beauty of civil service, at that time; no matter what you did, it seemed you couldn't be fired.

Ambushes and Triple Fatal's

THE LAW OF AVERAGES

I APPRECIATED BUD ROWLEY SUPPORTING ME during the Hempe situation. I soon had a chance to repay the favor. A couple of weeks later, in the wee hours of the night I heard Sergeant Rowley on the radio asking for cover. Bud was at the service station on 28 and Holgate Street. I punched the gas on my screamer in an effort to get there as soon as I could, instantly concerned. When I sped into the parking lot, I could see that the glass was smashed out of the front door of the service station. Bud was on the ground outside, on his back, with a large white man straddling him. The man was punching him rapidly in the face, with both fists, as if he were punching a boxer's punching bag. I jumped out of the car, with my lead-weighted sap gripped tight in my hand, and ran up behind the burglar. I tried to position myself so I could hit the bastard in the back of the neck, in an attempt to knock him unconscious. This was something I'd done before to resisters, and it worked. The guy heard me coming though, and quickly turned, looking up. Now, the back of his neck became the front of his face, and I bashed out a few teeth instead. The poor sergeant was huffing and puffing and damned glad to see me, as we overpowered the guy and put him in hand cuffs. "Doing a little police work, Sergeant?" I chided breathlessly.

Seeing Bud in trouble like that, underscored the fact that even an old, experienced, street sergeant like Bud Rowley, could be taken by surprise. I made a mental note to be more careful and patted my chrome plated silent partner. Soon I got another call. "Car 350, take a 12-1, 12-9, code 3, car into a mobile home, 8500 block on Union," cracked the radio. "10-4, 350 copies," I said. That address was a long way from my part of town but no other traffic cars were available. By now, Bud had the burglar who had attacked him handcuffed and in the backseat of his car, with his head bent over, bleeding into his lap and minus about four teeth. He told me to go ahead, the situation was under control, I could go on to the new call.

In only a few minutes, I was pulling up to 8500 and Union and Columbia. I could see that a car had left the traffic lane and driven half under a double-wide mobile home on the corner of a motor home sales lot. As the car slid under the mobile home, the hood peeled up and rolled back, like the lid from a can of sardines. The hood pushed through the windshield and crushed the man and woman in the front seat to death. It was very bloody. Broken windshield glass had been crushed into their faces, making them unrecognizable pulp. The forward momentum had stopped just short of the back seat, but laying there was another dead man. His eyes were wide-open and there was a small, neat hole punched through his skull, right between the eyes. At first it looked as if he'd been shot in the head, but upon closer inspection I realized he had not been shot. I picked up the radio, "350, I don't need an ambulance. This is a triple fatal. Send the fire department rescue. Two of these bodies will have to be cut out of the car. Go ahead and contact the morgue." After talking to dispatch, I took another look at the dead man in the back seat. The sharp metal rod holding the sun visor had turned toward the backseat on impact and as the man was propelled forward, the visor punched a narrow, even hole through his skull. As I stood there, bent over and looking into the car, the visor glistened, wrapped as it was, in a red sheath of blood.

It hit the man before he could shut his eyes, and after impact, his body was slammed back into the back seat area, where I found him. The scene was so horrible, I fought the feeling that I might vomit and had to take some deep breaths and turn away, walking several feet away. The smell emanating from the vehicle was the heady, overpowering and metallic scent of large quantities of blood. It was a gruesome sight that I'll never forget. In a few minutes a wrecker arrived, and pulled the car out from under the mobile home so the fire department could work on it. Three people were killed in this accident, two so badly maimed their mothers wouldn't know them. What a horrible waste I thought. God, how I hated fatals!

During the years I worked traffic, I wrote hundreds of traffic tickets and got involved in lots of high speed chases that ended in violent crashes. One of the worst things that ever happened while working traffic occurred June 9, 1963. During a wild chase, I hit a family of five, broadsiding their small Opel station wagon and rolling them over. Miraculously, no one was injured. Mother, father and their three boys, Byron, seven, Dennis, five, and Mitchell, three, were not sent to the hospital, and the parents refused all medical treatment. They weren't doing anything wrong, they just didn't see a cop chasing a speeder, as I came up behind them and attempted to pass. None in the family were seriously injured and thankfully, all survived. The city bought the family a new car and replaced the police car I'd totaled. That was the end of *shop 122* and represented the second car I'd wrecked while working Traffic. I was very shaken up as I recall, because of what *could* have been a needless tragedy, a tragedy involving three innocent children and their parents. All the unintended victims of a high speed police pursuit. I was also very safety conscious, at a time, when it wasn't popular to wear seat belts. The accident illustrated to me, the value of a seat belt, and reinforced my habit of always wearing one when I was working. The impact of the accident, which resulted in ninety seven feet of skid mark before making impact, left a wide strip of deep bruising on my lower abdomen, from where the lap seat belt had been fastened. My lower belly was black and blue, and painful for over a week. Had I not been wearing that seat belt I would have been thrown through the windshield and possibly killed.

The stress of the chase, for a police officer, can sometimes seem insurmountable. Anger and frustration can make a good cop do things they wouldn't ordinarily do when they're overworked, challenged by a violent offender, or simply burnt-out from the job. For example, when I was a street cop in my late twenties I tried to stop a guy who ran a red light at 60th and Fremont street and continued to speed west on Fremont. I was driving a blue 1957 Ford, unmarked car, the one I had previously smacked into the wall, one hell of a good car, but it had a manual siren. I had to push one of two buttons, the button on the dashboard, with my finger or the button on the floor with my braking foot, to keep the siren going, all while I was trying to drive and talk on the radio too. As I followed the eluder, I reached down and put the red light up on the magnetic stand, on the dashboard, so it would show through the car windshield. I tried to get alongside of him, to pull him over, but when he saw the red light flashing, he hit the gas, speeding away and grabbing a quick left to turn into the Alameda district, a residential area of winding streets and family homes.

I chased him around and around the neighborhood, all the way to Wisteria Drive. He finally got down to 42nd street, sped over to Sandy, and then sped down Sandy to Broadway, where he tried to lose me in the Lloyd Center Mall area. There was no way I was going to let him get away. I just stayed behind him poking the siren button, and watching him make bigger and bigger mistakes, until he crashed into a tree, in front of a house, trying to make a corner. Good, I thought to myself! That will stop the asshole. After running to his car, I jerked open the driver's door and dragged him out, throwing him on the ground.

I was so angry, I kicked him twice in the chest, before I realized he was unconscious from the crash. I rolled him on his face, checked that he was still breathing, handcuffed him and sat on him until the wagon arrived. Clearly, I shouldn't have kicked him, but the adrenalin and anger overcame my reason. I was angry because he wouldn't stop and I had to chase him for over twenty minutes, through a neighborhood where kids lived, putting innocent civilian's lives in danger, not to mention my own life! It's scenarios like this that can make an officer so angry they will do things they normally wouldn't. Like kick an unconscious offender and then sit on him until the wagon or ambulance arrives. I vividly remember the sense of satisfaction, however, as I sat on the man, watching the steam and smelling it, as it rose from his smashed radiator, after his car had collided with the tree. I felt smug and smart. I had won.

I always felt insulted when an offender thought he could outrun me and like most cops, I hated to lose. This chase was the longest of any chase in my career and extremely frustrating for me, not to mention very dangerous for any unsuspecting bystanders. By the time it was over, I was covered in sweat, breathing hard, spent and furious.

We don't allow police officers to fire a shotgun down a crowded city street. That would be an improper use of deadly force. The level of danger seems similar when a 3000 pound police car is hurtling through the streets at high speeds. That could easily become an improper use of deadly force. After the accident with the young family, I re-evaluated chasing speeders, and I wasn't quite as aggressive as I'd been before. The highest speed I ever clocked *anyone* was on the Banfield freeway, interstate 84. The car was going 104 mph and the driver turned out to be an off-duty cop, named Bob Wiskoff. Bob was on his way home from the Police Club and very drunk, and though I pulled him over, I did let him go. I was angry, however, because 104 mph *is* fast and dangerous, but after my experience apprehending Sergeant George Hempe, and not being allowed to tell my side of the story, I didn't want to chase Wiskoff's drunk ass all over the freeway and have my superiors look at me sideways for my efforts. Wiskoff also didn't try to outrun me, and so I cut him a break. If he had tried to outrun me, it would have been a different story, but he pulled over and was embarrassed, polite and cooperative. As one police officer dealing with another police officer, who had crossed the line, I appreciated his conduct very much and let him go. As it turned out, after I pulled him over, and then let him go, he later repaid the favor by giving me free gas and several oil changes over a one year period. His part time job was at a gas station located at 102nd and NE Glisan Street.

Vice Squad

WHAT PRICE PUSSY?

THE VICE SQUAD WAS ALWAYS looking for new faces. Working vice can be tricky though. After a few months, you get "burned," even if you use a code name. Certain individuals end up knowing who you are. *You're a cop.* And you can't work under cover any longer, and sometimes you even get death threats from people you helped put away. I was getting tired and bored working traffic; the horrible fatalities and the likelihood of chasing down drunk cops was starting to wear on me. I had a reputation as a hard worker and it was suggested by Sergeant Bud Rowley that I join vice.

"I'm getting *really* tired of traffic," I mumbled quietly to Bud, as I sat filling out my time card one cold, winter, morning. He leaned in closer and nodded his head as if he understood, cupping his hands around his hot mug of coffee and taking small sips.

"I'm tired of the dead bodies and the fucking mess."

"So, have you thought of working vice, Don?"

"Do they need anybody?"

"They *always* need new faces. You should look into it."

I thought about Bud's suggestion for a day or two and realized, I was ready for a change. On December 27, 1962, I was transferred to the vice squad working for Lieutenant Carl Crisp. From the outside, vice seemed to be a dream job, plain clothes, unmarked cars, hanging around the clubs and getting paid to drink. All while on duty. Let me tell you what it was *really* like. My partner was Officer Danny Stohl. Danny was an experienced officer and a veteran in vice investigations. I found him to be laid back, friendly, and easy to work with. Our favorite car was a two-tone green and white 1957 Ford. The siren and radio were hidden and the back seat was full of kids' toys and a baby seat. The car looked pretty straight. Our shift hours were eight at night, to four in the morning and I usually dressed in slacks or jeans, with a casual shirt.

The badge was too bulky to conceal, so I carried only my police ID card tucked inside a pack of cigarettes. My small, chrome-plated automatic pistol was also in my pocket. We were assigned to work morals crimes. That would include arresting prostitutes and "queers," as gay people were referred to then, along with handling other common crimes. Referring to homosexuals as *queers* in a derogatory fashion is offensive now, but in the middle 1960s being openly gay was looked down on by the vast majority of the public and engaging in homosexual sex was considered a crime of disorderly conduct.

After picking up our car, we would cruise the downtown tenderloin area looking for prostitutes. Trolling, it was called. Citizens would call in and report active vice locations where drugs and prostitution were common, and we concentrated on those areas. Danny would pick up about $25 a night in "drinking money," from our vice Lieutenant Carl Crisp, to get us started. Back then, that was a lot of money for alcohol, and kept a guy drinking most of the night. The Old Glory, located at 118 SW Madison, was a crummy bar where the hookers were getting out of hand. There were reports that they were fighting, yelling at passing cars, and strutting on the avenue, showing off their attributes. Danny and I were sitting and drinking beer one night, trying to act like two guys from out of town, looking for some action. A black girl with a short skirt came up and sat down next to me. She was bony, unattractive and high on something. "Hey baby, you interested in a woman?" she slurred. "Yeah," I said, "We're both looking."

"I don't got a friend but I'll take you both for a hundred."

"Look honey," I said, "we ain't got but $75 between us to spend for pussy."

"All right baby," she responded, "but it'll have to be a quickie; who wants to go first?"

We looked at each other for a split second and then Danny gave me the nudge. We had worked it out so that he would try to follow me, just out of sight, and be close by for the arrest. I stood up and escorted the girl out the front door. She was tipsy but was able to walk the two blocks down the street to the flea bag hotel where she was staying, which turned out to be The Lotus Hotel on 3rd Avenue. Her room was on the second floor, unit number ten, with a window looking south. The glass was covered in a thick film of decades of city grime and car exhaust. As we walked up the rickety, old staircase, I could smell the pungent odor of urine, and spilled alcohol. The clerk didn't look up, as we passed him in the hall.

Outside of her room door, we agreed on a blow job and a straight lay (half and half) for Danny and me, for eighty five dollars. That's how much money she *really* needed for a fix. Her small room was filthy and smelled like cheap perfume, cigarettes and stale, closed-in air. On a rickety breakfast table lay a bent spoon and cotton ball next to a small pile of burned paper matches. In the corner, near the closet was a sink and a two burner gas grill. She removed a skillet dotted with mold from the grill and put on a bent aluminum pan, filled with water to heat. From her purse she took a small folded piece of paper. It contained a brown powder that she mixed with water in the spoon. As I sat and watched, morbidly fascinated, she lit a book of matches and cooked the mixture. The brown substance began to boil and she dipped in a small cotton ball, which would act as a filter. She fished around in her purse and found a metal Sucrets throat lozenge box. In the box was an eyedropper that had been fitted with a hypodermic needle. She filled the eye dropper with the fluid in the spoon, and then handed me a towel and pointed to the pan of hot water. "Baby, take off your pants and wash your dick off real good. Peel back the skin and wash that too."

I smiled to myself, thinking, *I'm not uncircumcised,* as I began to slowly undo my fly. I was playing the part of a John and pretending to comply with her request. I watched her tie a nylon stocking around her arm, tightly, and inject the drug into her vein. "Be right witcha baby," she said, "be right witcha." I had seen enough. There is an old rule in vice, as told to me by Lieutenant Carl Crisp, (who would have known better than most) "If you're gonna arrest em' don't fuck em'! And if you're gonna fuck em' don't arrest em'!" Though, I never would have touched this one. I re-zipped my fly, slid my ID card out of the cigarette pack, showing it to her. "Ah sheeit!" she said in surprise, acting defeated. I approached and she offered no resistance as I handcuffed her and retrieved the $40 front money from her purse. "If you gonna take the money back at least lemme shoot some more dope. Please baybeeee please?" she begged. "You knows I'm gum-be sick."

I ignored her pleas, stony faced, and took her out of the building, down the stairwell where Danny was waiting with the car. We put the girl in the back seat and drove directly to jail. She was charged with prostitution and possession of narcotics, and as she was a prostitute we placed a health hold on her, which would deny her bail until we saw the results of a mandatory blood test for venereal disease. Friday night was the best night to arrest prostitutes. It allowed us to keep them off the streets for the weekend, and gave them an opportunity to sober up and maybe choose to turn their lives around. This prostitute would be in jail until Tuesday waiting for the VD blood test to come back. After she was locked up, Danny and I went back and ransacked her room at the Lotus. We found her little black "trick book," and not much else. We arrested two more such ladies operating out of the Old Glory that night, but after drinking seven or eight beers over the evening, it was a little hard to get serious about the phone numbers or the names in their trick books. We would save them for the next shift, when we weren't so drunk or so tired.

Danny and I would cruise by the known whorehouses and park nearby to watch people coming in and going out. Obtaining registration information on the cars gave us a good idea who was in the neighborhood. We were always on the lookout for a *weak John* to come out of one of the whorehouses. In other words, a reputable citizen with a wife and kids, a good job, and a lot to lose. Someone who wouldn't want anyone to know he was visiting a prostitute, behind his wife's back. The idea was to get a weak John to take one of us back inside the whorehouse and introduce us as an out of town friend. In return for getting us inside, we would agree *not* to arrest the John on the "after hours," charge that he would normally get, and not to tow his car. It was like plea bargaining on the street. Sometimes it worked and sometimes it didn't. If we had hopes of getting inside a whorehouse for a bust, we would lay back and be cool, watching and continuing to gather intelligence. If there was no hope of getting in, we would harass the place; we'd break out the parking ticket book and write tickets for being parked over a foot from the curb, whether they were or not. We'd stop and talk to everybody going in or coming out, writing parking tickets and towing cars and generally disrupting business. Harassing people was one of the ways we did our job. I could almost hear Fred Brock whispering in my ear, "We have a job to do, law or no law."

One particularly busy whorehouse was in a private residence on 14th and NE Killingsworth. It was operated by a black madam named Mary Taylor. Mary was one of two black Madam's both with the first name Mary who we dealt with. She'd been in business a long time and her clientèle was well established. Few newcomers were admitted. Most of Mary's regular customers were Asian workers, cooks, waiters and owners of the local Chinese restaurants. Mary felt safe with Asians as there were no Asian police officers at the time employed with the police bureau. She allowed very few white customers because a white man *could* be a police officer but not an Asian. One of her few Caucasian customers was the president of a major soda pop bottling company. He showed up about twice a week, this being 1963. When I worked the ghetto as a patrolman, all during the 1960s, I was always amazed at the number of white men who solicited sex with young attractive black women. I also noticed the black men who worked as pimps for the North End whorehouses were never customers. This is what I was told and what I observed. Black guys didn't pay for pussy and they laughed at white guys who did. "Paddys!' they called them, and "fools."

One of the other officers I worked with, was a hardworking

cop named Lou. He worked the vice shift and was good at playing poker. One of his favorite pinches involved conning his way into a good poker game, in order to bust the players. Playing poker was against the law, in the 1950s and 1960s, and to gamble for money, even while at home, was a crime. Lou's mother owned The Wooden Shoe tavern on Union Avenue, which was a white tavern in a black neighborhood. Beer was on the house when we were in Lou's company. Some nights when it was slow we would go to The Wooden Shoe, drink beer and shoot pool. One night, our poker playing vice buddy was scheduled to play in an after-hours game at a house in the ghetto just off Vancouver and Fremont Avenue. If he could get some marked money in the game, we could all make a gambling bust. We waited at The Shoe, drinking beer and shooting pool until it was time for the bust. When the tavern closed at one in the morning, we chased all the customers out and locked the doors. We continued to drink beer, shoot pool and wait. At about three thirty, we left the tavern and took up our positions outside the gambling house. Danny and I could see the lights were on in the house where the game was being held. We sneaked up to the window and hid in the shrubs, listening. *Hello Walls*, by Faron Young was playing loudly on the radio, and we could hear Lou and the other players talking pretty well, laughing and joking as they slapped down the cards. Everything was going according to plan.

    Jesus, I had to take a piss though. I crept behind the bushes into the back yard trying to be quiet, and urinated in a corner. What I was doing *bothered* me. Here I am, I thought, half drunk, sneaking around in someone's backyard, pissing in the corner, waiting to break in and arrest some guys for playing poker? I could see the paddy wagon waiting down the street, lights off, ready to take the card playing criminals to jail. Danny was moving around in the dark and also took a piss in the corner, near the shrubs. When he returned he brought the sledge hammer from the car, the one I would use to break through the front door, which was a flimsy, old, wood-frame door. When the signal came, Danny covered the back door. I went to the front door and hit it with the twelve pound sledge hammer. The door flew open splintering wood and breaking glass. I rushed in bellowing, "Police officers! You're all under arrest!" Danny came in the back door yelling too and this is how the card players discovered to their astonishment, that one of the gamblers, now pointing a gun, was a vice cop. We crowded seven arrested card players into wagon 99, including the owner of the house.

They were all charged with "visiting an unlicensed establishment." Bail was set at $25 per person. Three were white businessmen, two were Asian men, one was the black owner of the house and the other was a black pimp who called himself Buck Owens. During the game, I listened outside the window, as Buck bragged about one of his new girls, a 19-year-old named Pam. He was going on and on about how pretty she was.

Over at the police headquarters Jail, we found some mug shots of Pam and a couple of his other girls. Pam Owens, as she called herself, had been arrested in Portland for prostitution and had a mug shot on file. She used her pimp's last name but of course, they had never been married. I pulled Pam and Buck's mug shots and added them to my growing file of known pimps and prostitutes, which I kept in a small file folder, in the back seat of my unmarked car. Later, when I met Pam in person, I found her to be heartbreakingly young. She was only 19-years old and she was surrounded by vipers. She had no direction, no parental involvement and no moral compass. Pam stood about five feet, eight inches, was very slender and had the fine boned features of an Ethiopian woman. She always wore a full makeup, expertly applied, that consisted of false eye lashes, creamy pancake makeup, bright red lipstick and lots of Tabu perfume. Pam was extremely pretty, seductive, cunning and a hopeless heroin addict.

Queers were the other part of the regular trolling operation we were required to do, and it was expected that we arrest several every month. It was what we were told to do. To go out there and arrest queers and prostitutes. Portland culture has since made many positive improvements towards gaining a greater understanding and acceptance of diverse sexual preferences and sexual identity. And Portland is particularly supportive of sexual diversity, *now*. But Portland in the 1960s was very different and a far less tolerant place. I remember one of my first nights, working vice and being told how important it was to arrest queers. "The more queers you arrest, the safer the children will be!" they lectured us more than once. We parked close to the gay bar at second and Yamhill and wrote a few jaywalking tickets to the customers flowing out onto the street. It seemed odd to me, to be writing jaywalking tickets from a car with a baby seat in the back.

We were given instructions to cruise two or three gay bars, all located in the downtown area. Eventually we wound up at the Globe Theater on Forth and Morrison. The Globe Theater was located at 626 Fourth Street on Morrison, and had been called The Blue Mouse Theater years earlier. Danny said it was a "great place," to "pinch queers," and that he hadn't been there for a while. He told me he'd show me the ropes. We went in and bought a twenty five cent Coke. We stood in the aisle letting our eyes adjust to the dark, as we slowly finished drinking our soda. Then Danny said, almost jokingly, "Come on, I'll show you the men's room." The men's room in the Globe was a scary place. Fifteen or twenty guys standing around in a four urinal rest room and not too many were interested in taking a piss. They would stand against the wall, just standing, posing, and looking. Eye contact would be made and then someone would lick his lips. Two sets of feet would show beneath one toilet stall door. The atmosphere was very intense. After we went in, Danny smiled and winked at a guy standing over in the corner and nudged me to do the same. I picked out a guy, winked and blew a kiss. I felt ridiculous and awkward because the deception was so blatant and it was hard to fake being something I wasn't.

After a few minutes, Danny and I left the rest room and went to buy some popcorn at the concession stand. When we returned to the darkened theater rows, we picked two seats as close to the men's room door as possible, and sat watching. When we finished eating the popcorn, I went back into the rest room and Danny sat by the door. The guy I had winked at was still there, leaning against the wall and he gave me the nod. We made eye contact and he crossed the room, sauntering slowly. While standing in front of me, he turned around seductively and backed up against me. I felt his left hand groping my privates. I encouraged his other hand and when I had them both, I quickly pushed him against the wall to the right and then handcuffed them together. The six or seven other men still in the room casually ignored the fact that I was arresting one of their own, who offered no resistance. I pushed the guy out of the rest room, as he groaned, mumbling "Ah shit!" Danny stood up and we whisked the man out a side exit and into our unmarked car. We drove him directly to jail and booked him for disorderly conduct, morals. Bail set at one hundred dollars. We went right back to the theater and that night we took four more queers out of the theater rest room the same way. It was like fishing in a pond, a real "cherry patch," as the guys called it. We continued trolling until the bars closed and then we turned our efforts towards the other night people, out breaking the law. At that time, we were told that queers were child molesters and predators by our sergeant's and that we were doing the right thing by arresting them and keeping them away from the youth of Portland.

 Lying in bed after getting home from work gave me time to think about my profession in all its many facets, dangers and contradictions. It became apparent to me that I was having increasing difficulties reconciling the morality of vice work. At first, drinking at night on city money was fun, but gradually, *having* to drink every night was getting to be a drag. It was adversely effecting my health. I could always feel the effects of the alcohol after the third or fourth beer, and so could the guys I was working with. I thought, "Here I am going to work every night, drinking, driving a police car and arresting people, *while* I'm drunk?" Vice work was just the opposite of my police work in uniform. Should a cop who has been drinking be out arresting people? And what about the complexity of drug cases? A vice cop always had to take a hit off the joint that was passed around, just so no one would be suspicious of him. Should he be arresting people when he's high? As a uniformed cop, I was upfront about what I *was* and what I was doing. As a vice cop I had to lie to everyone and *deny* what I was and what I was doing. I was getting confused about which me *was* me and I didn't have a good feeling about it anymore. The moral dilemma was beginning to bother me. Just what did this badge stand for anyway?

Van's Olympic Room

VICE, SIN AND BROKEN BONES

About three weeks after the poker game bust, I noticed a teletype on the clip board, in the vice office. It was from the Seattle Police Department. It indicated that Buck Owens was now "wanted for promoting prostitution," and since I knew what he looked like, I decided to keep my eye out for him. Normally I didn't work alone, but that night was an exception. My partner Danny Stohl had done something unbelievable. He had accidentally shot himself in the *balls!* Danny normally carried a .38 revolver pushed down inside his waist band. On his way to work, a few weeks after the gambling bust, Danny grabbed his gun and pushed it inside his belt, as he always did. Later that night, (September 19, 1963) after he'd arrived home, Danny had... "started to remove his .38-caliber revolver from a belt holster when the weapon discharged. Stohl then placed the gun on a shelf and asked his wife to call police headquarters for an ambulance." (Oregon Journal, 1963).

Sometime during his shift, the hammer had caught on Danny's pants and cocked the gun. Later, when he was home, as he pulled the gun out, it went off. It could have been a devastating injury. Fortunately for Danny it was only minor, and he was still intact, but he would be off work for a few days and unable to walk. Danny was so afraid to come back to work, for fear of the ruthless razzing he would get from the guys, that he asked me, "Do you think they're gonna start callin' me shortie?" I had called him on the telephone, to inquire about his health and his question caught me off guard. I laughed out loud, his question was so funny and finally asked him what we were *all* wondering, "Whaddaya got left Danny? Six inches or only four?" He grumbled into the phone and said, "It's alright, it only got nicked but I can see I'm gonna get a lot of sympathy from *you!*" He did receive a merciless razzing from the guys for a few days but he was always good natured about it and soon the controversy over the shot-up remains of Danny's private parts died down.

After looking at Seattle's teletype about Buck Owens being wanted, I decided to see if he might be hanging around at Van's. I hadn't been to Van's Olympic Room since my probation days at East Precinct, and decided to check it out. I didn't think anyone in the club would recognize me in plain clothes, but that presumption was a mistake. Parking the unmarked car in a darkened alley near Van's, I walked in and ordered a drink. Van himself wasn't around but LeRoy was tending bar and Big Jim was preparing the few food orders that came in. They both recognized me right away, following me with their eyes. Still, I walked to a table in the shadows, so I could see the action but remain unobtrusive and perhaps even unnoticed. Van's was busy that evening. Two exotic dancers, Thelma and Pam, were sharing equal time on the grand piano top that served as a stage. I noticed I was the only white person in the place and thought about leaving. I *should* have. Instead I ordered another drink and sat back, entranced, watching the nearly nude Thelma and Pam dancing in bare feet. They wore only pink, sparkly, tasseled pasties and G-string's and they both looked gorgeous.

I had been in the club about an hour and was starting to notice the effects of the alcohol. Feeling the urge, I worked my way through the crowd to the men's room in the back and took a piss. As I was washing my hands at the sink, Buck Owens entered the rest room and sidled up to the urinal. Well, well! I couldn't believe my good fortune. He had come to watch out for his girl Pam, as she danced on the Grand Piano, with Thelma. Buck unzipped his pants. Now is my chance, I thought. He's by himself and I can take him, caught literally with his pants down. I waited until I could hear him do the shake, and then zip up his pants and then rushed up behind him. I pushed him hard against the wall to the right of the urinal, putting him in a choke hold, and dragging him back away from the urinal. I relished being able to surprise Buck Owens, with his pants down, so to speak. After he stopped resisting, I got both his hands cuffed behind his back, then fished out my ID card to show to him, flashing it in his face for a brief second or two. I told him he was under arrest on a "pimping warrant out of Seattle" at which point he told me, "Fuck off! You don't know who you messin' with man!" I laughed, "Yeah, right! Shut the hell up, and do what I tell ya!" Now that I had Buck in custody, all I had to do was get him out of the club and back to the police car. I knew it wouldn't be easy. I eased Buck back through the men's room door and out into the crowd. As soon as I did, Buck flopped face down on the floor and started wailing, "This white motherfuckin' pig's trying to bust me on a humbug!" He kept yelling the phrase, over and over, and I couldn't get him up off the floor.

The piano music stopped and the all black crowd stopped what they were doing and started to gather around me, as I held onto my prisoner. Some had curious looks on their faces and other's had looks of pure hatred on their faces. I saw LeRoy disappear into the back room and Big Jim emerge with an ancient looking, meat cleaver. I felt certain that Big Jim would remember me and I yelled at him, "I'm a police officer and this man is under arrest! We're going out the front door!" Buck wouldn't move so I grabbed him by the handcuffs and reefed his arms up, managing to drag him a few feet closer to the door. He screamed obscenities at me, but still refused to move, forcing me to drag him by the handcuffs, even farther. Big Jim positioned himself and the meat cleaver between me and the front door. There was no sign of recognition in his eyes. I made sure he saw my ID in my right hand. I cocked the automatic and pointed it right at him. "I'm a police officer and I'm taking this prisoner out the front door!" Big Jim didn't budge and I wondered desperately, what I should do next.

God damn it, I thought, *do I have to shoot my way out of here?* Just then the front door crashed open. The cavalry had arrived. Two beautiful blue uniforms rushed in, guns drawn. It was Fred Brock, my old coach and friend, and a scared looking, young, rookie patrolman with big terrified eyes. LeRoy had called the cops, thank God. We put Buck Owens in Fred's black and white and drove him to Emanuel hospital. He couldn't move his left arm. X-ray's showed I had broken Buck's left collar bone trying to reef him out the door, while he was resisting. Things had not gone well. I had almost bitten off more than I could chew. I was mad at myself for getting in over my head without a partner and mad that I had injured my prisoner—even though he *was* an asshole pimp who preyed on women and routinely broke the law. Besides the warrant, I would add the charge of resisting arrest. I had to, as that would explain Buck's injury.

Fool's Errand in Old Town

WHEN BEGGING WAS AGAINST THE LAW

When Danny could walk and piss without screaming, about ten days after his accidental, self-inflicted injury, he came back to work. I noticed he now carried his gun in a holster, like the rest of us. The poor boy took a hell of a razzing, but it *was* funny and we were all genuinely glad he was okay. Several weeks later, the vice lieutenant, Carl Crisp, handed Danny and I a report from the mayor's office. One of the mayor's staff members had been accosted by a black prostitute while he was strolling through skid-row. Heaven forbid this should happen in *our* town, that one of the Mayor's employees might be accosted. We weren't given much of a description to work with. She was a black female, tight blue jeans, drunk and unattractive. We were assigned to troll the skid-row bars and arrest her, find out who she was and then report back to the mayor's office. It turned out to be a fool's errand. We parked the police car on Third Avenue and Everett Street and began checking the bars. There were a lot of crummy bars on skid row at that time, so I knew this was not going to be an easy job. After three hours of drinking beer and looking for the girl, we decided to split up so we could cover more ground. We agreed to meet back at the car shortly after midnight and I started working the bars on the main drag. For the first time ever, the entire area seemed completely without prostitutes of any color. Bar after bar and beer after beer, no unattractive black girl in tight jeans crossed my path.

By now I was drunk and frustrated and the bars would be closing soon. I had spent all evening in this crummy part of town, drinking in smelly bars and had no arrests to show for it. Finally, I gave up the search and started to walk back to the car on unsteady feet. Maybe Danny had found the girl, I hoped. A couple of blocks from the car, near Third and Burnside, two bums walking together staggered up to me on the street and drunkenly asked for some spare change. My alcohol fogged brain thought, well, what the hell! So that the whole night should not be a total waste, I said, "I'm a police officer and you're both under arrest for vagrancy by begging!" I quickly handcuffed one of the bums and grabbed the other one by the seat of his pants. With one prisoner in each hand, I continued toward the police car, pushing them forward, in front of me. Quickly, bum number two realized my critical error. I only had *one* set of handcuffs. He turned and hit me hard on the chest, trying to struggle free. I was having a Jesus of a time controlling the two at once and realized I could be in trouble. Fuck no! I thought, getting angry. Both of these bastards are going to jail! I hated to lose and after all, wasn't begging a serious crime? My supervisors had *never* downplayed the crime of begging. It made our city look bad they told us repeatedly. And where the hell was Danny? I needed some help, or a new strategy, so I dragged both men out into the middle of the intersection. Right there at West Third and Burnside, across from the Viking Tavern (now Dante's Tavern), continuing the fight and stopping traffic.

As drunk as I was, I realized my best bet was to attract as much attention as possible. Bum number one was handcuffed on his belly, and didn't present much of a problem, laying there in the middle of the street, no longer resisting. But bum number two was on his back, angry and fighting me. I was straddling him, as he kept punching me in the chest, and trying to punch up into my face, which only infuriated me. To get him to stop, I grabbed him by the hair with both hands and banged his head six or seven times on the hard pavement in rapid succession. Well, three guys fighting in the middle of a big intersection is bound to attract police attention. Shortly, a black and white police car with lights flashing pulled up and two officers jumped out, grabbed me and hoisted me up. They threw me against the car and patted me down finding the automatic. I knew they were fellow cops, from Central Precinct, and only doing their jobs. Realizing one guy was in handcuffs, one of the uniformed officers, looking confused, demanded, "Who the hell *are* you?"

"I'm DuPay, and I'm workin' vice!" I said, still frustrated and angry. After fishing out my ID card from the cigarette pack, I told the officers with growing impatience, "These two are my prisoners and gimme back my gun!" The guy on the pavement wasn't responding well, he was bleeding and drifting in and out of consciousness. We sent him to the hospital, where they performed an X-ray of his head. I had cracked his skull. Besides the vagrancy charge, I added the charge of resisting arrest. That would cover the reason for the injury. Once again, things had not gone well and I was left trying to figure out why.

Later that night, as I lay in bed, I replayed the scene with the two bums over and over in my mind. What could I have done differently? How could I have been a better police officer? I knew I was drunk, while trying to arrest them, but that was part of working vice. One of my supervisors had told me, "Drinking is a necessary part of the job in vice. You have to be okay with it." And yet, somehow I *knew* that was wrong. During the tussle with the bums, I remember vividly, the frustration of not being in my usual top form, because of how intoxicated I was. And all while on duty and carrying around a badge and a gun. I remembered the pathetic look of the man I'd assaulted, as he was carried away on the stretcher, with a fractured skull and a white sheet pulled to his chin, unconscious and bleeding. When I saw him on the stretcher, I felt instantly sorry and remorseful for what I'd done. I remembered my single minded determination to get him to comply and the way I'd slammed his head again and again on the dirty asphalt. Was I trying to punish myself by remembering these ugly details or gain some kind of understanding as to what had happened? I tried to recall the righteous anger I'd felt during the arrest but lying in bed, later, it wouldn't come to me.

More Trouble at Van's

SHOTS FIRED AND A TRIP TO THE HOSPITAL

A FEW NIGHTS LATER, I READ an intelligence report written by officers at East Precinct. They had developed an informant who told them that Buck Owens was carrying a gun and looking for me. He intended to shoot me on sight, I was told. "That white paddy pig ain't gonna get away with it!" Buck had been heard bragging to people. I handled all threats against my life the same way I handled everything else—offensively. Danny and I went looking for him. We parked the police car in the alleyway near Van's Olympic Room and walked inside. Danny picked a corner table, out of the way and had a couple of drinks sent over. Maybe *dumb-fuck Buck* would show up, as Danny and I liked to call him. Buck Owens was a pimp, a heroin dealer, a bully and a parasite. He would end up destroying the lives of several women he would turn into heroin addicts, so they could then prostitute for him. Danny and I despised him.

Van's was busy as usual. *Night Train* by Buddy Morrow was blasting from the Jute Box, as we walked in. LeRoy spotted me from his place behind the bar and we made eye contact. I could see Big Jim working in the back. Management knew the cops had arrived. Thelma, one of the beautiful exotic dancers who worked there was dancing on the piano, jiggling her tasseled boobs. Someone had stuck a ten dollar bill in her G-string, and she continued to dance and smile at the patrons seductively.

Two other white guys were in the place, sitting at a table near the piano. They had a black girl sitting between them and we could see she was putting on the hustle. I worked my way through the crowd, past the piano and back to the men's room. Although she had never seen me, I instantly recognized the black girl at the table hustling the two white men. She was 19-years-old, drinking, and her name was Pam Owens. The same Pam Owens who Buck

Owens had bragged about at the poker game and the same Pam Owens who had been dancing on the piano just a few days before, barefoot and in a G-string. When I came back from the men's room, I nudged Danny and told him the good news; that since Pam was at the bar maybe that meant Buck would show up too. We ordered another drink and sat back watching Thelma jiggle and waiting for Buck. It didn't work out the way we wanted though. Pam started getting up to leave with the two white johns and forced our hand. After Danny and I quickly walked over, we identified ourselves as police officers and placed Pam under arrest for being a minor in possession of alcohol. I pumped up my aura and flashed my most threatening look at LeRoy and Big Jim. It meant to stay behind the God damned bar and *don't* interfere.

Hurriedly, we took the handcuffed Pam out through the front door. We were immediately followed by four or five black guys and the two white johns. They intended to rescue the pretty girl from the pigs. Pam was struggling, trying to get away, and we soon found ourselves surrounded by attackers. I had a secure hold on Pam, but Danny and I were outnumbered. They began to crowd around us and before we knew it, there were seven guys beating on us. They were punching us, kicking at us and shouting "Let her loose! Turn her loose! She didn't *do* nuthin' Pig!" Our objective was to get Pam safely into the back seat of our unmarked car, but it became clear that would not happen easily. During the tumult, Pam and I had fallen onto the ground together. I quickly got to my knees and straddled her in my efforts to control her, as she lay on her side, on the ground. At that point the group of men circled around us, getting in closer and I had to lean over Pam and duck, to avoid some of the blows. Danny ended up on the ground with a couple of black guys pounding on him, several feet away. Determined to hang onto Pam, I couldn't help Danny, or even defend myself very well, and I was getting hurt.

I continued to hold onto Pam, with my left hand gripping the back of her belt and jeans, and my right hand free to move, trying to fend off the blows and protect myself. There were too many of them though and I could only lean forward and wait for it to end. Blood was running into my eyes and my mouth. I thought about shooting somebody but decided against it. So far they were only using their fists and feet. Then I heard—*POP-POP-POP-POP*—the unmistakable sound of a snub nosed .38 going off, but had no idea who was shooting it. I couldn't see much. Things were getting desperate.

Through the fog in my brain I heard a siren and a police radio cracking nearby. The cavalry had arrived again. Danny had fired the pistol shots, as a warning, into the side of a nearby tire dealership. It was enough to cause all the attackers to flee in a hurry. In due time, Pam was taken to jail and booked with a "health hold," to keep her for a while, so she could be tested for venereal disease.

Though it looked as if Danny was in real danger, which he was, he had not been seriously hurt. Most of the angst and violence had been directed at me. I was taken to the hospital emergency room, at Emanuel. Eight stitches closed the laceration over my right eye and my bloody nose was packed with cotton. My body was black and blue all over from being punched and kicked. My lower legs had been stomped and I couldn't walk very well. I was released, later and taken home to my wife. Not a pretty picture for her to see, no doubt. At the time, though I was being severely beaten, I didn't feel any reason to shoot my weapon. We were taught, that unless the criminal had a lethal weapon, like a gun or a knife, not to shoot them. Besides I was stubborn, there was *no* way I was going to get beat up *and* lose my prisoner too. In retrospect, I've always been grateful I never had to shoot anyone. During my career, there were many opportunities to pull the trigger, but I always chose not to. In my entire career, I only fired my weapon twice and no one was ever hurt or killed. I generally never felt the level of threat necessary to do so and I'm glad, because the last thing I ever wanted to do was kill someone.

Recuperating from my injuries at home provided me with a lot of time to think. Time to reflect on law enforcement in general and vice in particular. I knew that drinking and then arresting people was wrong. I felt that a citizen is entitled to *not* be arrested by a cop who is either drunk or high. The end never justifies the means, particularly in police work. Another aspect to police work that troubled me, was that any law that interferes with the sexual activities of consenting adults, whatever their sexual persuasion, is bullshit and unconscionable. It doesn't make any difference what your morality or religious beliefs may be, sex is a product and products obey only one law; the law of supply and demand. Trapping gay people and trapping prostitutes is wrong. It is the worst example of what police will do when given an impossible task. I think that if a solution to the prostitution problem existed, somebody would have figured it out a couple thousand years ago. Cops and citizens should give up arresting hookers. Sending a twenty-dollar-an-hour cop to hassle a fifty-dollar-an-hour hooker is dumb, really dumb. Prostitutes need social services, not arrest.

North Precinct

A SHOOTING A WEEK

POLICE CIVIL SERVICE IS A law unto itself. It hires and protects officers almost regardless of their conduct. It doesn't permit citizens to view or review their actions. Cops are often surrounded by a protective cocoon, a practice left over from the dark ages of police work, around the turn of the century, wherein corruption blossomed without restraint, in places like New York and Chicago. The same forms of corruption in those places, also existed and were tolerated in Portland, Oregon. The system protects officers from the very laws they enforce against citizens. Only when a cop kills does the action get pulled before a citizen grand jury. Almost all other officer misconduct is reviewed only by other officers in secret proceedings, conducted by internal affairs. If a penalty is deemed necessary, after an investigation by internal affairs, it usually amounts to a temporary suspension from duty without pay and little else, such as what occurred with Sergeant George Hempe.

Offenses such as drunk driving, theft, and minor assault are usually not enough to prosecute a police officer; or at least they weren't in my day. They are often not even a bar to future promotion, as has been demonstrated by the bureau in recent years. The police fraternity, as I experienced it, was above the law and broke many laws regular citizens would have received stiff sentences for, had they broken those very laws. What do you do then, with the officers who have forsaken their integrity? The drunks, the thieves, and the assaulters? The answer in my time, according to command staff, was to *transfer* them. Transfer them someplace out of sight, and out of mind. Transfer them to *North Precinct*.

In the early 1960s, North was commanded by a permanent civil service police captain, an ex-chief of police forced out of his chief's job by allegations of corruption during the 1956 Vice Scandal. The commander was Jim Purcell Jr.

Have you ever watched the animated television program, The Simpsons? Are you familiar with the Joe Quimby character? The creator of the show, Matt Groening, based the Joe Quimby character (the Mayor of Springfield) on the notorious Diamond Jim Purcell. Only in real life, having to work for Jim Purcell wasn't a laughing matter. Everyone who worked for "Big Jim," knew one thing though; he didn't care what you did on the job. He didn't care if you drank, or did good police work or if you slept your shift away in the back seat of a patrol car, in a park somewhere. He simply didn't care.

I spent a week recuperating from my vice injuries from the parking lot attack, and during that week, I made a decision. I wanted to work at North Precinct. The city's police patrol districts had been redrawn and the area of town I wanted to work was now the responsibility of North and Big Jim Purcell. It was one of the toughest, most crime ridden part of town, but I wanted to make some changes for the better, was still dedicated to the idea of public safety and considered the prospect a challenge. I knew it would be tough establishing my own turf with all the misfit cops out there, but decided that hard work and honesty would prevail. If I could find another good partner like Frank, police work might be fun again. Knowing I would not return to Vice, I requested a transfer to North Precinct and was transferred July 30, 1964. It would be my last precinct assignment, before I was promoted to detective.

St. Johns had once been a small, very tough mill town a few miles down the Willamette River from Portland. Even though it was now a part of the city of Portland, St. Johns was still tough, independent, and the locals called the cops there "The St. Johns Police." The precinct was located in the old St. Johns city hall building, right at the east end of the St. Johns bridge, where the building still stands today. The police cars were parked outside by the gas pumps, in the parking lot. The desk officer's counter was just inside the big glass front doors, and to the right. Across the hallway, to the left, were some snack machines and the public restrooms.

The duty sergeant worked in a small cubicle that connected to the lieutenant's office. Captain Purcell had a private office in the back of the building near the roll call room. The officers lounge area, with lockers and pool tables was located upstairs, on the second floor. The back of the lounge had a good view of the wooded hills across the river and the Forest Park area, and was used as a forest fire watch station in summer. The basement had a small holding cell that had been constructed of thick flat metal bars and was covered with about six coats of different colored peeling paint. It looked like a cage in a prisoner of war movie, and over time, I locked up literally hundreds of prisoners behind those bars. This holding cell is now located in the Portland Police Museum at the Justice Center in downtown Portland.

That first day, since I had never worked at the precinct before, I showed up an hour early, to look the place over and read the crime reports. Each patrol district maintained a clipboard of its own reports and activities and I wanted to get familiar with their routine. I was feeling good because I'd requested North Precinct and the graveyard shift and had gotten both. So far so good, I remember thinking.

Since I was early, arriving a little after ten p.m., the swing shift lieutenant and the desk officer (who was on the phone trying to explain to a drunk lady why her car was being towed) were the only two people in the building. The door to Lieutenant Ohren's office was partially open and he was sitting with his feet propped up on his desk. Ohren was the swing shift commander and he was openly drinking beer from a quart bottle in a brown paper sack, set in his lap. He was also reading a nudie magazine. He nodded nonchalantly as I passed by. "To your health, Lieutenant!" I muttered under my breath, sarcastically. Putting on a clean uniform, I poured myself a cup of coffee and sat down in the roll-call room to wait. One by one, six or seven officers filed in and sat down, followed by the shift sergeant, Blackwood, with his clipboard under his arm. The sergeant introduced me around to the crew.

Some of their faces were familiar, and all were old timers. Two of the officers were grossly overweight brothers. They looked for all the world like Humpty and Dumpty. They operated an auto parts store during the day, over in the North End on Union Avenue, and were known for sleeping their night shifts away on a regular basis. A red-faced pot belly named Glen was my assigned partner for the evening. Sergeant Blackwood, by comparison was built fairly thin for a cop, though he was taller than six feet. Blackwood was always carefully dressed, had grey hair and a perfectly trimmed grey mustache. He looked out of place, but then so did I for that matter. I was young, fit, fresh-faced and eager to get to work. The potbelly and I had been assigned the patrol area nearest the precinct, District 43. It was large for a prowl district and included Pier Park. Glen picked up the keys to the police car and we went out to gas up. The main drag through St Johns on Lombard Street was dotted with bars, cafes, taverns, storefronts and more bars.

After clearing with the dispatcher, Glen drove three blocks to a local club called, The Wishing Well. We parked and went in the back door, walking up to the bar. The bartender at The Wishing Well greeted my partner by name and set two coffee cups down. He filled one cup half full of whiskey and topped it off with black coffee. He then looked at me.

"You want the same?" he asked.

"No thanks, I'll take cream and sugar with mine," I said.

The bartender shrugged as he went to collect the sugar and cream for my coffee. The juke box blasted country music and the blue collar crowd was having a good time. We drank two cups of coffee fixed the same way and walked back to the car. Glen cleared with radio and then drove the car directly into Pier Park. We didn't talk or chat. He went up over the curb, around the pool building, stopping short near a grove of trees, and then turned off the engine and killed the lights. Glen took off his gun belt and got a blanket and pillow out of the trunk. "Answer the radio, but don't volunteer for nothin' kid!" he said, lying down in the back seat. Jesus! I felt like I was having a flashback! Glen had a full-time job doing Formica and vinyl floors during the day. With two cups of whiskey in him, he was asleep in five minutes. I sat in the front seat stony faced, and as soon as he started snoring, I reached over and set the electronic siren switch to the yelp position, got out of the car, quietly closed the door and walked away. When he woke up and turned on the ignition, the siren would go on instantly. It was a prank cops played on each other, for one reason or another and I relished that I was doing it to him. He was after all a fuck-off cop. I walked the mile and a half back to the precinct cussing most of the way. Mentally, I was preparing myself for Sergeant Blackwood. I had to set him straight right off the bat. The sergeant was surprised to see me when I walked into his office, with a pissed off look on my face.

"What's going on? Where's your partner?" he asked.

"You can find that fat old drunk in Pier Park, sleepin' like a baby!" I responded, almost shouting.

"What?!" he said incredulously.

"I'm not going to work with a partner like that! Not now! Not ever!" As I'd suspected he would, Sergeant Blackwood jumped up angry, and sputtering from behind his desk. "Listen kid, I'm in charge here and I make the assignments. You work where I tell you to work!" he told me. "Look Sergeant, I came out here to *work!* Not sleep with some lazy, drunk, fuck-off cop in the park. Now if you have a problem with me doin' good police work here, then you can call the captain, the chief or anybody else you like!" I pumped up my aura and glared directly into his eyes. Maintaining eye contact, I brazenly walked around and behind the counter and took the keys to the sergeant's own unmarked car off the key rack. I wrote myself in on the duty roster, as a wild-car, signing my name in an angry flourish, turned on my heel and stomped out to work. A wild-car is on duty, but not assigned to a specific area, so it's free to roam through all districts. The Sergeant didn't offer any protest and said nothing as I walked out the door with the keys to his unmarked patrol car. After getting into the car, I took a moment to gloat. I had stared down Sergeant Blackwood and won. I felt good about that, because I knew I'd done the right thing. I just wanted to work. I was a police officer. I wanted to go out and help citizens, arrest criminals and make a difference. I was 28-years old and still young enough to be an idealist. As soon as I turned on the radio, within only a couple of seconds, a call came out. "Any car to cover a motorcycle accident?" asked the dispatcher, "4500 block on North Columbia?" No answer. What the hell, I'm probably the only cop *awake*, I thought to myself.

"Any car for a 12-9 on this accident?" cracked the radio.

"49, I'll take the call, 12-9 on a cycle down," I said.

The motorcycle was down on the pavement, crumpled up at the base of a power pole. The rider was off the road in some blackberry brambles about sixty feet away. He had died instantly. I could tell by the way the body was positioned that several leg bones were broken, as well as his neck and there was just a bloody mess left inside the poor guy's helmet. Motorcycle helmets were good for one thing; it kept the remains in a container. And it made the coroners job just a little easier. "49, this is a single vehicle fatal," I said to the dispatcher. "Send the coroner and a traffic car."

In about five minutes, the traffic officer arrived. How nice, I thought, to be able to turn this mess over to a traffic cop. I hated fatals, and was glad I didn't have to work this one. I never got used to seeing the blood and the gore and this accident was a bloody mess. I put some flares out for the traffic officer and left. The coroners van was just arriving, as I pulled away. I felt sorry for him having to see what I'd just seen, as I nodded to him, grimly.

By now it was five in the morning so I drove to the Burger Barn for coffee and a cheeseburger. It was the only all night coffee and greasy hamburger place open on Union Avenue. They had a little gambling in the back room on weekends, but it was a popular coffee stop for hungry cops late at night, working graveyard. We looked the other way about the intermittent gambling that occurred there and never did anything about it. The owners and their friends never got into any serious trouble or made any problems, which accounted for our leniency. As I sipped the hot coffee and scarfed the cheese burger, I thought about my first shift at North. The swing shift lieutenant was drinking beer in his office and looking at porn when I came to work and making no attempt to hide it. I left a drinking-and-driving partner asleep in Pier Park and had a shouting match with another old timer sergeant. And then I got to see another mangled dead body. I had to have another cup of coffee on that one. What the hell! I knew it wasn't going to be easy. It would take some time to establish myself at North, but time was on my side. I paid for my coffee and cheeseburger and left. It bothered the waitress; she stood there confused, looked down at the bill, back up at me, then down at the bill again. I smiled and waved as I walked out the door. It was clear, this lady wasn't used to seeing a cop pay for anything. She was a skinny, elderly black woman and who knows how many years she had poured free coffee and laid down free cheese burgers for Portland's Finest.

    I spent the time driving to work the next night psyching myself up for my next encounter with the sergeant. I was unsure what might happen after the previous night's yelling match, but I wanted to be mentally ready for anything. I got all pumped up for nothing. It was almost a letdown. It was potbelly Glen's regular night off, and Sergeant Blackwood was decent, with a polite demeanor. It was like he didn't remember the previous night. When he read through the district assignments he looked right at me and said, "DuPay, you'll be car 49, wild." Right on! I thought to myself. He's decided not to fuck with me. He's made the right decision and he's going to let me work! Of course the real reason Blackwood gave me the wild car was because word had gotten around about my outburst the night before and no one wanted to work with me. These guys were all old timers with day jobs and they used the profession of police work to get money for basically doing nothing or very little. They were afraid I might keep them awake doing police work when they wanted to sleep at night.

    As soon as I turned on the car ignition, the radio cracked, "Any car for a shooting, 7900 block North Jersey?" I took a deep breath. "49, I'll cover the call," I said, hitting the red light as I took off. I could handle it. My equipment was ready. My new five-cell flashlight was reinforced with hack saw blades and electrical tape. My .38 was loaded with hot loads. My .25 automatic back-up gun was in my pocket and I had a new night stick. I was ready. When I approached the address, I saw a middle-aged, thin, white woman waving frantically and yelling for help, crying that her daughter had been shot. "She's been shot! Oh, God, she's been shot! My little girl! My little girl!" She was completely naked, terrified and hysterical. I slammed the car into park, jumped out and opened the trunk, knowing there would be a grey wool blanket inside. I retrieved the blanket, covered her, and led her into the back seat of the squad car, telling her to stay put until I could come back.

I entered the home, with my gun drawn, and seeing the first floor was clear, I raced upstairs. After finding the location of the bathroom I discovered a young woman's body slumped over and wedged between the empty bath tub and the toilet. She was wearing a tattered and now bloody pink nightgown and had been shot in the head at close range. A .30 .30 rifle casing lay on the floor. The bullet passed through the right side of her skull, near the temple and blew away the entire back portion of her skull. The damage to the back of her head made her face and facial bones appear as if they had collapsed. She no longer looked human, but rather like the bloody fright mask of someone with a deformed and concave face. The bullet passing through the daughter's skull had sprayed small, white, bone fragments and brain tissue up against the tile wall and mirror. The blood and brain matter dripped slowly down the bathroom mirror.

The woman told me her son in-law had shot her daughter in the upstairs bathroom of the home they all lived in. "And then he shot at me, too!" she cried, "As I was gettin' ready for bed and before he ran outa the house!" The dead girl's mother was crying her eyes out and I tried to comfort her as best I could. It was not easy. I was a 28-year old kid trying to comfort a woman in her fifties who had just seen her daughter murdered with a rifle at close range. She told me her daughter had wanted to get out of an unhappy marriage, but the husband had killed her daughter, rather than let her go. Well, she was out of the relationship now. Back at the car, I told radio, "49, this is a homicide, get the detectives out here!" Detectives covered all homicide scenes and they were welcome to this one. In a few minutes the homicide Dicks arrived and took over. The picture of the bone chips and blood running down the mirror, it still sticks in my mind to this day. The bastard must have been crazy. He blew his wife's brains out in the bathroom with a .30 .30 hunting rifle. Didn't they believe in divorce in St. Johns?

Headstones and Traffic Tickets

BEATING THE QUOTA

North Precinct had the same traffic ticket quota as the other precincts, twelve per man, per month. I never had any trouble writing twelve tickets per month because I was always out working and looking for violators. Once in a while, someone would show up in traffic court to contest one of my tickets. That was pretty normal for me. I noticed however, that the other officers on my crew rarely had a violator show up, and that could *not* have been normal. I couldn't figure it out for the longest time, why so many other officers never had anyone show up to contest their tickets. It took me a while but the mystery was soon solved. Working alone at night, I often spent a lot of time patrolling deserted alleys, side streets and parks in the darkest hours of the night, with my car lights off. I was always trying to sneak up on any potential bad guys. I would drive around slowly, looking for stolen cars, stolen TVs, or burglars on the prowl. I'd also look for any storefront doors or back doors pried open, along with other night people who might be up to no good. The whole time lamenting the fact that I was handicapped by having to drive an obvious marked car. I made the most of it, by turning off my lights as I snooped around neighborhoods and kept an eye out.

One night, as I was patrolling the Pioneer Cemetery, just off Columbia Boulevard, with my lights off as usual, I noticed a North Precinct police car parked at the far end of the cemetery, about a block away. The cars had a precinct letter designation painted on the trunk. For example, C for central, E for East and N for North. On this particular car, I saw an N, designating it a North precinct car, and I recognized the officer. He was one of the pot bellied, old timers and he was standing near a headstone writing something on a clip board, and completely oblivious to my presence a block away. He had his flashlight on and it was tucked under his left arm, pointed at the headstone, so he could see. Suddenly it clicked; this officer was writing down the names engraved on the headstones. For a moment I just sat there, astonished. I couldn't believe what I was seeing. This would explain so much. I then quietly backed out of the cemetery and he never knew I'd been there watching him.

Some of the cops at the precinct were writing traffic tickets and pedestrian citations to dead people! Of course. That's why no one showed up in court. The warrants were being issued to dead people. This practice was common knowledge, I later came to find out, among patrolman, but it took me a while to figure out what was going on. I don't know how many of the sergeants or lieutenants knew about this practice but all the patrolmen knew, so it's safe to presume they *all* knew. Seeing that officer, writing down bogus names on a clipboard added to my level of disgust at the relentless shenanigans going on at North Precinct. I had requested a transfer to work at North because I wanted to work the geographical area but I was fully aware it was also where most of the misfit cops worked, doing no work at all and wasting taxpayers' dollars. A warrant for a dead person! It was the old timers' way of dealing with the quota and still being able to sleep all night on their shifts, so they could work day jobs and get paid double. If you missed your traffic quota, then you worked desk duty. If you had desk duty, you had to stay *awake*. Thanks to those resting in peace in the cemetery, the old timers could rest in peace in the back seat of their patrol cars. I always felt that was adding insult to injury: you're dead and now there's a warrant out for you too? Boy, the citizens sure were taking it in the shorts.

New Blood

FINALLY SOME HELP

Another new officer soon showed up on the graveyard shift. His name was Ray Jones and I wondered out loud why he had transferred to North. We were in the officers' lounge dressing for work, when I asked him. "What's a nice guy like you doing in a screwed up precinct like this?" Ray chuckled and said "I live a few miles up the river in Scappoose, and this is the closest precinct to my house. It's as simple as that." I gave him a rundown on what to expect; the sleeping, the drinking and the trips to the cemetery for bogus names—unless he wanted to work with *me*. His options were simple, work all night with me? Or sleep all night with one of the old timers, in a stuffy car. Ray wanted to work. We went downstairs to talk it over with Sergeant Blackwood.

The swing shift lieutenant, Lieutenant Ohren, was in his office drinking beer and reading porno magazines as usual. Sergeant Blackwood was making up the duty assignments for the next week in an adjacent office, and as Ray and I walked in, he closed the door for privacy. I had no trouble convincing Sergeant Blackwood to let Ray and I work together, but I wanted to work the ghetto, which was district 72 over in the North End. The sergeant frowned. He didn't think we had enough experience to handle it. "Bullshit!" I told him, "I can handle it!" I pumped myself up, sticking my chest out and raising my chin slightly in defiance. I wanted him to see that I was capable, aggressive and confident. What was he going to say anyway? That I should work with Potbelly Glen or some other *sleeping beauty*? Seeing my determination, he said "I'll make you guys a deal, okay? Take the downtown St. Johns district for a few weeks and if you do a good job with it, I'll give you the ghetto." It seemed fair. "It's a deal," I said and we all shook hands on it. The Sergeant didn't want another, young hard charger, like DuPay, annoying the guys who wanted to sleep at night, so he gladly allowed Ray and I to work together, if only to get us off his back.

Ray and I would start our shift by checking many of the area bars and taverns all through St. Johns proper. In many of these dives, the bartenders would serve alcohol until the customers fell off the stools and passed out. Those who hadn't passed out in their beer would drive home drunk. We would pick out two or three of the drunkest each night, and arrest them for being drunk in public. Then the state liquor commission would come out and give the bartender a ticket for serving drunks. Three tickets for the same thing, and the commission would lock the tavern doors for a couple of weeks. This action hurt the owners in their wallet and gradually they started to pay attention when Ray and I walked through the door. The cab drivers loved us though, because they got more fares from all the drunks.

A Troubled Teen

FOOTPRINTS IN THE SNOW

"Car 43, take a burglary of the service station, 8500 block North Lombard," the radio cracked. "Car 43 copies," said Ray. We saw the service station owner standing by the front door. He had discovered the break-in and called us. The burglar had entered the station by climbing up a pile of old tires, near the outside of the building, and breaking out a top window. He climbed through the broken window and jumped down into the service bay. I noticed a wallet on the floor below the broken window, and a few drops of blood. "Does this wallet belong to anybody you know?" I asked the owner, showing him the wallet.

"Sure don't," he said.

Maybe this one would be easy, I thought. Ray went through the papers in the wallet, and discovered it belonged to a 17-year-old boy who lived about ten blocks away. We drove to the address provided by the wallet and woke up the boy's parents. The father was standing in the doorway wearing an old burgundy colored robe. The mother was behind him looking over his shoulder, fearfully. We introduced ourselves and handed the wallet to the father.

"That's my son's wallet," he said, "Where'd you get it?"

"He left it inside the service station he burglarized down on Lombard Street," said Ray.

"Now wait a minute, officers! That couldn't be *my* son!"

"And you'll find that he's cut his hand, too," continued Ray.

We followed the boy's father upstairs to his son's bedroom. The boy hadn't been home long. He was still sweaty and his face was flushed a bright pink. Toilet paper was wrapped around his thumb stemming the flow of blood, as he lay in bed with the covers pulled to his chin, fully clothed. "Where's your wallet son?" asked Ray. The boy sat up but didn't respond, and simply hung his head, as he grasped his thumb. I felt really bad for the parents. They had no idea their son was a burglar in his spare time. The dad began yelling at the kid, and the mother was crying and yelling at him, too. We took the boy into custody and booked him into juvenile hall. Dad would miss a day of work to be in court, we knew. A few weeks later we caught the same boy again. Apparently, he hadn't learned his lesson. The boy had pried open the back alley door of the neighborhood theater and broken in. Ray and I discovered the door ajar when we cruised through the alley. This kid wasn't having any luck at all. While he was inside burglarizing the theater, it had started to snow outside, quite heavily in fact, as it was the middle of winter. When the boy walked out the back door, with what little money he could find in the theater, and a bag of popcorn, he left fresh foot prints in the snow—all the way home. "Your son's got a problem," I told the boy's father, as I stood in his living room, with my arms crossed over my chest.

"He's a burglar, but not a very smart one yet—because he walked home in the snow which led us directly to him. We just kept following his footprints. I'd watch him, if I were you. Watch him close." Later, as I led the boy to the patrol car, I looked over at the father. He seemed like any typical, exhausted, working man, trying to do the right thing and take care of his family. "You need to know where he is at night," I told the father, over my shoulder. "He needs better supervision than he's getting," I added, as I approached the patrol car. The father nodded his head and said nothing, as he slowly closed the front door to his home. I never saw the boy again and never heard any more about him. There are always calls that stand out in the mind of a cop; what happened to that person? How are they doing? The reality is, there are generally too many calls to follow up on. I wondered about the boy every now and then and never forgot the amusement that Ray and I felt, while we casually followed those footprints in the snow, to where they would lead us.

Going Back to the Ghetto

THE OLD GANG

During the first month Ray and I worked together, we served thirty-nine warrants for theft, burglary, and larceny. I couldn't believe so many people were just out walking around, or sitting on bar stools, in St. Johns, *wanted* like that. Not for murder or rape maybe, but wanted just the same. It was a tough neighborhood, St. Johns. But the neighborhood I wanted was even tougher. After about a month, I got it. We were called into Sergeant Blackwood's office one day in early spring. The sergeant began to congratulate Ray and I on having done a good job together in St. Johns, and having done "good police work," there. It was a useful but slightly dishonest show of support. Sergeant Blackwood merely tolerated Ray and I, and did what he could to keep us out of the way of the old timers, who were his friends and who openly disliked us for our gung-ho, superior attitude. We took police work seriously and took pride in our profession, whereas they apparently, did not.

I *knew* the old timers disliked us, (there were about eight of them) and they were often grumbling that Ray and I were making them look bad. *It wasn't hard.* These guys hadn't served thirty nine warrants all year. The Sergeant kept his promise, though, because he wanted nothing more than to be rid of us. But in this instance, two goals were aligned. Sergeant Blackwood kept his promise to us and gave us District 72, *and* got us out of his hair at the same time. District 72, as my old training grounds, was an area of town I liked and felt at home in. It had Van's Olympic Room, on Vancouver and Fremont, The Red Sands, The Theme, Kings Tavern, The Paragon Club and all the trouble makers I'd gotten to know, and arrest. Trouble makers like LeRoy Clark, Big Jim, Thelma Moody, Pam Owens, Candy Canyon, Buck Owens and an assortment of other small time crooks. There was more going on in District 72, than in almost all the other districts. It was where the hookers and the drugs were at, and if you were an ambitious cop, and wanted to make arrests, District 72 was the place to be. I wanted to get back to where the action was at, because it was not in St. Johns.

A cop is only as good as his information, so I set out to keep good note-books. Good basic files, added to a little bit at a time. I kept copies of mugshots of known criminals and a list of their associates and the cars they drove, a file of street names or nicknames, a list of after-hours joints, gambling houses, prostitutes and their *cribs* where they lived. As people crossed our path, they were added to my growing files. Already in the files were people we had met, like Buck Owens, Pam, Thelma, LeRoy, and Big Jim. Ah yes, Big Jim! We had some unfinished business to discuss. I wanted to stick a meat cleaver up his ass. But more on that later.

All night we drove the streets and back alleys of our district. I wanted to know the location of all the dead ends and the alleys and short cuts through the streets. No surprises. Soon we were comfortable with the area and knew most of the regulars and all the cars. When a new face or car drove through the neighborhood, we made it our business to know who was in it, by pulling them over. I always tried to be the kind of cop I'd want in my own neighborhood. The kind of cop who knew what was going on, where anything might be happening, and why. We knew we had three bars that were trouble spots and we set out to know who the patrons were and what kind of action went on inside.

Van's Olympic Room was the first stop. We parked in the alley behind Van's and went in the front door. Van was sitting at the end of the bar, drinking coffee and chain smoking. LeRoy was behind the bar fixing drinks and Thelma was sitting on the piano taking a break. I could see Big Jim working in the kitchen. It was like old times. I introduced Ray to Van, as "My new partner, Ray." We told him we were the new regular district officers and would be by often. Van motioned for LeRoy to come over and meet us. LeRoy didn't seem very happy to see me, saying only "Yeah, we've met." He was remembering a ticket from the liquor commission for serving alcohol to Pam. "Who's the new face?" I asked, nodding towards another exotic dancer I hadn't seen before.

"That's Myra," LeRoy said, smiling dreamily. "Her name is Myra." We paid for our coffee and left. "Well, what do you think about Van's?" I asked Ray as we drove off. "I don't know about Van himself," Ray said, "but LeRoy is into something heavy. Big Jim is just there. Thelma is a convicted prostitute and I'll bet Myra is too." I couldn't help but smile. Ray had gotten it all spot-on. After checking with records, we found Myra had a mug shot and a record for prostitution, going back to when she was a minor. Myra was 21-years old, and though she was not as pretty as Thelma or Pam, she had a great body and was an energetic and cheerful piano dancer. Unlike some of the other dancers, Myra was friendly and flirtatious with the police. We added her to our files. Van now had *two* prostitutes working in the place.

"Car 72?" asked the dispatcher.

"Go ahead," said Ray.

"Car 72, take a knifing outside the Paragon Club, 800 block of North Killingsworth."

"72 copies, we're on the way," said Ray.

The Paragon Club, was one of our three problem bars on our list. We were headed there already, we might just as well start with a knifing, I thought to myself. When we arrived, we saw a drunk man out in front of the club waving a paring knife around and swearing incoherently. He was cussing at another man who was sitting at the curb holding a handkerchief around his cut hand. "Drop the knife and come over here!" I ordered loudly. The guy was too drunk to be *really* dangerous. He staggered toward me, mumbling obscenities under his breath and at the last minute, he lunged at me with the knife. I was ready for him and hit his knife hand with my night stick. He let go of the knife, which went flying and looked surprised, too drunk to feel much pain. Ray had put a temporary bandage on the victim's knife wound, using a first-aid kit from the trunk of the patrol car. "Car 72," Ray said to the dispatcher, "send us the paddy wagon and an ambulance. The victim will need some stitches."

We arrested the knifer for being drunk and disorderly and for assault. When 99 came rolling up and the ambulance left, we went inside to talk to the club owner. The Paragon Club was a blue collar bar catering mostly to white truckers and laborers. The front door opened directly onto Killingsworth Street and as you walked in the door, you had to negotiate two foos-ball tables, two pool tables, and a shuffleboard table, before you could get close enough to the bar to sit down. It was a dump. The shuffleboard table was always busy and the bar stools were all filled. This was another operation where alcohol was served on demand regardless of the drunken condition of the patrons. Ray and I introduced ourselves to the owner and told him what we expected of him.

"You can't keep serving patrons until they get this drunk" I told the man firmly, motioning outside to the area of the fight.

"Are you crazy?" he asked me sarcastically.

"This is a bar, people come in here to get drunk—that's how I make my money!"

"Not anymore! Don't serve *anybody* already intoxicated or else!" I ordered.

"Or else what?" the bar owner challenged, not realizing our power to close down the bar. I bent over the counter and motioned him over, with my right hand. He sullenly ambled over and leaned forward across the counter. I whispered into his ear, with as much sarcasm and threat as I could muster, "Or else you'll have to find another way to make a living! And we'd like two cups of coffee please!" The owner's bad attitude was the direct result of a district cop never having been in the place or laying down the rules of appropriate conduct. He continued to act defiant and insulted, as he turned his back and started to walk away to get our coffee. Here this guy was, serving drinks to people visibly drunk, resulting in bloody knife fights and general chaos in the street, and defending *his* right to serve alcohol to any adult who had the price of a drink. "Hey! You get back here!" I shouted. He turned around and walked back. "We just had a knife-fight out front, with one of your God damned Beer Bottle Tigers! Someone could have been killed! I'm gonna tell you again, do NOT serve anyone already intoxicated! DO you understand me?!"

He slid the coffee cups across the bar to us, his mouth a tight line and gave us a reluctant, terse nod. He wasn't used to being told how to conduct his business by cops and was clearly embarrassed, as the other patrons watched the exchange curiously. We stood by the front door of the tavern, leaning into the wall, for another twenty minutes, nonchalantly drinking our coffee and making people nervous. We were determined to make some changes in this part of town. Ray put a dollar on the bar to cover the coffee and we left.

Later, in the car the radio cracked, "Car 72, cover a silent alarm at the Lampus store on NE Union, 2500 block," said the dispatcher. The department store was just over the precinct boundary in east territory and we would be covering the East Precinct officers who had already been called. It was a large store, set on an entire city block which sold things as varied as perfume, skin cream, lingerie and furniture. When we arrived, Ray ran in back to cover the loading dock and I climbed a steep fire access ladder to the roof.

I noticed an East Precinct officer, Phil Todd, was already on the roof. Just then we heard glass shattering from down below and the burglar broke out through a glass front door and ran down Knott Street. Todd fired three rounds after the burglar, as he fled down the street. CABOOM! CABOOM! CABOOM! Each shot echoed across the street and into the dark night. Magnum hits. I could see the slugs hitting the sidewalk and leaving sparks in their wake, but as it turned out, the burglar escaped into the shadows. When I climbed down from the roof, a burly East sergeant in his fifties pulled up in his car. "What the hell you firing up there? It sounded like heavies to me!" he said to Officer Todd accusingly. "Bullshit Sergeant. You know we can't carry magnums," Todd replied calmly, as he looked down at the sergeant on the street. "Well, see that you *don't!*" yelled the sergeant out the car window. The sergeant drove away, clearly not wanting to know the truth. Ray and I walked to the sidewalk where the burglar had been running. We could see the gouges in the concrete where the slugs had hit. We chuckled to ourselves. They were magnums alright.

Walking the Alleys

CROWBARS AND BACK DOORS

NORTH MISSISSIPPI AVENUE RAN FOR about ten blocks through our ghetto district. It was dotted with taverns and boarded up store fronts, and an old abandoned neighborhood theater. Mom and Pop Opperman, an old white couple, ran a small grocery store on Mississippi and Skidmore. Opperman was having trouble making ends meet and started keeping the store open longer hours. An alley ran behind these taverns and stores and often customers would park in the back. During the hours between three and five in the morning, the streets and sidewalks were deserted. You could fire a cannon down the avenue and it wouldn't hit anything. During this time of the night, Ray and I would search the alleys and back streets, looking for burglars and other night people up to no good. We often parked the car on a side street and would walk down the alleys quietly in the dark. Ray would take the opposite end of the alley and we would walk towards each other, hoping to flush someone out.

One night, we were walking the alley behind Mississippi Avenue. I saw a cigarette glow in the dark behind Opperman's store. We stopped to watch and were able to make out a black man wearing dark clothing standing in the shadows. We turned on our flashlights at the same time. "Police officers! Put your hands where we can see them!" Ray ordered. As the guy's hands went up, a 36-inch crow bar fell out from under his jacket, clattering loudly on the ground. "Whacha doin' at four in the morning behind a grocery store with a crow bar?" I asked the man, my voice dripping with sarcasm. "Fuck you! I ain't doin' nothin!" he muttered. "Turn your ass around!" I ordered. He was arrested without incident and we put him in jail for violation of the after-hours ordinance and threw his crow bar in the trash. While I rarely arrested people for the after-hours law—because I believed it to be unconstitutional,

I did use it to arrest *this* man. "That fucker was gonna hit old man Opperman's grocery store!" Ray said indignantly. We both felt good about catching *this* bad guy.

Tying up Loose Ends

AND ABOUT THAT MEAT CLEAVER!

One night after Van's had closed, we saw LeRoy's tan Cadillac and Big Jim's beater Chevy leave the parking lot together. Big Jim's tail light was out. "Now's your chance to talk to Jim alone," Ray suggested with a wry smile. "Don't you have a bone to pick with him? Something about a meat cleaver?" Ray asked, with a smile. I nodded solemnly. "Yeah, I do. But wait a minute," I said, "Let's follow them first and see where they go." I turned off the car lights and we followed them, keeping a safe distance away. The two cars stayed in traffic together and drove directly to one of the known after-hour's clubs; Mary's Place on 14th and Killingsworth. "There must be something happening. Let's hang around and see who else shows up," I suggested. Ray parked the car about a block away and we sat back, leaning into the seats to watch. A black Cadillac pulled on by and went around the block and came back again. It parked about a block away and the driver got out and went in. We recognized the woman as Mary Taylor—the notorious Madam. She was with an Asian man I also recognized as a Chef who worked in one of the Chinese restaurants in the North End. "An interesting crowd," I said to Ray. "Let's send a short report to the narcs on this meeting. They're probably dealing heroin and the guys in narc are gonna wanna know." As we watched, Big Jim came out and drove off in his old Chevy, with one tail light out. We stopped him about ten blocks away. He pulled over when he saw the flashing light.

"Hey, Jim, remember *me*?" I asked brightly, smiling big.

"Your tail lights out! Gimme your driver's license!" I demanded, the smile instantly leaving my face. "And by the way, who are you visiting this time of night?"

"Sorry," he began pleasantly, "bout the tail light bein' broke. Been meanin' to get that fixed."

"Is that right?"

"Jes' stopped by to visit some friends over at Mary's after work."

"You know Mary's a convicted prostitute don't you?"

"Nah, she jus a workin' woman. She good people."

He handed me a social security card with a hopeful smile on his face.

"This *isn't* a license!"

"Well, y'all *know* who I am, and I can't find it right now."

"I'm gonna ticket you for that one, Jim! Driving without a license, and having a burnt-out tail light." Then I got down to why I'd really stopped him.

"And while we're at it, WHY did you bar the door, and wave that meat cleaver at me that night at Van's?!" I asked aggressively, leaning into the window and getting into his face. "Gee, Mr. Don, I'm real sorry 'bout that night. I jus' wasn't sure 'bout your intentions is all."

"Do you know I coulda *shot* you?!"

"Well, I knew LeRoy called fer the police to come, and you couldn't have hurt me with that little pop gun you had," he said, smiling up at me.

"Jesus Jim, you're crazy! Get your tail light fixed and go home." Ray motioned for me to come back to the police car. I glowered at Big Jim, before turning my back to walk back to the patrol car. "Come on!" Ray said, "we've got a call; a 12-9 on a wreck on Interstate Street and Killingsworth." When we arrived, we could tell somebody must be dead, even before we stopped. One car had hit another broadside at the intersection. There were parts all over the street—just parts. Car parts here and body parts there. It was the worst accident I'd ever seen. One driver was crushed in his car and the other driver was all over the street. "72, we're 10-97. This is a double fatal. We need a traffic car and the coroner," said Ray. "On the way 72," said dispatch. After looking over the accident scene, I walked back to the car and called the dispatcher. "72, we need the Fire Department out here to wash down some of this blood and tissue," I told him. "10-4," said the dispatcher.

After looking around I could see that there was a large pool of blood on the sidewalk. Hair, blood and body parts were everywhere. I walked to a nearby telephone pole and reached up with my right arm extended, placing my palm flat against it for support as I took in the horrendous scene and tried to figure out how to proceed. Suddenly, I felt the heavy, thick sound of something dripping on me. I looked up, directly above me and saw a chunk of cream colored brain tissue, dripping blood, and clinging to the middle of a nearby telephone pole. I stepped out of the way, to avoid more blood falling on me, and took out my handkerchief to wipe off the droplets that had landed on my right wrist. The feeling of blood falling on me from such a distance was grotesque and unnerving. I couldn't wipe it off fast enough. The guy had been hit so hard he just *blew* up. We roped off the scene, to keep everyone away and let the fire department and the coroner do their jobs.

Two more mangled bodies to remember, I thought, in the back of my mind. When I got home and into bed all I could do was toss and turn. I couldn't sleep. I got out of bed, put on my robe and poured some coffee. I had to fill my mind with something besides dead people. When I couldn't sleep at night, I studied. I was studying for promotion to detective. Officers qualified for promotion after five years' service, and I definitely planned on being a detective. Outside of the chief's job, a detective was the most prestigious position within the bureau. I always enjoyed working the streets but I had no intention of being a career patrolman. I wanted to become a detective. I had a detectives study guide, and another more detailed reading list I had typed up, that was taped to my work desk at home. I opened the biggest book I'd recently purchased, a book entitled "Police Administration," by O. W. Wilson, and started reading and taking notes. I also had another book, about forensic science that I studied, which included photos of gunshot wounds, stab wounds, bitten off nipples and other gruesome death photos. Working nights, sleeping days and trying to study for detective too, was hard, but I would be prepared come test date—I'd be ready.

In my police career, I began to encounter two opposite societies, co-existing in the same city in Portland; the night world and the straight working world, with one culture barely aware of the other's existence. Day people, are those folks hustling and bustling to work, then scurrying home at night. Time to fix dinner, pick the kids up from band practice, watch the six o'clock news, and hope there was enough money in the checking account to pay the car insurance. Night people had different concerns, more pressing than kids and car insurance. Most were driven by their addiction to drugs, alcohol and fast money. "Why work when I can get bitches to bring me money?" one pimp asked me smugly during an interrogation. "Shit man, I can make three-four hundred dollars a day hookin' and no taxes!" boasted a prostitute I sometimes talked to.

"I can make more money in a day than straight people make in a week," said a dope dealer.

"I'm jes a business man," said one of the after-hours operators. "People don't wanna quit drinkin' and dancin' just cause the legit bars is closed!" Supply and demand; it's the only law the night people understand. And there's an army of them. Hookers worked not only out of Van's Olympic Room but also The Cotton Club, The Texas Playhouse, The Paradise Club, The Theme, The Top Hat, and The BelAire. They worked the fancy hotels and clubs downtown, and they walked the streets, working out of an endless stream of cheap motels on the Avenue.

"Moody," was a pimp who ran a regular trap line of girls and that included Thelma and Myra. His real name was Jaynolen Moody. But we preferred calling him Moody, because that was his last name and he had a bad attitude about cops. He kept a girl or two working in some of these clubs, like Van's and The Cotton Club. He'd run back and forth in his black Cadillac Eldorado convertible, collecting the cash and keeping his stable in line. Ray and I succeeded in this environment because we were pragmatic about it. The hookers and pimps knew that as long as they didn't beat or rob the tricks, we'd treat them fairly. But drug addiction drives the need for cash, fast cash and lots of it.

Blood and Spit

ON THE AVENUE

King's Tavern on North Williams Avenue, was a haven for drug dealers, and was the worst of all the dump taverns in our district. It was one of three hot spots, that Ray and I had scheduled for improvement and we considered it one of our special projects. Prior to our taking over district 72, where King's Tavern was located, there was a stabbing or a shooting there, at least once a week. With no parking lot for customers, any trouble spilled right onto Williams Avenue. Driving by we'd see people milling around, couples fighting, cussing, drinking out of beer bottles and causing general chaos. The first time Ray and I went into King's Tavern was in late 1965. We parked the police car by the front door, for effect. We elbowed our way through the crowd milling around outside by the front door and pushed our way inside. We could tell it had been a long time since any policemen had been in the tavern, because the bartender asked nervously, "Uh, what can I get for you guys?"

"Nothing, thank you. We're just here to introduce ourselves and see what's going on," I said cheerfully.

"Oh, okay" he said, with apprehension written all over his face.

"I'm Officer Don DuPay and this is my partner Ray Jones. We're going to be coming around from now on, to make sure there's no trouble here."

"Okay, uh, are you sure I can't get you anything? You want some coffee, or maybe a beer?"

"No. We don't drink on duty." I told him.

The bar had about fifteen stools and was just inside the door to the right. Behind the bar was a food preparation area, and a chalk board menu advertising chili, hot dogs, and cold sandwiches. An old grey tomcat was snoozing in a basket of folded bar towels, near some loaves of bread and containers of mustard. Real sanitary, I thought. Regular pool and a bumper pool table shared space in the corner with a foosball table and a juke box. The tavern was crowded with too many people who were drunk. Shortly after we walked in, a Mexican guy wearing a dirty Army fatigue jacket spotted us. He appeared nervous, and began to move away from us toward the men's room. I quickly worked my way through the crowd of drunks toward him to see why he wanted to avoid the police. I found him in the restroom hurriedly taking something out of his jacket pocket. When he saw me come in, he put whatever was in his hand into his mouth. I pushed him into the corner by the urinal and grabbed him by the throat, choking him hard. "Spit it out!" I ordered. "Spit it out or I'll *strangle* you!" We struggled and he tried desperately to swallow, but it wouldn't go down. I dug my thumbs into his carotid artery and finally he gave up and spit. Out came five, small, round, blue rubber balloons. I handcuffed him and as he stood there panting in the corner, I took my knife out and cut one of the balloons open. It was full of a brown powder. Three more balloons and a switch blade were in his pocket.

"I'll bet this is heroin! What's your name?" I demanded.

"None of your fuckin' business!"

"Do you know what smack *does* to kids?!"

"Kiss my ass, pig-face. Let me loose and I'll cut your throat!" he said as he tried to spit on me. I backhanded him hard. The black leather sap gloves I was wearing helped. He decided to stop giving me shit. I was tired of low-life criminals either trying to spit on me or smear their blood on me, when I tried to execute a legitimate arrest. I hustled him out of the restroom and pushed him through the crowd. My mind flashed back to all the times I'd been spit on by drunks, drug addicts, wife beaters, and prostitutes. I remembered all the people who had tried to flick or smear their blood on me, after getting their asses kicked due to resisting and I could feel my blood pressure rise. I was glad I had arrested this loser. He was going to jail. The police car was parked close to the front door and Ray had a passed out drunk in custody in the back seat. "My guy's got eight balloons of heroin on him. What'd your guy do?" I asked. "He was passed out in his beer," Ray said with a laugh.

As soon as wagon 99 left with our prisoners, we went back inside and cornered the bartender. We gave him our standard lecture on not serving customers who were already visibly intoxicated, and warned him that the liquor commission would be out to explain the rules later in the week. "You can expect us to be in here *every* night until things change around here!" I said. "And take the damned cat home. You can't have a cat in the tavern, sleeping on the cutting board!" The bartender didn't hear a word I said. He stood there looking scared but it was like talking to the wall. It went in one ear and out the other.

On the next shift, Ray and I wanted the sergeant to check out the action at King's Tavern *with* us. "Car 72, can you have our sergeant meet us at King's?" Ray asked the dispatcher. "Sergeant Blackwood is on the way from the office, 72," said dispatch. When the sergeant arrived, we briefed him on yesterday's events and the three of us walked in together. Three uniformed cops walking in together at once really tightened up the atmosphere. The bartender threw down his bar towel in disgust when he saw us all walking in and copped an attitude. The tomcat was once again curled up asleep on the sandwich cutting board. I nudged Sergeant Blackwood, "Hey Sarge, wanna get a bowl of chili and a sandwich?" I asked him. "I'll buy!" He smirked, "Christ, you'll make me gag!" he said, as he noticed the cat sleeping on the cutting board. We walked around the tavern and picked three of the drunkest customers, taking them into custody for being drunk in public. The next day, the city health department locked the tavern doors. They didn't approve of the tomcat sleeping with the sandwiches. The liquor commission followed up with another three weeks closure, but in the end our efforts were mostly wasted. For several months King's Tavern continued to have shootings and stabbings, mostly drug related, at least once a week.

Self-Defense

OVER A FIVE DOLLAR DEBT

How does a cop get used to seeing people shot up all the time? I saw the consequences of random violence regularly, on my shifts working the streets but I never got used to it. Being a police officer and having to resolve violent altercations every shift wears on you. It takes an emotional and mental toll. One shooting stands out in my mind. "72, take a shooting, 500 block on North Failing Street," cracked the radio. "72 copies, a shooting on Failing," Ray said.

As we pulled up in front of the address we recognized the house, at 511 North Failing Street, as one of the after-hours joints we occasionally had problems with. When we walked up the steps, "Candy," aged forty-six, met us at the door. Candy's real name was Herman J. Canyon, of 84 NE Broadway, and he was known as the vending machine king of NE Portland. He also operated several after-hours clubs. His candy machines, cigarette, pop and snack vending machines were in every black owned business in the North End. Not only was he well-known for his after-hours joints, but he was also very well-liked, and thought of as a legitimate black business man who rarely got into trouble.

On this night, Candy met us at the front door holding the side of his cheek. He was bleeding from several razor slashes on his face and was sopping up the dripping blood with his handkerchief. Candy immediately handed me a snub nosed .38 and said, "The mother fucker tried to cut my throat with a straight razor! I had to kill him!" He was breathing hard, sweating, agitated and upset. He kept repeating, as if he needed us to understand, "I had to kill him. I had to!"

Candy pointed towards the kitchen of the old house, and there in the middle of the floor, lay a motionless black man. James T. Wooten, aged 34, of 543 North Brazee Street lay dead on the floor, flat on his back, legs apart, arms to his sides, with his eyes open and staring sightlessly at the smoke stained ceiling. A bloody straight razor was nearby, on the floor. Blood had oozed from a bullet hole in the center of the stomach, and there were two more obvious bullet holes in the floor. I wondered again, why people always die with their eyes open. It's such an eerie looking sight. I have seen too many people, dead with their eyes open and it was always unnerving.

After walking to the car, I reached in for the mic. "72, get the coroner over here. It might be self-defense, but we're going to take the shooter downtown to talk to the detectives, anyway," I said. Once we got downtown, I handed Candy over to Detective John Terleski. He was on duty and took over the death investigation. Terleski was one of two permanently assigned graveyard detectives who followed up on murders, robberies and various felony arrests. He was a thin, balding old-timer, who believed in doing good police work and had a great deal of experience being an all around good detective.

According to the witnesses we interviewed, the dead man, James Wooten, insisted on collecting five dollars he believed Candy owed him. Candy denied the debt, but Wooten kept after him and finally pulled out a straight razor which he proceeded to threaten Candy with. Candy fled into the kitchen to get away from Wooten, and was pursued and that's when Candy pulled out his .38 and fired two warning shots into the floor. Wooten ignored the gun and lunged at him. After Candy had been slashed in the face several times, he was through trying to reason with the man and shot Wooten in the stomach, killing him.

Candy was originally charged with murder, but then later released from custody and set free by the municipal court judge, a Judge J. J. Labadie, the next morning. The murder charge was dismissed, on the grounds of justifiable homicide. If you are a student of criminal law, this homicide was a textbook case of self-defense and that made Candy's release just and legal. Later, I couldn't help wondering why in hell a man with a razor would attack another man with a .38. And all over a five dollar debt. There are some crazy people in the world and they sometimes wind up dead over a five dollar debt.

Behind Opperman's Store

RANDOM TV'S IN THE MIDDLE OF THE NIGHT

Ray and I were having a lot of success making quality arrests in the middle of the night. Checking side-streets and alleys paid off. We were continually finding thieves trying to break into a store or parked in an alleyway with a carload of TV sets they didn't own and couldn't explain. For instance, the night of January 6, 1967, it was 5:20 am and we had just finished a check of the alley behind Opperman's store. We were exiting the alley, when we observed an old Chevy with no license plate light, driving on Skidmore Street. We pulled it over. The car was occupied by one Caldwell Goodspeed and his brother, Hizedis Goodspeed, and we noticed three brand new TV sets in the back seat. While the Goodspeed brothers waited, we asked radio if they were aware of any burglaries where any new TV's were stolen.

District car 18 reported they had just discovered the Colonial Appliance Center on 2135 SE Division Street had been recently burglarized and several TV sets were missing from the display window. The crime was being reported to dispatch, when Ray and I caught these thieves only minutes after their smash and grab. Almost always it was the need for drugs that were involved in these burglaries. Break into a store and steal some TV's, then sell the TV's for money to a fence, take the money and buy drugs. Like wiping your ass with a hoop, there's no end to it. Ray and I received a written commendation for the arrest of the Goodspeed brothers by Sergeant Phil Smith, and signed by Captain Jim Purcell on September 15, 1967. "...when the officers made this arrest the B & E had not been reported. As a direct result of their work the case was cleared."

I always felt Sergeant Smith gave us that commendation partly because he knew we were awake and working, at 5:20 in the morning, and probably one of few precinct officers that *were* still up and working. Our written commendation's continued, for at least six narcotics arrests. We received mention by two different sergeants. One of the Sergeants, John Roe, wrote a letter of commendation, concerning a narcotics arrest of one Samuel Walker. He wrote on March 4, 1966: "This is typical of the continuous attention to the proper performance of their duties, and more, on the part of these officers. This is just one of numerous instances in which their work is worthy of commendation."

    These commendations were always signed by the North Precinct Captain before being added to our permanent personnel files. The commendations may have looked good on paper, (with Purcell's signature on them) but the North Precinct Captain, Jim Purcell, was a two-faced motherfucker and we couldn't stand each other. I had already been called into his office for a private conversation a few weeks before he'd had to sign the commendation for Ray Jones and me, on capturing the TV thieves. During that short meeting, Purcell told me flatly to "stay away," from a certain black Madam; Miss Mary Williams, whom we knew as Fat Mary and any whorehouse she might be operating. Purcell ended our meeting by asking me sarcastically, as he leaned back in his captain's chair, with his paunch spilling over his too-tight belt, "Do I make myself perfectly clear, DuPay?" I stood in front of him, with my arms clasped behind my back. With my chin raised and my mouth pursed, I said nothing. I looked down my nose at him and we glared at each other with open hostility. The room was quiet. When he realized I would not answer him, he spat out, "dismissed!" I turned on my heel and left.

    This was the second police captain who had tried to make himself "perfectly clear," to me. I had listened politely, realizing that I had just been *ordered* to ignore certain criminal activity. I intended to ignore Captain Jim Purcell Junior instead. I decided neither this captain nor any other captain would *ever* tell me whom not to arrest. I wasn't that kind of cop. I didn't work for *them*; I worked for the citizens. We were clear alright, Purcell was a pimp with a police car and no different than Buck Owens or any other lowlife pimp who would prey on women and live off their suffering, rather than work an honest job. Ultimately, it was Jim Purcell's *leadership* that allowed sleeping on the job, drinking on the job and not only ignoring police work but engaging in criminal activity like creating, maintaining and organizing houses of prostitution in the North End.

One of the few freedoms we have in life is the freedom of choice. We may not want to pay the consequences, but we always have freedom of choice. This private meeting with Captain Purcell made me even *more* determined to make detective and I took a couple extra days off to study and prepare for the exam.

Fat Mary and Sergeant Rich

PROSTITUTION AND REPORT WRITING

A NEW SERGEANT, SHOWED UP ON the graveyard shift and was assigned to supervise the ghetto area. That meant he would be my boss. Whenever a new face transferred into North Precinct, I always tried to find out what they had done wrong to get there, particularly if they might be working with me. "Rich," looked clean-cut and communicated intelligently enough, maybe he would be okay. I would reserve judgment. It was just about ten days later, as I cruised the district, that I noticed a late model, Cadillac sedan that I knew belonged to a convicted prostitute, pull out of the parking lot at Van's Olympic Room. I decided to follow the Cadillac and see where it was going. After about a mile, the driver noticed me following and pulled over to the curb. I drove on by, going slowly and saw the driver was not the black high class hooker, Octavine P. Harrington I had dealt with before—an older, dark skinned and very beautiful prostitute who owned the car—but rather my new sergeant! Fuck! I thought. Another pimp on the police force to deal with.

It had always been hard to do an honest night's work at North Precinct, but two bosses into the hookers was a bit much. To celebrate, I decided to park my police car in front of a certain Madam's whorehouse on North Commercial Street, and do some paper work. "Fat Mary" Williams was not too happy to see my black and white parked right in front of her door again. She stomped out on the front porch and yelled over, "Captain Jim's gonna hear bout dis! You better get outa here DuPay!"

I sat in the driver's seat, my face expressionless, as I slapped my left palm loudly against the outside of the car door two or three times. Then a moment later, I turned on the overhead red flasher and let it spin for a few minutes. Fat Mary stood there in disbelief and finally stomped back into her house, slamming the door behind her and muttering obscenities. Fat Mary was a former prostitute and her habits of dress hadn't changed much. She wore a thick layer of pancake make-up that was too light, bright red lipstick, false eye lashes, and revealing clothing that didn't flatter her obese frame. She generally showed too much cleavage and too much bare belly.

Animals on the Night Shift

OPOSSUMS AND AN ANGRY WOMAN

Ray Jones and I got a call for help one night to a house on fourteenth Avenue, just off Prescott Street. I was still working the North End at this time and the nature of some calls never ceased to amaze me. A woman was yelling at the radio dispatcher about a wild animal stuck under her front porch, hissing and spitting at her, and could the police come and take care of it? We parked in front of the house and walked to the front door where she met us, yelling that there was a wild-looking rat, with a long tail hissing and threatening her. She had a long broomstick she had been poking it with, until it scared her, in its effort to defend itself. "It has a lot of sharp teeth!" she exclaimed, "and it's hairy! How did it get under there anyway?" she demanded. I assured her that I had no idea how it got under her porch or even exactly what the thing was. I'd never seen an animal like it before. Ray and I shined both our flashlights under the porch and saw two frightened, glittering black, beady eyes looking back. It was as far away from us as it could get, trying to get comfortable under the wooden stairs of the front porch. I poked at it and it moved toward me a little, threateningly, with its mouth wide open, glaring and indeed hissing. It scared me too.

From the time I was eleven-years-old, in 1947, I'd been raised in Portland, and had never seen an opossum in the wild. My only remembrance of opossums was from the movie "Bambi," that my family and I saw at the Hollywood Theater, back when I was a kid. The film showed a family of smiling, happy opossums hanging by their tails in a tree. Opossums, apparently, became well-known in Portland in about 1964 when the police began getting calls about "large rats," that were being squashed in the middle of the street by cars. I remember it well.

After a minute or two of discussing the situation with Ray, we realized this animal must be one of those opossum's we'd been hearing about. We then had to figure out how we were going to get it out from under the porch. We poked. It hissed. We poked. It spit, and then hissed more. "It looks like it wants to bite us," said Ray. "Have you got a longer stick?" he asked the lady.

"No! I'm scared of it *too!*" she replied. Just then it hissed again, sounding very cat-like.

"Shoot it! Shoot it! Kill it!" the lady yelled frantically.

Ray and I looked at each other for clues, trying to figure out how to deal with this new, unexpected dilemma. What exactly were we supposed to *do* with this hairy, long tailed monster? "We can't just *shoot* it." I told the woman, growing exasperated with her impatience.

"It'll die right there and stink up the place," I offered, hoping she'd calm down.

"You officers are supposed to DO *something!*" she exclaimed, disappointed that we didn't have our guns out, and wouldn't readily start firing Willy Nilly at the terrified animal. "We need a longer stick," explained Ray. "I'll go find one," he said and disappeared into the street, returning not long after, with a fallen tree branch with some desiccated foliage on the end. We threaded the long Y shaped branch under the porch and succeeded in cornering the now snarling and still very scary looking creature. I kept it pinned down with the longer of the two sticks, while Ray opened the trunk of the police car and retrieved a yellow rain poncho. Ray tore off a few dilapidated slats from the underside of the old porch and made an opening. Now I was able to maneuver the unhappy and very vocal opossum over toward the hole, where it slipped through. Ray captured it in the raincoat on the other side, wrapping it up in the coat, as the animal hissed and struggled. He hurried with the unwanted bundle in his arms and hastily threw it into the trunk of the police car and slammed the lid shut.

The lady was now quite happy that the opossum was gone, smiling, thanking us, and smoothing down her light blue house dress, but we were left with the new dilemma of what the hell we were going to *do* with the animal. After driving around for a while, we drove to a park on Killingsworth Street, drove up over the curb and well into the park. Ray and I got out of the car and stood in front of the trunk, flashlights raised.

"How are we gonna get that thing out?" Ray asked.

"Poke it, maybe it'll jump out," I suggested.

"Why don't you use your night stick?" Ray said.

"Why do they always call *us* for this stuff? Isn't this the Humane Society's job?"

"Let's just get the damn thing outa the car, Don!"

"Alright, I'm gonna do it—you cover me—don't let that thing bite me!"

I opened the trunk with one deft motion. Up close we could see that the opossum did indeed have long, sharp, catlike teeth, and it hissed like a cat too. This was a feral animal and both Ray and I tried to keep our distance and at the same time encourage it to jump out of the trunk. We poked at it with our night sticks until it finally got the hint and jumped out. It waddled off with a hurried, comical gait, into the darkness of the park, a little worse for wear, but still very much alive and unharmed. Ray and I both felt smug. I felt more smug though, because the animal was gone, no shots were fired and it was *Ray's* raincoat that had opossum poop on it.

Killing the Animal of Another

HEARTBREAK IN ST. JOHN'S

COLUMBIA VILLA WAS BASICALLY A slum located in St. Johns, along with University Housing, which was located on the far north side of Columbia Villa and just as seedy and troublesome. St. Johns was so poorly thought of as a neighborhood, at the time, this being the middle 1960s, that the city dump was located there. The Villa was cheaply constructed during WWII as temporary housing for the burgeoning number of workers coming to build Liberty ships at the Swan Island shipyard. Columbia Villa had long ago ceased to be temporary housing by the time Ray and I were working as street cops there. And the complex had deteriorated into slum conditions with low income neighbors constantly fighting and drinking, and drinking and fighting, with a huge domestic violence problem.

Come summertime, folks would sit on their small front stoop, drinking and yelling at their neighbors, or yelling at their numerous neighbor's dogs who would run through anyone's yard, sniffing, peeing and pooping, and generally running wild. Ray and I could count on at least two calls a shift when we were assigned to District 42 where Columbia Villa was located. During one of those shifts, radio gave us a call to *see the man*. I hated calls that came out as just *see the man*. This meant the dispatcher wasn't able to get sufficient information from the caller, but knew he should send the district car to *see the man* anyway.

The address was located in Columbia Villa near Portsmouth Street and when we arrived we found a tall, thin, middle-aged man wearing worn blue jeans, and a gas station attendant's uniform shirt, stained with motor oil. The man was kneeling by his dog, on the overgrown front lawn of the house. The dog was bleeding from a wound on the back of its neck that appeared to be a simple flesh wound.

The shaggy brown dog looked up at me, whimpered and coughed.

"What happened?" I asked.

"That bastard shot my dog!" He pointed to a rundown, splotchy, blue house next door and up at a second story window. The window was open and a tattered, dirty white curtain hung out far enough to catch the breeze. "That bastard shot my dog," the man repeated "and I don't have a car to take Buddy to the vet" he said despairingly, with tears welling in his eyes.

"What kind of a dog is it?"

"He's just a mutt terrier. I've had him since he was little," he told me, wiping his eyes with the back of his hand. "He's like family, ya know? I just came home from work and found him right there on the grass."

"Did you see who shot Buddy?"

"I didn't actually *see* it happen but that asshole has threatened to shoot Buddy before." The man pointed to the rundown blue house.

"Why would he threaten to shoot your dog?"

"Oh, ya know, sometimes buddy goes over and pees on his grass. I can't keep him locked up during the day, when I'm at work. It just happens sometimes." I looked over at the sparse, overgrown, dry crab grass that the neighbor's lawn represented and wondered why the guy would even care. Ray, and I helped the man carefully lift the still bleeding dog, and place it on the back seat of the police car, on a thin, wool blanket that was kept in the trunk of the car. The man sat next to his dog, petting him and generally trying to comfort him on the drive over. We transported the animal to a veterinary clinic on Interstate Avenue where the owner said his dog had been treated before. We left the dog in the care of the veterinarian after I made sure the doctor understood I wanted the bullet after he removed it. We gave the poor dog owner a lift home, with a promise from *me* that I would follow up on the case. The man stood on the concrete step, leading up to the wooden stairs of his home and with his hands in his pockets, he quietly thanked me, saying, "I know he's only a dog but he's my pal. He's all I've got, you know?"

I knew that shooting someone's animal was definitely against the law, but more than that it was just such a senseless act of cruelty. At times it seemed to me that some of the people who lived in St. Johns were just meaner than folks who lived in other parts of Portland. How could anyone shoot a poor dog who was just sniffing around in someone's yard, even if he *was* peeing? I could understand yelling at a dog, to get it to scram, but I couldn't understand shooting a dog for such a minor offense. The picture in my mind of the poor mutt bleeding and looking up at me, bewildered and in pain bothered me almost more than seeing a human being bleeding and in pain. More than I wanted to admit to myself anyway.

The next day, our first stop after going on shift was the vet's office. "How's the shaggy dog we brought in yesterday, the one who was shot?" I asked the doctor. The doctor sighed and shook his head. "Sorry, but the dog died. There was a problem with the surgery, more bleeding than we anticipated. My assistant forgot to tie off a very small blood vessel and the dog bled to death." He shrugged his shoulders sadly, and looked at the floor. I was pretty much stunned and just stood there, trying to take in this new information. What the hell was this? A dog survives a gunshot wound, only to die on the operating table due to medical carelessness?! Now I was angry and felt even sorrier for the owner, who clearly hadn't deserved to have his dog shot and killed by a cowardly man with a gun. I knew this was not a case that would be important to other cops, given the times, but I was determined to get the shooter if I could. In the middle 1960s animal's rights were not valued in the same way they are today, in the state of Oregon. However, it was important for *me* to make sure that the lowlife who did this went to jail, even if only for a little while.

As I stood in the veterinarian's office, I was handed the .22 caliber lead bullet that had been removed from the dog's neck. The veterinarian apologized profusely, murmuring, "We're sorry, we're really very sorry," along with "Surgeries don't always go well. It's not what we intended." I was now more determined than ever to get the guy who shot this dog named Buddy. Ray and I delivered the spent bullet to the lab at Central Precinct for analysis. "Find me the rifle that fired it," said the lab technician, as we stood there, "and I'll see what I can do." Ray and I decided to take the bull by the horns on this case, because we knew that most of the detectives were too busy working cases more important than a dead dog. Killing a dog who was doing nothing more than sniffing the grass looking for a place to pee, in an already overgrown, unattractive and neglected front yard, was a petty crime that really pissed me off. I was going to do something about it.

We drove directly to the guy's ramshackle, dumpy, old house by North Portsmouth Street and knocked on his front door. The glass in the door window was cracked and held in place by duct tape. One of the house address numbers originally nailed above the door, had lost one nail and now hung vertically, pointing to the porch. The place was a hazard. Two or three boards on the porch were rotted and broken. "Watch where you step," I advised Ray who was following me. "This porch is a potential trap." I knocked again, loudly this time. "Police officers! Open the door!" I yelled. I could see an old man shuffling his way toward the door and I knocked again impatiently. "Open the damned door!" I demanded as he reached for the deadbolt latch. When he finally opened the door, I could see by his appearance that he matched the ramshackle house, in almost every detail. He appeared to be a man in his early sixties, but easily looked ten years older and looked like a typical, St. Johns alcoholic. He hadn't shaved in months and scraggly gray hair hung just above his collar. A few strands were more or less combed over the shiny bald spot on the top of his head. His blue, farmer overalls were held up by only one strap and covered dirty long johns underneath. I pushed my way inside and stood in the doorway, looking around, with Ray standing right behind me. The inside of the house smelled like it looked. Similar to a chicken coop.

"You got a .22 rifle?"

"Yep," he replied.

"Give it to me!"

The old man turned around and shuffled away a few steps, retrieving his rifle from behind a nearby sofa, with the stuffing falling out in clumps. He handed me an old Remington .22 caliber, bolt action, single shot rifle, with iron sights. The barrel was pitted with small rust spots and the wooden stock was scratched and dinged. Surprised by the lack of resistance from the old man, I took the rifle out into the front yard and fired one round into a soft mushy spot in the yellow, crabgrass. I looked around for a sharp stick to dig out the bullet. Finding none, I sacrificed my ball point pen and dug around in the small hole looking for the slug. It came out a little flattened from the impact but I could see the grooves were still visible. Making sure the rifle was now empty, I walked back into the house and returned it to the old man, who was waiting in the living room.

"You shot your neighbor's dog, didn't you?" I asked quietly.

"I didn't shoot nuthin."

"If this bullet matches the one we got from your neighbor's dead dog, I'm going to arrest you. Do you understand me?" I pulled the bill of my cap down a little more over my eyes and glared at him. "DO you understand me?!" I repeated. The old man nodded, turned around and shuffled off into the depths of another dingy room. I slammed the front door, and Ray and I jumped into our patrol car and headed directly to the Central Precinct lab. It took about three days for the comparison lab to get around to my case, but finally they left a message for me at North Precinct. "The bullets match," read the memo, from my in-box. "The slug that came from the dog matches the slug turned in for examination by Officer DuPay. Both slugs were fired from the same gun."

"Okay Ray, let's go get him!"

We told the sergeant that we would be out of service for a while on a follow-up. Not much later, we were once again standing in front of the beat up, old front door of the shooter's house.

I banged on the door with my night stick, trying to be as loud as possible.

"Police! Open up!" I demanded.

Ray un-holstered his gun and stood close behind me. We knew the old geezer had a rifle and had already used it, so we wanted to be ready for him just in case. After a moment or two of knocking on the door with my night stick and demanding entry, I saw the old guy again shuffling his way toward the door empty-handed. When he finally got the door open, I told him he was under arrest for killing the animal of another. Ray and I stepped inside and I turned the man around and hand cuffed him. I found the old rifle behind the couch where it had been the last time we were there. After stuffing the old man in the back seat of the police car and putting the rifle in the trunk, we transported him to North Precinct in St. Johns. My partner and I both knew that we still had work to do on this case. Yes, we had the rifle that killed the dog and both slugs matched. But as we learned in the academy, no crime exists if no one *saw* anyone do anything. No one saw the old man pull the trigger. He had to confess and sign a statement that he shot the dog. Only then could we lock him up.

At the precinct I set things up in the upstairs roll call room. I piled up a bunch of official looking law books that would sit in front of the old man, on the table, during the interrogation. Once he shuffled in the room and sat down in a chair, I put a statement form and a pen in front of him. Then, after picking up the gun where it stood propped in a corner, I slammed the rifle down on the table with the big "Evidence" tag tied to it. The old man blinked from the noise. I picked the rifle up and slammed it down again loudly, for effect. From the other side of the roll call table, I leaned over, glowering, with my palms flat on the table, almost on top of the guy and yelled at him. "You shot the dog with this rifle didn't you?!"

"I didn't shoot nuthin!"

"We both know you shot the dog! *Everybody* knows you shot the dog!"

I hunched over him as close as I could get, invading his personal space and breathing on him. I had a pretty good glare going on and I smothered him with it. Moving back to his side of the table I sat next to him, crowding up against him. "Tell me what happened," I whispered in his ear. "I know you didn't *mean* to kill the dog, but just tell me what happened, okay?" Finally the old man sighed, and sat back in his chair. He looked over at me and then at Ray. It was then, I knew we had defeated him.

"What happened?!" I yelled impatiently, "Tell me the truth!"

"I didn't *mean* to kill him, I just meant to *burn* him a little."

"What do you mean, *burn* the dog?"

"I just meant to graze him and make him run away. I'm tired of the dog pissin' in my yard!" the man said in a pleading tone.

"Are you a crack shot?" I asked calmly. "Only a crack shot with a scope could have parted the hairs on that dog without really hitting him." He didn't answer.

"DID you pull the trigger and shoot the dog?" I banged the rifle on the table again for emphasis.

"Yes, but I didn't mean to kill it," he replied in exasperation, his voice now thin and shrill.

"I want your hand-written statement on what happened!" I demanded. "The pen is in front of you. Get going. I don't have all shift to fool with you!" As the old man began to write, Ray and I stood up and grinned at each other. We knew we had made the case and the old man would go to jail. The maximum penalty for this crime or something similar was three years but we knew he'd only spend a few months in county. We had solved a killing. It may not have been a human who died, but it was an unjust killing just the same. I had been a cop for almost six years and was only thirty-years-old, but my sense of satisfaction at *this* crime being solved was intense. The poor dog owner would be happy with the news that the shooter had been arrested, the dog was no longer suffering and could rest in peace and the case would be a lesson for the other residents in the area; Don't go and kill the animal of another. Or you might get arrested. As we left the precinct office, we had another radio call waiting. "Car 42, see the trouble. Naked man running west on North Willis, toward Berkeley."

Assault with an Electrical Cord

WE ALL WHUP OUR KIDS LIKE THAT

MOST OF MY TIME WORKING as a uniformed police officer was spent patrolling areas of the city in the North End, largely populated by black citizens. We called this area *the ghetto*, as our supervisors had called it and their supervisors before them. The ghetto was located from NE Broadway to NE Columbia Boulevard and from the River East to twenty fifth Avenue. The houses were wood frame, clapboard structures built in the 1920s and early 1930s. They were worn, dilapidated and old, always in need of paint or porch repair and surrounded by backyard wooden fencing that looked as if a mild breeze could topple it at any moment. The lawns were seldom mowed and there was never a lawn sprinkler in sight. As a cop there, I learned early on, that there are definite cultural differences between white and black populations. I learned, for example, that black people are not just white people in black skins; they are culturally and socially different. It seemed to me, from the hundreds of radio calls I received about domestic disputes, or the various and sundry family beefs, that black folks were quicker to react violently, quicker to assault, quicker to shoot, quicker to stab. I have no scientific studies to prove this, just my own working experience and my memories of countless situations I was called in to settle and resolve. This was an area of town where people struggled to survive, fought every kind of addiction and family dysfunction, and basically did the best they could under extremely grim social and economic circumstances.

More times than I can remember, I was called to a domestic dispute, usually by neighbors complaining of yelling and screaming coming from a nearby family. I would arrive to find an irate, usually drunk parent, beating on one of their kids with an electrical cord. The cords invariably came from a coffee pot or a steam iron, or an extension cord, and left bloody marks and welts reminiscent of the times when black slaves were beaten by white plantation owners from 200 years before. I can remember over twenty calls like this, in my six years as a street cop. These calls generally involved a young black youth, covered in marks, welts and abrasions that were bleeding and swelling, all up and down his or her back. One particular call of this nature was from a frightened neighbor who told the radio dispatcher that it sounded like someone was "gettin' killed" next door. The call came from an ancient rundown walk-up apartment that fronted on NE Union Avenue just south of Alberta Street. There were frequent calls for service from that apartment house and I had been in every single apartment unit—all three floors of it at one time or another. On this occasion, I could hear what sounded like a teenage boy, crying and pleading. I could hear him begging "Daddy! Don't hit me no mo!" Then the sound of loud whacks and more crying and whimpering. I shoved open the unlocked door and just stood there for a moment, taking in the situation.

In front of me and damned surprised to see a uniformed cop with a gun in his hand, was a boy of about thirteen, bleeding from the top of his head and all down his bare back. His white t-shirt was torn as if he had been fighting with his father, and hung in shreds. "This boy's plain outa control!" said the father, biting his lower lip and shaking. He was a burly, working man wearing dirty, railroad coveralls and no shoes, and I could smell the unmistakable odor of alcohol on his breath. "Runnin' the streets! Stayin' out late! Sassin' me! Gotta be whupped!" I jerked a six-foot extension cord out of the father's hands and put my gun back in the holster. "You can't beat on people with a weapon like this!" I said through gritted teeth. I then slapped the long cord down on a nearby ironing board—as hard as I could, to make my point. I was very angry that a father would beat on his own son so viciously. The father just stood there surprised, uncertain what I would do next and clearly afraid.

"But we all whup our kids like this," he tried to explain. "It's what *we* folks do round here."

"No you don't!" I yelled back at him, pushing him forcefully against the wall. "No you don't! Not anymore! Whether your boy deserved punishment is not the issue here. This boy is going to the hospital and *you're* going to jail. You're under arrest for assault. Turn around!" The man being much shorter than I was had to look up at me, as I told him the news. He was flabbergasted that I would arrest him and very unhappy about it, I could tell, mumbling that he was "Jus tryin' to keep ma boy in line." It was obvious he resented a white man telling him how to raise his child, but the law was the law and he was going to jail. I spun him around, shoved him up against the wall, and snapped on the cuffs, leading him outside and stuffing him into my patrol car. On my radio, I called an ambulance and the boy was soon taken to Emanuel Hospital for much needed medical treatment. I felt so sorry for the young boy and wanted to comfort him but it was always difficult for me, in my career, to assume that role. He was still crying, and hunched over, with his arms crossed over his thin chest and his head down as I approached him. All I could manage to say was, "The ambulance will be here soon and you'll be helped by some nice ladies at the hospital, okay?" He mumbled, "Thank you," and nodded his head, wiping his eyes with the back of his hand, straightening up and trying to be brave.

The boy may have deserved a swat on the butt, or loss of privileges, but whenever I ran into a case like this where the excuse for violent assault with an electrical cord was "It's our tradition," or "It's the way we always done it!" I responded with a definitive, *Bullshit!* Not on *my* watch! Time in jail was my answer for people like this, black or white, who broke the law by violently abusing their children with an electrical cord. After a while, word got around in my district that whacking a kid with an electrical cord or some other traditional weapon was something that would get you jail time. Officer DuPay would see to that.

The Watts Riots

PORTLAND'S LONG HOT SUMMER

August 1965 seemed to be the first of several long hot summers, of increasing racial tension nationwide. I worked the ghetto and could sense things were changing. We were being trained in riot control tactics, out at the Kelly Butte firing range on SE Powell. We were issued long, polished, hardwood batons and practiced different marching formations. We practiced marching in the wedge formation, a tactic used to open up and disperse an angry crowd. We used the batons like spearheads as we marched lock-step toward the crowd, shouting "Back up! Back up! Back up!" We were issued blue helmets, which looked similar to motorcycle helmets. They replaced the soft, blue, shiny-billed caps we normally wore, and we were expected to wear the damned helmets inside the police cars at all times. I guess it made us cops look more formidable, riding around in cars with helmets on all the time, but the truth is the helmets were too hot to wear inside a car with no air conditioning in the middle of August, and there were no air conditioned police cars in 1965.

The public watched, horrified, as riots broke out in the Watts area of Los Angeles that August of 1965. The images flooded our television screens, as a series of violent riots were covered by TV stations across the country. We saw building after building being burned down and Asian shop owners on top of their buildings with rifles, shooting at looters and arsonists who were trying to burn down their businesses. It set a tone, for cops in Portland, an attitude that if *they* tried anything here in Portland *we cops* would be ready for them. And as it turned out, things did get hot and heavy. It started when the Black Panthers became active in Portland in about 1965. They opened a ramshackle office, at 3639 NE Union Avenue right smack dab in the middle of my district. The headquarters was located in an old, rundown house, painted dark blue with worn wooden steps leading up to the front porch. Before the Panthers moved in, it had been a second-hand clothing store of sorts that catered to low income single mothers. We watched the place constantly and stopped and talked to as many people as we could. Who were these people, and what were they doing we wanted to know? Rumor was they were gathering guns and explosives and that they called themselves The Black Panthers.

The summer of August 1967 was when Portland got its taste of the riots and the rampant social unrest that was happening all through California. It started as a political rally in Irving Park at NE Seventh Avenue and Fremont Street. When my shift came to work at about 3:30 p.m. the unruly crowd spilled out of Irving Park and onto Union Avenue. Each district car had been issued a shotgun and plenty of 00-buck-shot ammunition. At Kelly Butte, during training, we had practiced firing our shotguns at the pavement, a few yards in front of an imaginary crowd. The idea was to bounce the slugs off the pavement so they would rise about two or three feet and take out the legs of the first few crowd members. With practice at Kelly Butte I was consistently able to bounce slugs about knee high, so I was ready. The unspoken message we officers received from our superiors, was to shoot the first three or four rioters in the front of the crowd and then see if the rest of the rioters still wanted to participate. This could have resulted in fatalities. At the time it seemed to be a good tactic, an immediate and overwhelming response, like a good, hard, back-hand that demanded compliance, but it made me and my fellow officers uneasy. I didn't want to kill anyone and neither did any of the other men I worked with.

As the crowds spilled onto NE Union Avenue, just a few blocks from Irving Park we parked our car on Fremont near Union, close to the McDonald's restaurant on the corner. We locked the car, got out with our helmets strapped on tight and the long batons swinging from our belts. Salty sweat ran down from under my blue helmet and into my eyes and I kept wiping it away with my arm. My hands were sweating on the metal of my 12 gauge, and the gathering crowds were shouting at us, calling us the usual things: pigs, motherfuckers and sons of bitches. I was scared but confident. We had been well-trained in crowd control and I knew what my shotgun could do. I also knew that the National Guard would be called out as well, and a bunch of state troopers if it turned out we needed *more* help after that. A few rioters were throwing rocks, but with very little damage. As the evening heat wore on, all semblance of normal police work stopped. We took no calls. We just watched the crowd, dodged an occasional rock, and perspired under the hot sun and stifling helmets.

Looking farther north on Union Avenue from my location, we could see smoke rising from a fire. The radio dispatcher advised us that a grocery store had been set on fire near Union and North Portland Boulevard with a Molotov cocktail, and that more store windows were being smashed. After the fire started all hell seemed to break loose. One of our officers shot a black rioter in the act of throwing a firebomb into a furniture store. The shotgun blast struck but did not kill the fire bomber, who was later taken to the hospital. The gasoline bomb fell short of the store and burned harmlessly in the grass. The fire department responded and the police had to make sure our Portland firemen were not attacked by rioters while they tried to put out two more small, arson fires. "Burn baby burn!" seemed to echo all the way from Watts to Portland, and as innocent fireman in the Watts area were being shot at by rioters, it was very important to the Portland cops to protect *our* fireman, who were just trying to do their jobs.

I was ordered to remain in the area of NE Union and Fremont. The main business at that location was the McDonald's and it was almost directly across the street from the Black Panthers' office. I was glad that so far the worst of the mess was a half mile north of my location. I kept my eyes focused on the Black Panther office, not knowing what might happen or who might come bursting out the front door. We thought they had a lot of guns and might come out shooting. Well, so what! I thought to myself. *I've got three guns. My .38 service revolver, the 12 gauge shotgun and a backup .25 automatic in my pocket. Besides, I'm hot and tired. Don't fuck with me!*

We worked two hours overtime that night, keeping fireman safe and the crowds calm. I got back to North Precinct at around one in the morning. I was soaked from sweat, my uniform shirt was wet, and my trousers were damp under my gun belt. I was exhausted from the stress and emotionally drained. My body had been on high alert for more than ten hours. At that time, my wife and I lived in an apartment on SE 122nd Avenue near Division Street and I stopped off on the way home to a neighborhood bar slamming down three strong drinks before last call. At home, I barely said two words to my wife, before stumbling past her in the hallway, and into the bedroom, where I collapsed into bed. She knew I was completely spent; she had been listening to our police scanner in the kitchen the whole evening and knew what I had been through that day.

The civil unrest continued into the next day and night, before everyone just seemed to get tired of it all and go home. The damage to buildings on Union Avenue with the broken glass and debris scattered everywhere reminded me of the Columbus Day storm of 1962 and the havoc it had caused to our community. I felt sorry for the local grocery store owner, whose business had been destroyed by a firebomb. The building was simply gone. He would have to start over. The McDonald's at NE Union and Fremont would also be bombed a few years later, in the early morning hours of August 22nd 1970. That never made sense to me. Their burgers weren't all that bad.

HONORABLE MENTION

During the time of the 1965 riots, Officer Stan Harmon, of the Portland Police, also worked my district, usually on my days off. Stan was a big, tall, stern looking, muscular tough guy, with short-cropped, black hair, who rarely flashed a smile. He was quite intimidating in his uniform, especially with his helmet on. Harmon had worked in a meat packing plant lifting sides of beef for a living before becoming an officer, so hoisting up a 150 pound suspect and throwing him in the back of a police car was no trouble for Stan. Stan developed a reputation for being aggressive, productive and fair. Some people thought Stan was too aggressive, but I personally thought Stan Harmon was a damn good cop and I was happy to have him around. You could trust and depend on the guy. I never knew Stan very well, and we weren't close friends but he wouldn't run on you, never showed any fear and was always right there in a hot second if you needed him to provide cover on a difficult call. He was a friendly, professional and cool under fire cop and always an asset to the bureau.

Tragically, August 14, 1977, Stan was shot in some kind of fracas in his district, by a sniper on a sweltering, summer afternoon. His injuries left him paralyzed from the waist down and ended his police career. Two cops, one a veteran officer and the other a female recruit, were called to investigate a sniper, shooting from the second story apartment of a converted house, on SE thirty fourth and Belmont. They had just arrived and were awaiting backup when Stan pulled up in his patrol car ready to assist. It was about five in the afternoon and a very hot and humid day. The officers had both tried to warn Stan, shouting and waving at him, but apparently he didn't hear them and was shot by the sniper as soon as he exited his vehicle. He had only just looked up to the second story apartment, when he was shot and went down, falling beside his car. I've often thought it could just as well have been me, or any number of the other good men I worked with. Stan Harmon had guts. He was a brave man and I was glad to have worked with him. Now few people, other than retired law enforcement, even remember his name.

Instant Extradition

STREET JUSTICE VPD STYLE

During late August 1967, on a hot and particularly sticky humid day, it was almost impossible to sleep. Even though I had a box-fan in the bedroom window, all it did was blow in the hot air. I was hoping it would cool down before I had to go to work again at midnight (out in the North End) but of course it didn't. When I showed up to work, I found my partner Ray Jones dressed in his coolest, short sleeve uniform shirt. I myself dressed without an undershirt and left an additional button at the top of the shirt undone. The roll call sergeant also had the front of his shirt unbuttoned, with his clip-on tie hanging down lopsided from one side of his shirt collar. Everyone was hot and miserable and spit and polish was not the order of the day. I was driving the patrol car that night, and Ray kept his head near the open window trying to keep cool. As I was driving, I suddenly remembered the 1946 Plymouth I'd had when I went to Grant High School. It had wind-wings: those wonderful little hinged windows that allowed cool air in. I wondered why cars didn't seem to have them anymore.

"Do you remember when cars had wind-wings?" I asked Ray.

"I had a 1950 Ford," Ray replied forlornly, "It had wind-wings, yeah, I remember."

"Yeah."

"Why were you thinking about wind-wings Don?"

"Oh, I dunno. Just wishing it wasn't so damn hot."

"Wind-wings wouldn't help *this* heat much," Ray concluded.

By about 2:30 a.m. it was still hot, so Ray and I decided to roll all four windows down and do a little speeding. We agreed *that* would be our air conditioning. We drove slowly through the Kenton district on North Denver Avenue and continued toward the Interstate Bridge on North Interstate Avenue. There, I punched the gas pedal and got the car up to about 70 mph. The wind started blowing all our papers around, so I slowed down until Ray was able to gather them into his brief case. With the papers secure I took off again, flying north on Interstate. We whizzed by a few other cars on the road and sat up looking straight ahead, as if we were on official business. As I neared the Interstate Bridge we exited onto Jantzen Beach, passed Waddles Restaurant, cruised under the bridge and back up onto the on-ramp heading south again. I hesitated for a second, slowing down a bit, and came to a stop. I was hoping for a late-night speeder from Washington State, when suddenly radio told us that the Vancouver police were chasing a black 1966 Ford Mustang. All over downtown Vancouver they chased him, for running a bunch of red lights and still, they couldn't seem to catch the guy.

VPD were talking with dispatch, trying to get a squad car in place to prevent the eluder from gaining access to Interstate Bridge. With our windows rolled down, just idling at the on-ramp and within only a few seconds, we could hear the distant wail of sirens just across the river. The Vancouver cops were hot after the Mustang. While Ray and I were listening to the radio for more information on speed and direction, we saw the Mustang come flying off the Interstate Bridge, heading south. My partner and I looked at each other quickly, smiling, knowing we were in the right place at the right time. I fell in behind the Mustang and clocked him at a steady 80 mph. He was thirty miles an hour over the speed limit. I realized that as the speeding Mustang approached Kenton he would not be able to negotiate the sharp left turn, and then the right dog-leg at the Paul Bunyan statue. The car would have to either slow down or wreck at its present speed. By now, three Vancouver police cars were following us, just barely keeping up.

The speeding Mustang didn't take the dog-leg onto Interstate but slowed entering Kenton, which was now a straight shot for him on Denver Avenue. By now I could arrest the speeder for attempting to elude a police officer, along with speeding and probably reckless driving as well. The speeder, however, refused to stop and turned west into an alley, coming out near Brandon

Street and Kenton Park. As the Mustang approached the park, I overtook him, by driving alongside, crowding him, and forcing him off the road into Kenton Park itself. I had him now, and he pulled over near the Public Restroom building. Ray jumped out of the car, ran over and pulled the driver out by his jacket. He pushed him down, face first onto the hood of the Mustang, telling him, "Put your hands behind your back, NOW!" After I jumped out of the car, I reached for my citation book to start writing the traffic citations. At that point, three Vancouver police cars skidded into the park and boxed-in the Mustang and Ray and I with our prisoner.

Three really mad, big, burly Vancouver cops nudged Ray aside and dragged the speeder about fifty feet to their cruiser and one of them threw the young man against the back door of the car. I heard a low thud as the suspects head hit the metal. "Oh, I guess we should open the door first, huh?" I heard one of the angry officers say in mock, girlish concern. When the backseat door was finally opened, they tossed the now half-conscious violator into the vehicle. He lay collapsed and handcuffed across the seat, with his knees drawn close to his chest, looking like a lumpy bag of discarded potatoes. One of the officers looked over and lifted his hand quickly in a gesture of reluctant acknowledgment, mumbling, "Thanks guys," as they got into their cars, to head back to Vancouver. We watched all three cars, with their red lights still flashing, disappearing down the road. They were barely out of sight when a Vancouver tow-truck they had ordered showed up and the Mustang soon disappeared over the bridge, also heading back to Vancouver. Ray and I just looked at each other, dumbfounded, with our mouths kind of hanging open. Everything seemed to happen so fast. I caught the speeder, the VPD snatched him up and it was all over and done with, before we could catch our breath. I felt a little like the fisherman who just caught a big fish only to have it snatched away by a couple of big bears. About five minutes after the VPD officers completed their instant extradition, our duty sergeant rolled up with his car windows rolled down and his tie still hanging askew.

"Where's your prisoner? What happened?" he asked, with a perplexed look on his face.

"I caught him and then the Vancouver cops just snatched him up and took em' back to Vancouver!" I said shrugging my shoulders and tossing my ticket book into the front seat of the cruiser. Ray laughed disgustedly, and ran his hand through his hair. The sergeant shook his head, disappointed, and looking back over his shoulder said, "Well, I won't write anything down then. And you don't have to either," he said, referring to report writing. He rolled slowly away disappearing into the darkness a few blocks down the street. Ray and I were kind of mad for a while, as we stood there ruminating over the injustice of it all, but we realized the Vancouver cops were even madder. They were mad at the guy in the Mustang for getting away. They were mad they couldn't catch him. They were mad he made it into Oregon, and I knew they were mad at me because I did catch him when they couldn't.

After shift and on the way out the precinct door the same sergeant told us not to worry about what had happened. "That was just an example of old fashioned street justice," he explained good naturedly. "Don't let it bother ya!" Ordinarily Ray and I went straight home after shift, but it was still warm, and so we stopped at Patti's Perch on Lombard, a tavern a few blocks from North Precinct, and ordered some ice cold beers. Halfway through his beer Ray began to wax philosophical and in his best *Cool Hand Luke* kind of voice he said, "What we have here is a failure of the judicial system. That boy should have been properly extradited. Yes sir, a failure of the system!" We both laughed heartily at his joke and agreed that sometimes street justice was the only justice available, what with the new Miranda warnings we now had to deal with. Before 1966, we just arrested criminals who broke the law and never had to advise them of their rights. But since the Miranda vs. Arizona Supreme Court decision, (June 13th of 1966) all police officers had to then read suspects their rights after arresting them. And in our collective naivety we all felt this new change was troublesome, and a waste of valuable time. After another cold beer, Ray and I both went home to bed. I slept comfortably in front of the fan. It had cooled off and I remember feeling grateful, that I'd once more come home alive and in one piece to my wife and son.

Thelma and the Trick

THE FAST LIFE WAS A BURNER

"Car 72, see the man at the phone booth on Union and Alberta Avenue. He says he's been beaten and robbed," cracked the radio. "10-4, 72 has it," I said, as I hit the gas. We could see the man sitting on the curb by the phone booth. He had a cut on the back of his head and another cut on the bridge of his nose and was sopping at the blood with a handkerchief. He had a sad story we had heard *many* times before. He was a business man from Seattle and was alone in town for a few days. He'd picked up a black girl at The Cotton Club and agreed to pay her $100 for sex. They took a taxi to her apartment near North Portland Blvd. Once inside, the woman dropped all pretense of sex and demanded *all* his money and jewelry. She had made him bleed pretty well, and also managed to get his wallet away from him with $600 in it, before he escaped out the back door. "Well, you're a grown man," I said philosophically, and somewhat annoyed. "A white guy like you is just a piece of meat in this part of town, anyway. Whaddaya wanna do about it?" I asked blandly. "I want her *arrested* and I want my wallet and my money back!" the man replied indignantly, as if this was the first time this had happened to *any* man, ever, on a business trip in Portland. "Okay, if you can identify her," I began, "*and* if you'll testify against her in court? Then I'll see what we can do for you."

We put the trick in the car, and I got on radio. "Car 72, this is a trick-roll. We're going to see if we can find her." The trick directed us to her duplex apartment. From the description he provided us with, the black girl sounded an awful lot like Thelma. We all got out of the car and walked up to the building. As we walked up the cement stairs, I told the trick he'd have to wait on the porch, while we went inside. On the porch, we could see that the lights were on in the apartment and we could see into the front living room. A broken lamp was on the floor, and the coffee table was overturned.

"She hit me with that lamp!" the trick yelled, as he peeked through the window.

"You're lucky you're alive!" Ray said, becoming impatient, "Now go over and wait where we told you!"

"Police officers! Open the door!" I yelled, banging loudly on the glass with my flashlight. We could hear someone crashing around in the bedroom. "Police officers! Open the door!" I yelled again. Ray went around the side and banged on the bedroom window, but couldn't see in. I broke out a pane of glass in the old French style door with my leather sap, reached in and unlocked the deadbolt. We went in through the front door to see that the place was in a shambles. Another broken lamp was in the corner, a picture frame and broken glass scattered all over the davenport, and two more overturned chairs in the dining room. This guy was damned lucky, I thought to myself. It could have ended very differently for him. "We're police officers!" I said loudly, "Come on out and talk to us!" No answer. We started checking every nook or cranny in the apartment, where a small woman could hide. "Police officers! Come on out and talk to us!" I yelled again.

Finally, we found her hiding, curled up under some old wool blankets in the bedroom closet. Recognizing her, I bent down and began to gently pull her out by the wrist. "That's her! That's her!" the trick exclaimed, from behind me, having wandered into the house and into the bedroom. "You get outa here!" I told him in an angry, terse whisper. "We told you to stay outside, now get OUTA here!" Ray yelled, pointing to the bedroom door imperiously. The man turned around and walked out, sulking. The girl was Thelma, alright, and she was completely naked as she stood in front of me, looking up at me with fiery eyes. I flashed back to a couple of years ago when Thelma had been beautiful, in her G-string and pasties. But she was no beauty now. This girl was hollow-eyed and skinny. Heavy blue and purple needle marks showed on the veins of both arms. Her breasts were small and sagging, and her skinny thighs didn't touch anymore. The fast life was a burner and Thelma didn't have much left to work with.

Ray fished around and found a clean red and white, flared, polka-dot dance dress lying on the closet floor. He picked it up and handed it to Thelma without a word. She took it, shook it out and then slipped into it in one motion. She turned to me and asked me to help her zip it up, which I did. "I need my panties too," she said in a high, girlish voice. I waved my arm, giving her permission to go and look for her panties. She found a pair of red satin and lace panties on a closet shelf and slipped them on, looking back at me seductively. Then she turned toward Ray and I and smoothed down the folds of the flared skirt, with a smile, as if she was going to the prom. I walked over and took her wrist in my hand. "Come on Thelma, let's go," I said with gentle familiarity. "You're going to jail for assaulting and robbing this man. Where's the guys money and wallet?" Her demeanor changed instantly, as she shouted, "Fuck you! You pigs! I've never *seen* this cracker before!"

"Back over here, Don," I heard Ray call out from the dirty, bathroom, cluttered with trash and discarded clothes. As Thelma had been locating her panties, Ray had found the wallet and most of the tricks money floating in the toilet tank, where Thelma had carelessly tossed it in her haste. Ray fished out the wet, soggy, mess of legal tender and put it in a wad of toilet tissue. Hiding money and guns in a toilet tank was common in those days and also the first place that cops would look. I never did figure out why crooks thought it was a good idea, because it was never very smart. We later booked Thelma into jail and then drove the trick back to his hotel. "You be at the district attorney's office at 9:00 a.m. to sign a complaint on her or she'll go free," I warned the man. "I'll be there. That bitch could have killed me," he said indignantly. Nine o'clock, the next day, came and went. The trick never showed, Thelma walked free at ten o'clock and we weren't surprised: as that's the way it usually worked. *Caveat emptor.*

Perspective

IMAGINE WHAT IT'S LIKE

Police officers are witnesses to the personal tragedy of others' lives, sometimes through violence, sometimes through natural causes, and accidents, but tragedy just the same. Why don't you join me, reader, in the police car for a couple of shifts? It may change your perspective.

Have you all turned over in your bed in the night and sleepily touched your mate for warmth or reassurance? Imagine your horror if you found your mate cold, stiff, and dead under the covers with you. It happened to one poor older lady in the middle of the night and she jumped up and called the police. The call comes out over the radio as a "possible dead one." When you pull up to the address, you notice an older one story bungalow house sitting back off the street. You walk up the long driveway and knock on the door. The woman greets you in tears and frantically points to the bedroom. "My husband! My husband! I think there's something wrong with him. He won't wake up. Please officers, please save him!" she sobs. As you enter the bedroom, you see a still figure lying in the bed under the covers. Hesitantly, you pull the covers back. Her husband is laying on his side, with his knees pulled up in the fetal position. Touching his wrists you notice he is cold, as you look for signs of a pulse. There is no pulse. Pulling the covers back a little more, you notice that the lower half of the body is red and discolored. You know that in death, gravity pulls the body fluids to the lowest level and that's where the blood collects. The pillow is wet with drool, and urine and feces soil the bed sheets from an involuntary elimination caused by death. The woman shrieks, "Please save him! Oh God! Is he dead?! Oh God! Oh God!" You pull the covers back up over the body and turn to face her.

You know that you're talking to the city's newest widow and

you're wondering how to tell her what she already knows. That her husband died peacefully in his sleep and there's nothing you can do. That's all most of us can hope for, anyway, is to die in our sleep. But now this poor woman is left to face her future, alone, and starting *now*. "Ma'am, I'm *really* sorry," you hear yourself saying, "Do you have any relatives, a son or daughter we can call for you?" Soon the morgue will arrive to get the husbands body and relatives will come to comfort the sobbing widow. Well, it's time for us to go. Your job is done except for the report. Write it on a "Dead Body, Natural Causes," report form and start it out: "Sir, Received a call on a possible dead one at....."

More Perspective

BEDLAM AT THE DOODLE BUG

The Doodle Bug Tavern was located on North Interstate Avenue, which was one of the main streets that passed through the ghetto. It was a neighborhood tavern in the truest sense, where the locals gathered to drink beer, and play shuffleboard and pool. The responsible owner, and always a nice guy, enjoyed a thriving business and was never a problem for us. On this night a horror happened there. Your call comes out as "A shooting at the Doodle Bug." The shooters are two black males that left on foot, direction unknown. See if an ambulance might be needed. You're driving, so go ahead and park the police car directly in front of the tavern door. Inside, you see two young white men, who appeared to be in their early thirties, lying on the linoleum tiled floor near the end of the bar, shot to death at point blank range. The men are dressed in working class clothing and look like any blue collar working man you might see on the street, walking home from work. They are both lying in shallow pools of blood that gather around their heads, in small arcs. Both are shot cleanly in the right temples.

All twenty five of the remaining patrons have been forced to the floor and robbed. You arrive only minutes after the shooting. The atmosphere is bedlam, with screaming weeping women, yelling and general panic. Go ahead and cover the bodies with some bar towels. It's *your* job to protect the crime scene from contamination and potential damage, so the detectives can do *their* job. Now, try and get all of these people to calm down. They are not only robbery victims, but some of them actually saw the shootings and may be able to identify the shooters. That makes them material witnesses to a double homicide. Get the bartenders name and see if you can get a better description of the shooters. When you get that information, contact dispatch and get the information broadcast, so other officers can be looking, city wide. You hear yourself yelling to someone, over the noise, "Hey! Don't let that victim leave the tavern yet! No one can leave until they've been interviewed by the detectives! Yes, we can hold him against his will! He's a material witness!"

I know this is a lot of pressure for you, two dead bodies on the floor and twenty odd more people yelling at you too, that they were robbed and could have been killed, and they all want you to get their money back. But you're the one wearing the uniform and these people are looking to *you*. Remember, until the detectives get here, *you're* in charge. Good. Here comes a team of four detectives now. The rest will be up to them. Go ahead and write a regular officer report. Just cover the basic facts: Two black men walked in the busy tavern and announced, "This is a hold-up! Everyone on the floor!" The tavern was so noisy that no one paid any attention. So, they shot the closest two guys off their bar stools and that got everyone's attention. Then they robbed everyone of wallets and jewelry and fled. That's about it for us. Just be glad you're not taking all the detailed statements from that crowd, like the detectives. Oh, here comes the coroners van. Let's move the police car out of the way so he can park. We can leave now. I'll buy you coffee if you'd like some. *Perspective.* How did I get used to seeing three dead bodies in two days? I *never* got used to it.

The .25 Caliber Semi-automatic Pistol

I KNOWD I SHUDDA BOT THE THUTY EIGHT!

THE .25 CALIBER SEMI-AUTOMATIC PISTOL, because of its small size and conceal-ability, has been a long time favorite pocket gun of many cultures. It will fit in a pocket, purse or the palm of a hand and it can be quite lethal. It does, however, have its limitations. It is, because of its small caliber, necessarily and solely a point blank weapon. The best range for serious damage is three to five feet from the end of the barrel to the target. For several years, I personally carried a .25 semi-automatic as my back up gun, while working as a street cop, both in the Traffic Division and as a prowl officer at North Precinct. I am well aware of its potential and its limitations.

Ray and I had two calls at different times concerning victims who had been shot with a .25. The first call for help was from a twenty-five-year old black man who had been walking north on Williams Avenue, late one night after getting off the bus from work. Not long after exiting the bus, he felt someone "poke," him in the back. He looked around and could see no one on the streets near him, but several cars *had* passed by. After Ray and I came to the house, we took the man's statement. He told us his left kidney area hurt, but had no idea who had poked him or why.

In his kitchen, Ray helped the man take off his heavy jacket, a black Navy style P-coat. Laying the coat on the kitchen table we could see a small hole in the jacket material. The man pulled out his shirt tail and when he did a .25 caliber slug fell on the kitchen floor. He'd been shot, alright. The wound consisted of a small dimple about six inches above his belt line, which was exactly where his kidney hurt. There was no blood as the bullet had not penetrated the skin, but around the dimple, a dark discoloration was forming. The mark of impact was beginning to bruise. Since the injury was merely a bruise, the man declined medical treatment and we could tell he would be alright, because he appeared alert and calm. We surmised the shot had come from a passing car, at about a fifty foot distance.

Happy that he could now brag that he'd been shot in the back and lived to tell about it, he polished the slug on his pants and held it up to the light, looking at it in wonder. "Gonna keep *this* as a souvenir!" he bragged. "Maybe I'll hang it on a chain round my neck as a good luck charm, or make a tie-pin out of it," he mused. The man was on the phone to his girlfriend telling her all about it in no time, and rubbing his sore back when Ray and I left the house, shaking our heads but glad he was unhurt. He had been a very lucky man that night on Williams Avenue. The second shooting happened, several months later, at about 4:00 a.m. at an upstairs-downstairs duplex apartment. A very angry black woman had stayed up late waiting for her wayward husband to finally come home. We were called by the downstairs neighbors who reported the husband and wife were shouting at each other and reported they'd heard one shot fired.

The apartment was located on the west side of North Gantenbein Avenue. There were six wooden steps leading to the front porch. The right-hand door led to the upstairs apartment and the left-hand door led to the downstairs apartment. Both doors were largely glass, oval shaped with beveled edges. The wooden door frame had once been painted brown but now the grain of the wood was visible through the remaining paint. The once shiny doorknob had weathered to a sort of rusty patina. The right-hand door stood ajar and we entered to see the wife at the top of the stairs. She was wearing an old blue chenille robe tied together at the waist. Her brown opaque socks were rolled all the way down to the tops of her pink toe-less slippers. Her hair was up in big pink curlers, but my eyes were on the gun in her right hand. She held a blue steel .25 semi-automatic pistol and was waving it around and posturing in a threatening manner. Her other hand rested on her hip, all the while yelling obscenities at the man at the foot of the stairs right in front of me. "I tol you, don't try and sneak home this late. Git, or I'll chute ya again! Go on back to yer cheap lil hussy!"

Her husband, a black man with short greying hair and a thin grey mustache, viewed the arrival of the police with some surprise. Seeing us, he pointed to the top of the stairs and said, "She shot at me! I can't believe it, but that woman jus shot at me!" I bounded up the stairs, two at a time, and grabbed the small pistol, as she held it in her hand, with the barrel pointing toward the ceiling. She was still a very angry woman, but she had the sense to comply and not fight me. As semi-automatics are ready to fire again, with the hammer back and one in the chamber, I removed the clip and the shell from the chamber before putting it in my pocket.

"I'll chute him agin if he don't start actin' right!" she threatened.

"Mamn, you can't shoot your husband just for coming home late!"

"He's been gone all night! I know what he up to!"

"Did he hit you or try to hurt you?"

"No, but he can't stay out all night and then come home lookin' for some lovin' no mo! I'll kill him fust! He make me so mad. Let me chute him agin!" I shook my head indicating she could not shoot him again and after telling her to stay put at the top of the stairs, I returned to the landing to help Ray. My partner had turned the husband around a couple of times but couldn't see any blood.

"Where ya hit? I asked.

"There! She shot me in the back, right there."

The man pointed to an area on his back with his left hand, and rotated his right shoulder. Removing his suit jacket, we noticed a small hole in the fabric as well as a hole in his dress shirt. He removed both and when he did the slug fell out on the floor with a thud. Suddenly, I had a strong feeling of *Déjà vu*. Hadn't I seen this somewhere before? The man's right shoulder blade had a small dimple mark that was beginning to show bruising. From the top of the stairs to the bottom of the stairs, (a distance of about 25 feet) the bullet had hit solid bone and stopped. I was amazed. Ray and I had seen this situation with a .25 caliber semi-automatic pistol once before, and we couldn't help but look at each other and smile in sheer disbelief. This man had been *very* lucky. I picked up the slug off the floor and hefted it in my hand, tossing it in the air and catching it a couple times, glad that the man was unhurt.

"Are you willing to sign a complaint against your wife for shooting you?" I nonchalantly asked the husband. The two stared at each other for what seemed like a long time, while Ray and I waited patiently for his answer, knowing what it would be. We had small smiles on both our faces as I tossed the slug in the air one last time.

"Nah, she didn't get me," the man said quietly.

"Then you can keep this slug here, as a souvenir," I offered cheerfully.

"Okay-okay." he said looking at his feet, embarrassed and eager to comply.

"But you do have to find another place to spend the rest of the night," I insisted. "We can drop you off at a motel down on Interstate." As we escorted the husband out to the patrol car, I could hear the wife muttering to herself, "I know'd I shudda bot the thuty eight!" After we dropped the husband off at the Palms Motel, and watched him pay for and then enter his room, we drove to Central Precinct and put the .25 caliber semi-automatic pistol in the property room for safe keeping. I was happy that I was not entering it as a murder weapon. I was glad it hadn't killed anyone, and I was glad there had been no bloodshed for me to deal with either.

"Hell hath no fury like a woman scorned," Ray muttered as we returned to the police car.

"You can say that again!" I said with a chuckle.

"Car 72?" said the dispatcher. "Take a cold kick-in at the Opportunity Tavern. See the owner at North Vancouver and Ivy."

Man Down: Clarence's Sidewalk Demise

WHEN THE MOSS TURNED PURPLE

Before my career as a street cop ended, I fluctuated between having hope that I could make a difference in the world and feeling despondent over my role in law enforcement and how much good I could do. One shift I remember vividly. I was feeling good that night, convinced I could make Portland a better place and looking forward to going out and doing some police work. When I started my shift, I was feeling energetic. I'd gone out and had some cherry pie and coffee at the Bel Air and then I'd checked some of the local bars and taverns, like I did almost every shift. I hadn't been working long when I heard the call go out. I had just finished checking the Texas Playhouse and Van's Olympic Room to see which gangsters would be out on the streets looking to cause trouble. The usual suspects were missing, for the most part, from both establishments, so I strolled out to my car to resume patrol. My partner Ray had taken the night off and I was assigned Wild car 49, and ended up working alone.

As I was cruising around, I heard the radio call "Man down." The dispatcher repeated the call, "Man down," he said, "four hundred block of North Blandena." I listened intently, waiting for the district car to answer. "33, you available for a call?" The officers didn't answer, so I volunteered. "Man down, four hundred block on Blandena. 49 will take the call."

The weather had been good for a few nights but that night, it rained lightly on my way to work and the night air had that familiar smell of freshly rained on cement, earth and moss. I had my driver's window open wide, taking it all in, breathing deeply and enjoying the smell of Portland. The two cups of coffee I drank at the Bel Air were kicking in and I was ready to get to work.

Blandena Street runs east and west and the four hundred block was just west of North Williams Avenue. I didn't know who called the police, but suspected it was an annoyed neighbor or passing motorist. Either way, the streets were bare. Bare except for a man lying face down on the south sidewalk, head facing toward the river. His cheek was lying flat on the cold cement, and his arms were outstretched in front of him, with his palms flat on the pavement. He was dressed in dark, shabby clothing and wore a black overcoat too large for him that was half on and half off. He had definitely fallen on hard times. I got out of the car and jogged over to look at him, with my flashlight in my hand, quickly looking around to see if anyone else was nearby. No one was, so I knelt down, to access the situation, being careful not to place my knee in the huge amount of pooling blood collecting in front of him, and running down the sidewalk.

The blood had overrun the sidewalk and was running down the center cracks and into the bright green moss growing there. In the light of my flashlight, the scarlet blood turned the moss a glossy surreal purple color. I have never seen any color quite like it before or since. There was only one streetlight in the entire block and it was out. The houses were all rundown dumps, with tall grass and weeds crowding the front yard areas, along with an assortment of abandoned cars lining the street. The only light came from my car headlights and my flashlight, as I shone it over the man.

Of course, I knew him. The dying man was a long time Albina criminal named Clarence. He was one of the regular black gangsters I hadn't yet seen or come across that shift. I couldn't remember how many times I'd arrested Clarence, sometimes for assault, and sometimes for just being drunk and disorderly, but it was a lot. Looking down at him, I was instantly reminded of all the times I had arrested him over the years and how I had tried to keep him off the streets. The details of some of those arrests filtered back to me, filling my mind with images of Clarence resisting arrest, yelling profanities, trying to spit on me, calling me a "motherfucker" and smirking at his victims as they wept and told other covering officers what he'd done to them.

Clarence was a heroin dealer, a pimp, a thief and a robber. He was a very aggressive and brutal predator who spent a lot of time downtown picking up young women, both white and black at the dive bars that dotted the red-light district on Burnside. He would take them home to his apartment, have sex with them and then beat them up. When he was feeling more amiable, he would promise them the moon and the stars if they came with him, telling them he wanted them to be his "girlfriend." Then he would promptly do his best to get them addicted to his junk. He would turn them out as prostitutes and beat them mercilessly when and if they resisted, or tried to leave him or go back to their families.

I remember one of his prostitutes kept some of her earnings for herself; she was a young black underage girl, and when Clarence found out, he beat her so viciously she was in the hospital for two weeks recovering and yet she still refused to sign a complaint against him. That's how afraid people were of Clarence.

He was in his late thirties and had been a crook for a long time, since long before I'd signed on with PPB in 1961. I arrested him numerous times but never managed to get him more than about three months in jail. When Clarence ran short of cash he would rob, at gunpoint, the small Ma and Pop grocery stores in Albina and pistol whip any clerk who dared to talk back. In my mind, Clarence was pure evil and now it appeared he was getting his payback.

I bent down and tried to roll him over, lifting him up by the shoulders and turning him slightly, onto his side. I could see he'd been stabbed in the throat and the chest and most of the blood was coming from his neck. He opened his eyes, looking up at me in a daze, and I could tell, Clarence recognized me. "Call-a-am-bu-lance," he begged. The words came out of his mouth in a gurgled whisper. "It's too late, man, you're already dead," I said quietly, shaking my head.

He looked away from me, as I stood up. He had rolled back

onto his front, with his arms in front of him, and was trying to lift his head. He looked as if he were a man trying to swim, fully clothed in a sea of blood and concrete. I could see his eyes continued to blink and I knew he was considering what I'd just told him; that he was going to die. I suppose I could have called an ambulance, right at that moment. I suppose I could have told Clarence to hold on and everything would be all right, but I knew Clarence would be dead long before the ambulance arrived. And I wasn't going to lie to him, letting him think he had any kind of a fighting chance. I'd been around enough shot and stabbed up people to know he didn't have two minutes left. Maybe I did him a favor, by telling him he was "already dead." I guess I'll never know.

I returned to my car, sliding into the seat, and picked up the mic. "The man didn't make it. Send the coroner. I'll write a report for the dicks. 10-8." The radio cracked, "10-8, 49." Then I looked over at Clarence through the windshield, stretched out on the sidewalk and I could see his eyes were no longer blinking. His cheek was lying flat on the cold pavement again and his eyes were fixed and staring up at a sharp angle, into the dark night sky, dotted with glimmering stars. He was dead. I looked up and down the street, saw no one and didn't bother to look for whoever stabbed him. It didn't matter. Whoever they were, they had done the world a favor.

Captain Jim Purcell Junior

GOING THROUGH CHANNELS

About two weeks after Thelma walked free, after assaulting the businessman trick from Seattle, I found a memo in my in-box saying that Captain Jim Purcell wanted to see me again the following day. Purcell's status as captain resulted from being demoted, years earlier, after he'd been fired from his position as chief of police. The termination had occurred due to his involvement with corrupt associates in the late 1950s. By the time I came along, he was for all intents and purposes a laughing stock within the bureau, but he still retained a certain measure of undeniable power and influence as a police captain. I didn't care what Captain Purcell had to say to me, knowing as I did, that he could be both sarcastic and condescending.

I knew that he was just going to start harping about the numerous citizen complaints about me, that he claimed existed. The complaints represented nothing other than Fat Mary complaining about my presence, in my patrol car, outside of her whorehouse and how that interrupted her business. All that mattered to me was that Purcell couldn't keep me from being promoted to detective, but I needed to be certain of that. So, I called Lieutenant Andrew Crabtree at the chief's office, the following day. Crabtree was a hardworking, honest cop with a good reputation and I trusted him.

In the meeting, I expressed my intense disgust and frustration in dealing with Captain Purcell. I was tired of his blatant unprofessionalism, antagonism and flagrant deception, all while wearing a badge and a gun.

"All I wanna know is, can he can prevent me from being promoted to detective?"

"Jim Purcell *cannot* keep you from being promoted, Don. Don't worry about that. He has no further credibility here." Leaning over his desk earnestly, Crabtree sighed heavily, and folded his hands.

"Don, try to put up with Purcell, till an opening comes up in detectives, okay?"

"I don't know—he's just such a crook!"

"I know—I know, Don. Listen, if it gets too tough, I'll request a transfer, though channels, over the captain's head and I'll transfer you out myself."

"Thank you Sir," I said, rising from the chair, and smiling broadly. "You have no idea how much I appreciate this." Lieutenant Crabtree sighed again, and nodded his head wearily, returning to the paperwork on his desk. He said nothing more to me and I knew to take my leave. Lieutenant Crabtree was a man of few words. But it was clear, he respected me and I certainly respected him. He was one of the good guys in the bureau. This is great! I thought, as I walked down the hall, smiling down at the brown, spotted Asbestos tiles under my feet. I flipped Captain Purcell, a mental "bird," and ignored my appointment with him the next day. And then, at my very next opportunity, less than a week later, I once again parked my black and white in front of the very whorehouse Captain Purcell had warned me against watching. Fat Mary's whorehouse.

For a few minutes, as I sat there, I did some paperwork. I then turned on the flashing red light which illuminated the neighborhood. This scared off potential customers, and freaked out neighbors walking home from the local corner market. I sat in my car, smug, as I watched a young couple scurry off down the road, carrying bags of groceries, frightened by my flashing black and white. In only a few minutes, Fat Mary came stomping out on her front porch. She wore an ill-fitting, purple satin, too-tight blouse, and stood with her legs planted widely apart. She bellowed over at me, yelling, "Beat it! You get the hell outa here, DuPay!"

I smiled and tipped my cap at her, then ignoring her, I went back to my report writing, knowing there would be hell to pay. Fat Mary stomped back inside her house and slammed the door. Fuck Fat Mary and fuck Captain Purcell both, I thought to myself. As I continued to watch her house, I saw her pull aside the tattered

red draperies in her living room window. I could see she had her old black telephone pressed against her ear. She seemed animated and angry as she yelled into the receiver. She was letting me know she was calling Purcell. I sat in the patrol car, unmoved, refusing to leave for another twenty five minutes.

The situation with Captain Purcell was putting me under a lot of stress that my body and mind didn't need. I felt there was no hope for North Precinct and the citizens who lived in the area, so long as Captain Purcell remained in power. With few exceptions, the drinkers still drank on duty, the sleeping beauties still slept on duty, and traffic tickets were a joke—thanks to the cemetery on Columbia Boulevard. I had two weeks of vacation time coming, so I piled the family in the car and we drove to Disneyland. Getting away from the ghetto and the job made me realize what was happening to me on the inside. The people that had been head-shot, and gut-shot, all the crushed and scattered body parts lying in the streets from those horrendous accidents, the exhausted prostitutes who lived from one fix to the next, the parasite pimps who made their money keeping them hooked, the overall violence and the constant death; it was all taking its toll on me.

And on top of that, I was going head-to-head with a corrupt commander who wanted to destroy me. Captain Jim Purcell wanted to run houses of prostitution, without any interference from me. That interference was created by my desire to do good police work and enforce the law as I understood it. Some changes would have to be made, I decided. When I returned from our family vacation, however, I found that the changes had been made *for* me.

As I walked into the roll call room, one of my working sergeants was waiting for me with a funny look on his face. "Fat Mary's been complaining about you, DuPay," he told me smugly, as I came on shift. He was one of the old timers and had never liked me. "*And* Purcell says you're off the district," he concluded with a smirk.

"Well, what district am I working then?"

"You're not working the street anymore. You're working the desk, and at 7:00 a.m. you'll be directing rush hour traffic at the west end of the St. John's Bridge." I didn't give the sergeant the satisfaction of expressing surprise, anger or even disappointment. I just shrugged and walked away, all while I fumed internally. I knew where this had come from. Directly from Captain Jim Purcell, the ousted chief and laughing stock of the bureau. For the remainder of my time at North Precinct, close to a month, my only job would be to work the desk at night and then direct traffic at the end of the St. Johns Bridge during morning rush hour. There was an old expression back in those days, "A good cop doesn't get wet." Directing traffic in almost all cases is a punishment, or at least it was in my day. Every morning during this time, as he passed me in his car, on his way to work, Captain Jim Purcell would nod and smirk at me while I directed traffic. Now, he knew exactly where I was *and* what I was doing during my shift. I never gave him the satisfaction of letting him know just how much I hated him. I'd simply smile and wave him on by, because the truth was, I knew I was getting out and I wasn't afraid of him.

Purcell must have presumed that I had been humbled and now knew where I stood in the food chain. He must have presumed I would give him no further trouble or resistance. He was wrong. I had no intention of directing traffic so he could play with the hookers all night. I was beginning to thoroughly loathe the man and everything he stood for. Purcell came to represent everything I hated in a profession that I was genuinely proud of. I sometimes thought about plotting Purcell's demise and the fantasy preoccupied me, planning in my mind how I might do it. Such was the intensity of my hatred for him. He was after all trying to destroy me; he was trying to destroy my career and I despised him for it. What Purcell was doing was no different than what pimp, Jaynolen Moody had done. Purcell was running a trap line of prostitutes and collecting a percentage of the money they earned, to supplement his income, by providing protection from the police. The very police he worked with.

Before "Diamond Jim," Purcell was fired from his job as chief of police, due to blatant corruption, in the late 1950s, he was an associate of Jim Elkins, a notorious Portland mob boss and well-known criminal. Purcell's closest friend was a pimp by the name of George Bernard, and they spent a lot of time together. Some people say you can judge a person by the company they keep, and I've often found that to be true. After the 1952 mayoral election, the new mayor Fred Peterson, not known for being particularly honest, had allegedly been paid $100,000 by Jim Elkins to appoint Jim Purcell to the position of chief of police. (Stanford, 2004).

By the time I was working for the Portland Police Bureau, the rumor I heard, was that Jim Purcell was involved in providing protection for numerous houses of prostitution and he was paid handsomely for that protection. Purcell made sure that no police officers investigated those operations, or in any way harassed the women or madams who operated and worked in those establishments. Though Purcell had been demoted, from chief to captain, his power at the precinct remained unchallenged and it was that power that allowed Fat Mary to stomp out on her front porch and yell at me, a Portland police officer, to "beat it," and leave she and her working girls alone.

Having me direct traffic was Purcell's hole card, but now it was time to play mine. On September 15, 1967, I requested a transfer out of North Precinct. Lieutenant Crabtree kept his promise to me. I had taken and passed the necessary tests for promotion to detective. A letter came to my in-box from the civil service board, which said that my name would be "added to the list of those certified eligible for promotion." The long five year-wait for eligibility and the hours of hard study were over. All I had to do now was wait for an opening.

Eleven days later, I was transferred to East Precinct and then promoted to detective on November 9, 1967. I was just thirty one-years-old. My wife and I celebrated. We stripped the closet of the old blue uniforms and bought a few new suits. "Here's to Captain Purcell!" I said to my wife, while we drank red wine with our dinner. "Here's to him kissing my ass!"

Interlude

Well, how about it? Do you think crime pays? Are you wondering what happened to these real life characters I got to know so well? The ones who drove the Cadillacs? The schemers, the druggies, the con artists, and the hookers? And how about the blue uniformed crime stoppers at the St. Johns Police department? I know the endings to some of these stories. For instance, Buck Owens never did get *this* "white paddy pig," in his gun-sights and I heard later that he died under suspicious circumstances in California somewhere. Along with that, I heard through the police grapevine that shortly after Buck Owens had threatened to shoot me, two of my closet blue uniformed buddies, (Roy and John) had given Owens a ride down to Swan Island where, out on the end of a pier, they promptly kicked the shit out of him. All the while explaining to Buck that to shoot a policeman was probably not a good idea and to shoot DuPay was definitely not a good idea.

Pam Owens, tragically, died in Portland of a heroin overdose before she turned twenty one. In fact, Jaynolen Moody eventually lost several of the girls in his stable, including Thelma and Myra in one day, which had to have hurt his wallet. After an altercation at Van's Olympic Room, Thelma Zena Moody was shot and killed February 26, 1972 by Myra, whose full name was Margaret Parker. Thelma was only 29, and Myra 26, at the time of the shooting. They had gotten into a fight over the "quality" but more likely the ownership of a cheap $10 wig. What I heard is that Thelma pulled a knife on Myra and Myra happened to be armed that night. The knife flashed and Myra's gun fired and Thelma lay mortally wounded on the dance floor of Van's Olympic room, dying sometime later at Emmanuel Hospital. Myra was arrested with a man named Calvin Calhoun, who was held as an accessory to murder but then later released. "Police said patrons told them the two women were arguing over the quality of a wig when the incident occurred." (Oregonian Archives, 1972). Myra spent less than six months in jail and was released when she pled guilty to manslaughter, after the original murder charge was reduced. Myra was put on five years probation and fined $500. At the time of the shooting, Thelma went to the morgue and Myra went to jail for a few months, at which time, Moody took off to Las Vegas to try his luck and I never heard from him again after that.

Elwin Van Riper, or Van as he was commonly called, the owner of Van's Olympic Room, was never to my knowledge involved in any official criminal activity, despite the sordid reputation of his establishment, and I eventually heard that Van Riper died of natural causes. Although, in the twelve years, Van let LeRoy Clark run his place, as manager and bartender, Van *had* to have known about LeRoy's drug dealing and other possible criminal activity.

And what happened to LeRoy Clark? LeRoy was a tougher case. He was gunned down by members of the PPB SERT team, January 7, 1976 after a violent siege at Van's Olympic Room. I learned from an old informant of mine, that LeRoy had been upset about a "drug deal" gone bad. LeRoy blamed a narcotics sergeant for double crossing him. The situation would have led to considerable prison time LeRoy was not willing to accept, according to the informant, and a considerable loss of money had already been incurred, for whatever reason. LeRoy provoked a confrontation at the club after an eight hour standoff that would turn deadly. He felt he'd been screwed over and wanted to get even with the cops, hoping he might even kill a few. After several hours of refusing to come out and surrender, LeRoy turned out all the lights in Van's Olympic Room and stripped off his clothing. LeRoy lay on the floor behind the bar, a black man, naked in the darkness. He was waiting for the white policemen to come, his shotgun and his .38 ready. LeRoy was ready to kill. He was also ready to die.

After the police spent several hours calling for LeRoy to surrender with their loud speakers in the parking lot, and trying to reach him by phone, they heard no movement or sound and became concerned. They were concerned that LeRoy had killed himself and his wife Colleen, as he had allegedly threatened her life earlier while in the restaurant. The police entered the darkened club and one of the sergeant's, Sgt. Charles Hill, crept slowly across the floor, edging closer to the end of the bar. Unknowingly, Hill was crawling directly into LeRoy's sights.

As Hill crawled closer, LeRoy cut loose with his shotgun. The force of the blast spun the sergeant around and threw him to the floor, riddling his body with fifty two shotgun pellets. LeRoy jumped up, leaned over the bar and shot Hill again in the back, with his .38 revolver. The shot was a through and through and just barely missed Hill's heart. As Hill was attempting to escape, he got to his feet and put himself in the line of fire again. At that point, Patrolman, Dave Petry came to his aid with "a violent flying tackle that knocked Hill across the room and out the front door of the club." (Oregonian, 1-10-1976). Hill was reported as saying, "I think I owe my life to Petry. Dave's a big man and lucky for me he hits hard enough to move you. He moved me out of danger that night." (Oregonian, 1-10-1976).

After firing at Hill, LeRoy was then killed by gunfire from the rest of the SERT team, and bled to death from wounds received all below the waist. Sergeant Hill lived even though he had been hit by numerous shotgun pellets and shot in the back with a .38 pistol. The official story in the Oregonian, as related by the police, was that LeRoy had found God at the first of the year. That would have been January 1, 1976, *six* days before his death. They also claimed that several witnesses said LeRoy had been acting strangely for several days leading up to the siege. Elwin Van Riper claimed LeRoy had said, several days before the siege, "Van, I'm going to even up with God."

Sergeant Charles Hill also expressed deep regret that Clark had been killed, telling officers later, "I was shot by a friend of mine." LeRoy Clark was very well liked, despite his criminal activities, and had many friends on the police force. "Clark had a number of friends, including policemen, before he was shot to death Wednesday morning after holding officers at bay in the North Portland club for nearly eight hours." (Oregonian, 1-8-1976). A personal friend of LeRoy's, T.J. Olive claimed, "He got into religion about the first of the year. And it really snapped his mind. He sent away to California for some religious books and told me after the first of the year his whole body had turned over. I pleaded with him last night to give himself up, to throw out the guns, but he wouldn't listen. I don't think he knew what he was doing by then. He'd just rather die than come out. I never been around a man who went off so quick like that." (Oregonian, 1-8-1976).

Another witness claimed LeRoy had been using drugs shortly before he snapped. In my experience, people who deal drugs, as LeRoy did, also generally use drugs. It's very possible that was the case. It's also possible, as my former informant insisted, that LeRoy had been double crossed by someone in narcotics and wanted to get even. One cannot help but wonder, if LeRoy *had* found God, why would he then want to commit murder?

And poor Mr. and Mrs. Opperman. A month after I was promoted to detective, in middle December 1967, two young black men walked into Carl and Alice Oppermans store with the intention of robbing them. They loitered for about half an hour and then one of them trapped Mr. Opperman in a back aisle, demanding money in full view of several other customers who were in the store. "This is a stick-up!" the young man was quoted as saying by one eye witness. Old man Opperman was defiant and refused to give them the contents of the till. He had been pistol whipped less than a year before and his store had been robbed and vandalized several times in the past few years. Old man Opperman tried to fire his small .25 caliber hand gun at the young criminal but missed both times. The young man then shot Carl Opperman, who was 75-years-old in the head and chest, with a .38 caliber revolver, killing him instantly. Mrs. Opperman was shot in the chest and left to die. She didn't die though, she survived as her wound had been a "through and through" flesh wound. With Carl Opperman shot up and killed, and Alice Opperman in the hospital, it effectively ended the only white owned business on Mississippi Avenue at that time. (Oregonian archives, 1967).

Although Ray Jones and I remained friends, he was never able to pass a promotional exam and remained a patrol officer at North, where he continued to do good police work and honor the badge. And the captain? Less than six months after my promotion to detective, Captain Jim Purcell Junior, "Diamond Jim," died of natural causes following a surgery, March 7, 1968. He was buried with the honors befitting a former chief of police, which I never understood considering the reality of his career and the corruption he had always embraced. I requested a position as one of his pallbearers, by sending a written request, through channels, but was ultimately refused. Too bad, I thought. I had wanted to carry the bastard to his grave.

Don DuPay, as a young idealistic recruit, three weeks after signing on with the city. Circa late April 1961.

Don DuPay the day he was processed in as a new detective, November, 1967.

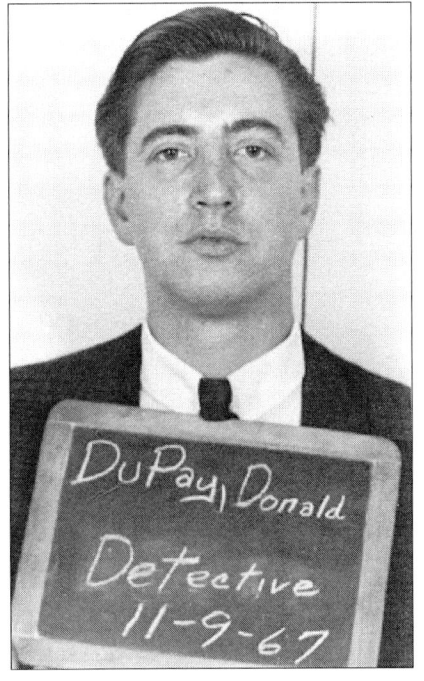

A typical structure at the old Columbia Villa located in the heart of the ghetto. Date and photographer unknown.

The Columbia Villa, too-small homes with a lot of grassy areas. Date and photogapher unknown.

Twentieth and Belmont, circa 1965, during the time Dupay worked that district. Photographer unknown.

Don DuPay in the burglary office, 1973. Photographer unknown.

Detective Don DuPay and Detective John Wayne Wesson in the burglary PPB office, 1970, examining a recently compromised Square door safe. Photographer unknown.

Above, left: Fred Brock, as a young recruit. DuPay's first coach and a good, fair cop. November of 1951.

Above, right: Frank Jozaitis, circa 1961. First partner of DuPay and a good all around cop. Committed suicide in 1965, depressed over the death of Bobby Ferron.

Left: Marlon "Ned" Nedderman was a great cop and detective. There was never any resistance when Ned was around. He got the job done, and was a jovial, dedicated and hardworking cop.

Above, left: Bobby Ferron, one of the first native American police officers hired with PPB. Ferron died in a car accident, while working in the vice squad, 1964. Photo taken July 16th, 1961.

Above: Leo Miller could have been the chief of police, if not for politics and burn-out. He worked as DuPay's traffic Sergeant and was one of the finest, most hardworking, idealistic, by the book cops ever employed with PPB. Photo date April 6th, 1954. Miller later committed suicide in 1975.

Left: Ray Jones, worked at North precinct and was DuPay's second partner and a fearless cop who always knew what to do and when to do it. Photo from Portland's Finest; Past and Present. 2000. Photo date 1982.

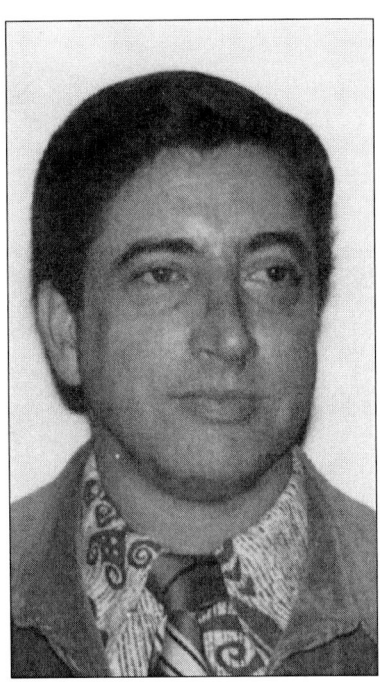

Above left: Detective Lieutenant Myron Warren hand picked DuPay as the youngest detective to work the Safe Detail with veteran detectives. Warren was a superbly honest police officer, with absolute integrity. He oversaw a staff of detectives proud and honored to work with him. Date of photo 1965.

Above right: Don DuPay, circa 1974, working the burglary detail.

Left: Phil Todd, a tough East Precinct patrol officer and later homicide detective who worked with DuPay. A good all around cop, tough, efficient, hard drinking and an often married, nice guy. Photo from Portland's Finest Past and Present, 2000. Photo date 1982.

Left: The notorious and nefarious Jim Purcell. Also known as Diamond Jim, he taught DuPay the meaning of corruption among the powerful command structure of PPB at the time. Circa 1944, photographer unknown.

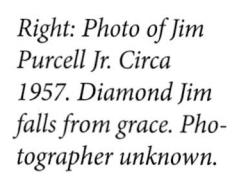

Right: Photo of Jim Purcell Jr. Circa 1957. Diamond Jim falls from grace. Photographer unknown.

Left: Carl Crisp in an early, 1931 photo. The good friend and associate of Jim Purcell, Crisp's well known corruption in the police bureau almost resulted in another cop killing him.

Right: Would you buy a used car from this man? Carl Crisp was one of the most ruthless and corrupt police lieutenants working for PPB at that time. Photo date, February 2nd, 1953.

209

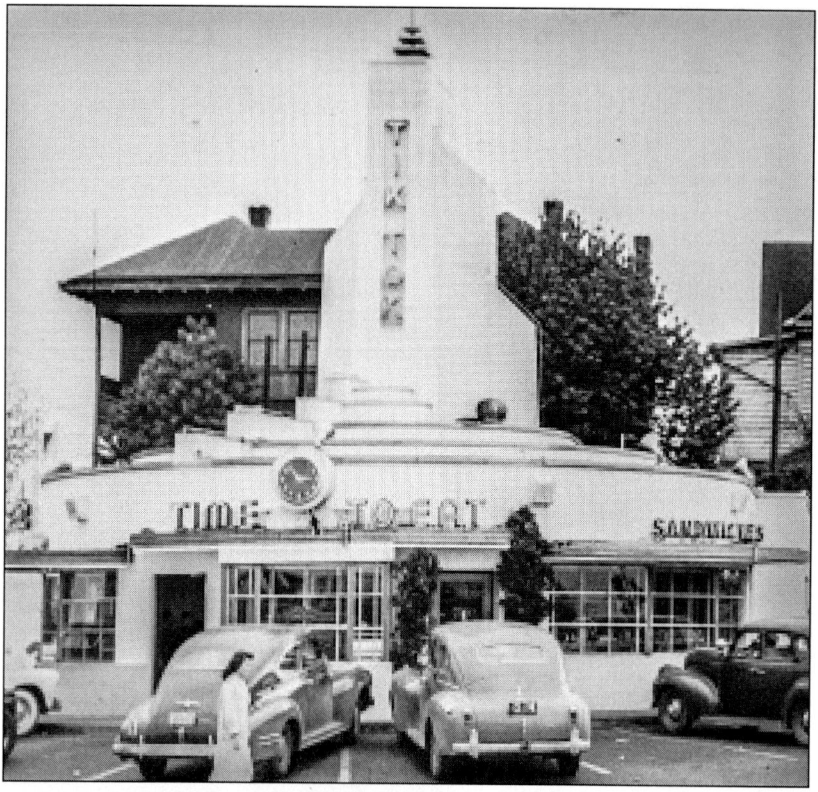
TIK TOK
TIME TO EAT
SANDWICHES

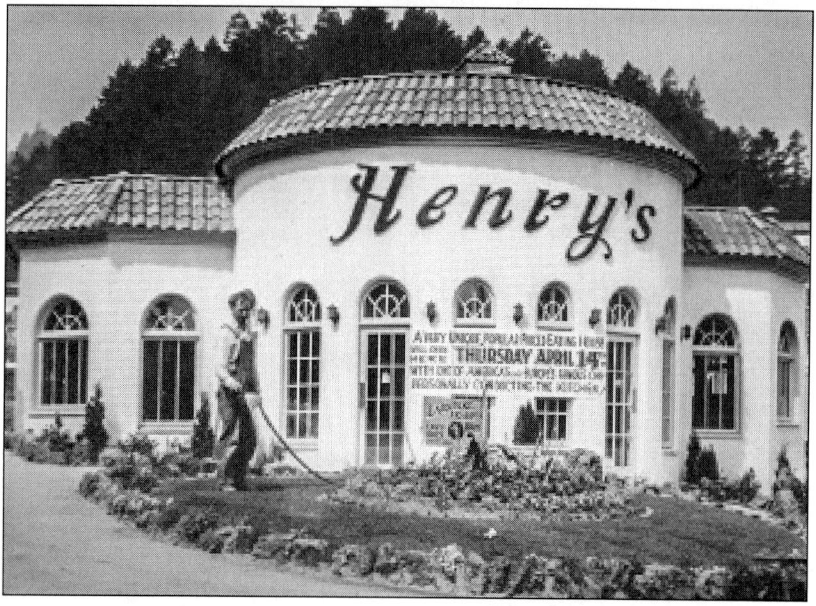
Henry's
THURSDAY APRIL 14

Left, top: The Tic Toc, one of the last drive-in restaurants, was located on 12th, where Burnside and NE Sandy Boulevard used to meet. Portland police officers regularly visited The Tic Toc for coffee. "22, 10-8, 10-10, Tic Toc."

Left, bottom: Henry Thiele's restaurant was another occasional coffee stop for Portland Police officers working in NW Portland and the downtown Central Precinct District.

Following page: Disturbance at Union and Fremont:
PPB officers Phil Todd and Don Kagy break up a fistfight at Union and Fremont, circa 1967. This photo shows Officer Phil Todd and Officer Don Kagy as they pull two black male youths apart, thereby breaking up a fistfight. This photo has been used in a biased fashion previously, in 2013, by PSU professors, Leanne Serbulo and Karen Gibson. In their essay, "Black and Blue," which details police civilian relations during the 1960s, they suggest the entire group of black youth in the photo were engaged in a conflict with the two officers present on the scene. They title the photo, "Black Youth Clash with Portland Police." The reality however is far less sinister. The photo depicts a large group of black youth, mostly males, with a small number of attractive females. Two black males are engaged in a fight, (note torn clothing and the way both the young men grip each other). Todd and Kagy were simply trying to break up a fistfight, which easily could have been a conflict over the affections of one of the pretty girls present. The fact that Phil Todd, on the left, has a cigarette in his mouth tells me that this was not a call that was radioed in, but rather a situation where Todd and Kagy were on patrol, just driving around and they happened to drive by. Phil jumped out of the car with the cigarette still in his mouth, which would not have happened if there had been a call radioed in to their patrol car. He would have disposed of the cigarette. I can remember several times this happened with me, as I smoked for the first four years of my career. When I happened to come across a crime in progress, the cigarette often stayed clamped in my mouth, as I jumped out of the patrol car, running. Trying to spin a straightforward image into something it is not is typical of those individuals who are critical of police no matter what the contrary may prove. I mention these things now because I worked with Phil Todd and Don Kagy, and they were both good police officers. Neither one of them deserved to have their integrity questioned or be judged potentially racist in Serbulo and Gibson's 2013 essay, Black and Blue, simply by virtue of a photo that was presented in a dishonest manner.

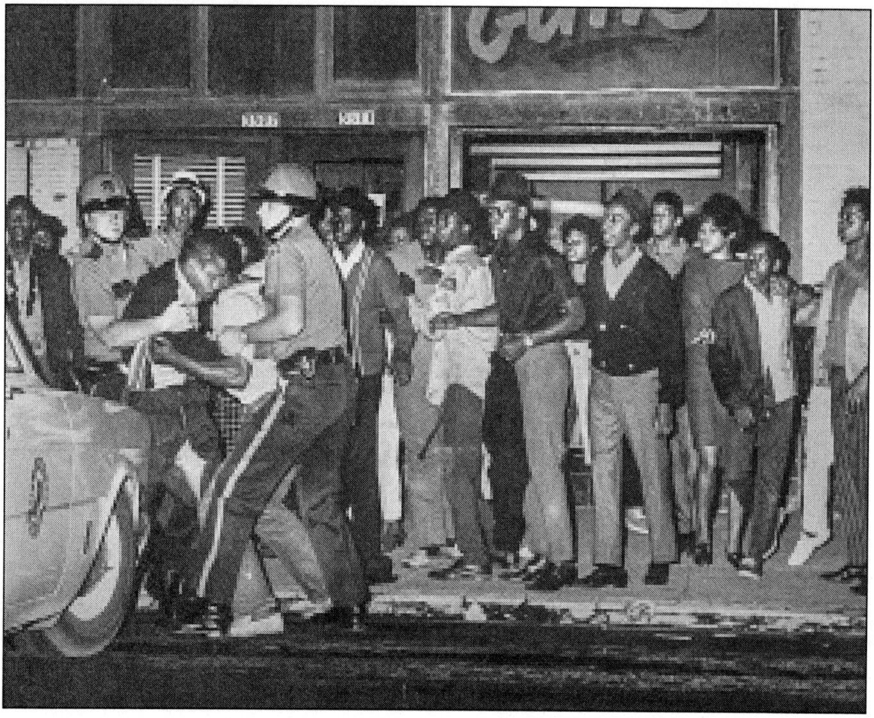

Some St John's Families;
a Retrospective

IN THE 1960s, ST. JOHNS was considered, by many local residents as a city apart from Portland. In a letter of commendation from that time frame, to the Portland Police Bureau regarding an officer's good conduct, a St. John's citizen complained about its poor reputation, writing, "Some people say St. Johns is like Siberia! And that doesn't sit well with me!" Many of the decent people of St. Johns resented its poor reputation. There were reasons for that though. The old city of St. Johns, had its own identity, flavor and people. It sat just a few miles up the river from Portland, and was a rough and tumble, mill town, filled with hardworking and hard drinking folks who sometimes liked to cause trouble. Many of the stories in this book, are predicated on the families with whom I came into contact as a street cop working the North End, including the entire St. Johns area. The citizens called us "The St. Johns police," even though we were all employed with Portland Police Bureau. Those of us who worked St. Johns were given that special nickname. Many of the families that settled in St. Johns remained there for decades, up to and including the time I worked there as a street cop during the 1960s. I came into contact with these families, sometimes on a daily basis, and it was always eventful and unusual.

This was a community of people who were proud of their mill town ways, as well as their many nefarious activities that brought in extra money on the sly. I encountered the younger members of these families, routinely, skipping school, violating curfew, ignoring the traffic laws, drinking alcohol, beating up other kids and shoplifting at the local Fred Meyers on Lombard and Ida. I can only give thanks to such St. Johns families as the Kemples, the Teeters, the Seacrests, the Longorias, the Banks, and the Bearcubs, for contributing in their own way, to the richness of detail I have described in my book and in the various stories I've been able to share with the reader. Though I have not named them specifically, several stories in my book involved some of the younger members of these families, and their antics, crimes and various escapades.

I can remember a specific teenage Longoria, out after curfew, drunk, smoking pot, yelling profanities, swaggering around, as he hung out at The Oak Pit, a hamburger joint on Lombard and North Ida. As an adult, this Longoria spent some serious time as a guest of the Oregon state penal institution, after spending years dealing drugs, stealing cars and parting them out in chop shops. He ran his own version of a Midnight Auto Supply Store, breaking the law on a regular basis and I often had to haul him into the precinct to spend time in the flat-barred holding cell that had probably been there, longer than both of us had been alive. I also remember a troubled teenager, Frankie Bearcub, doing the same thing. Frankie Bearcub was a defiant, angry, outspoken type of criminal I always knew would come to a bad end. He spent his time hanging out with his brothers and other low income kids from the neighborhood, drinking, smoking and shoplifting from the Fred Meyers.

Frankie stole constantly and he often wound up arrested. Just as many times he didn't get arrested and got away with it. He'd steal endless cartons of cigarettes, candy and beer, to sell to his friends for extra money. Sometimes, he'd get caught, and I'd be called to the Fred Meyer to take him to Juvenile Detention Hall, where he'd be home in three hours and back at the Fred Meyer to try his hand again. Bearcub later graduated to stealing cars regularly, for the local chop shops and became a habitual criminal. As Frankie grew up, he developed a hopeless addiction to alcohol, which only fueled his propensity for violence and predatory behavior. He was ultimately shot and killed by Portland police officer, Chuck Jensen, in 1985, after holding a Middle Eastern man hostage, at knife point, and refusing Jensen's repeated orders to drop the knife. When Bearcub said, "You've got three seconds or I'm gonna kill this guy!" Jensen fired two shots and Bearcub's unhappy life was finally over. Officer Jensen took a life that day, but he also saved a life. The scenario was a classic case of suicide by cop and represents the terrible dilemma that police officers face, when in a hostage situation with a desperate and unpredictable person who has nothing left to lose and wants to die.

Upon reflection it seems obvious that in spite of the time I spent both counseling and sending these kids through the criminal justice system, hopefully for some guidance, it was mostly to no avail. My sense of futility at seeing these kids repeated offenses and self-destructive behavior just added to my conviction that no matter how hard cops work, they won't make much of a difference. Despite the hundreds of arrests I made, of these youths, these St. Johns families provided some of the fabric through which this story is woven and the book would not be complete without mentioning them here.

The Detectives, Fall, 1967

BURGLARS 101

IN THE LATE 1960s, THE mood and temperament of society, concerning the employment of women and minorities was rapidly changing. The police department had always been almost exclusively male, white, tall and athletic. Regulations dictated a minimum height of no less than five feet nine inches. With a police force of over 650 sworn officers, less than ten were black and I don't remember an Asian ever being among them. The only Native Americans I can recall were Bobby Ferron, who was tragically killed in the line of duty in 1964, and Lieutenant Bill Taylor, who worked as my supervisor in traffic and was later promoted to Captain. Bill Taylor was a good guy and a great cop. The other officers respected him and he never got any flack, as far as I knew, because of his race.

Women, although allowed to join the police force, were restricted to the social work environment of the Women's Protective Division. They were not allowed to wear a uniform, work the street, or compete with male officers for higher rank. The attitude at the time, was that although women did have a place working in the Women's Protective Division, with children and female victims, street police work was still a man's job. And it was a big man's job at that. Cops wanted it to stay that way. So did I, as a matter of fact, for the simple reason that I could not imagine running after a dangerous, male criminal with a woman standing five feet four and weighing 125 pounds, struggling to keep up with me. Men are simply larger, stronger and faster and at the time, police work was considered the realm of men and only men.

Sinister forces, though, were at work to change the status quo. A couple of sisters, ball busters, as they were called behind their backs, by the men in the bureau, joined the police department in the middle 1960s. The more determined of the two sisters filed a civil rights lawsuit to force equal employment rights for women in police work. She ended up filing *many* lawsuits. She had no intention of wasting her talents away in the Women's Protective Division. As a detective during this time, I also worked as a coach, regularly teaching newbies the finer points of how to be good detectives. One of my young detectives was the younger of the two ball buster sisters. Ultimately I recommended, in my written coaching report, that she not be retained as a detective. I came to this decision, because her interest didn't seem to be in police work but more in promoting the feminist movement. While I had no problem with women promoting feminist ideology or the feminist movement, I did have a problem with any individual pushing their personal agenda at the expense of good police work. She also had only a few weeks experience working the streets as a patrol officer and I felt it would have been an insult to have such an inexperienced person promoted to detective. Unfortunately, command disregarded my recommendation and this woman continued to infect the bureau with her ambition and lack of commitment to doing adequate police work.

During this time, the department was buzzing with comments, and predictions of doom and gloom were everywhere. As might be expected, the idea of women working side by side with male officers was not popular with anyone on the force. One street cop I knew told me, "If I've got a dangerous problem on the street and I ask for a cover car and they send a woman, then I've got the *same* problem I had in the first place, plus a female to protect!"

"Hell no, I don't want another woman in the police car with my husband that many hours a day," said one cop's wife to a friend of mine. "You know how close partners can get?!" she concluded. "The next thing you know they'll be lowering the height-weight and intelligence standards! This is the beginning of the end," said an old-timer I had known for years. "They ought to leave things the way they are!" said someone else I knew. Most male police officers genuinely believed that women didn't belong in the ranks on the street, because they were smaller, weaker and less capable as fighters.

The view on African Americans was grim also. As far as blacks were concerned, it was generally felt that they didn't apply for police jobs for two reasons: blacks were basically anti-establishment, and didn't want to join up and become "the man." And it was commonly thought at the time that they weren't smart enough to pass the tests, which I always felt was bullshit. The Duke Brothers had been exemplary cops and had definitely passed the tests to become police officers, and I'd always been happy to work with them. "It'll be a sorry day for law enforcement when they let down the gate!" said Mike O'Leary, philosophically, one afternoon, as we all sat during our lunch break, drinking coffee and commiserating. O'Leary was an old, cynical, cigar-chomping Irish cop. He was a burglary detective I worked with early on after being promoted to detective and he always said the first thing that came into his head.

I sat with O'Leary and Fred Brock that afternoon, discussing the way things were changing and O'Leary finished his resentful diatribe by saying, as he blew out a smoke ring distractedly, "All they'll be hiring is cunts, runts and niggers!" We had all laughed at O'Leary's profane comments, but we kept our personal views to ourselves and said nothing. History will be the best judge of whether law enforcement has changed for the better and how. And in numerous respects, this remains to be seen. But I explain the mood here, and the opinions and perspectives of those men I worked with, because it reflected the mood and opinions of most cops at the time and not only in Portland either. And so, as I put away the uniform of my old working days as a street cop, the uniform I had been so proud to wear and that represented my idealism and naivety, I now joined the detectives, wearing a different uniform of plain clothes, and realized that things were rapidly changing. The clock could not be turned back.

The Initiation

WHO PUT SERGEANT HEMPE IN CHARGE?

THE DETECTIVE DIVISION OPERATED OUT of the second floor offices at the downtown police headquarters building and was home to about eighty detectives. A full shift of dicks worked days, a few less on the swing shift and three or four were assigned to graveyard to handle emergency cases such as murders, robberies and shootings. A detective's job was a laid back operation compared to the uniform. The uniform was rush-rush, answer the radio, get to the call and get on to the next one. As a detective, you went to work in an office, wore a suit and tie, and worked most of your cases from behind a desk, with the ever present telephone at the ready.

Each crime detail had separate office spaces, but shared the secretarial pool. Emma Jozaitis, Frank's widow, worked as a clerk typist for the detectives. She was continuing on with her life, and I always thought the bureau did a wonderful thing by giving her that job, and helping her support her four children after Frank's suicide. It was a wonderful thing to do for a new widow. It took one more worry off her mind and ensured that she would have a good way to support her children.

The work load of the burglary detail merited large office spaces and was divided into three sub-specialties; house burglaries, commercial and business burglaries, and the most prestigious was the safe burglary detail. When I joined the SMU or special missions unit, warrants had been issued for a number of active, city wide burglars, and the detectives were operating a temporary unit to bring them to trial. I was assigned to be the newest member of the SMU. Our unit was a portion of burglary detail guys, temporarily working to serve these warrants.

On my first working day, I showed up in a new dark blue suit. I had gotten a fresh haircut, and I knew I looked good. I stopped by the police photo lab to have my picture taken for my new ID card;

the one that said I was a detective. Detectives didn't have a stand up roll call, so after I walked into the squad room, I introduced myself to the shift commander and sat down at a table with a cup of hot coffee. The other detectives coming into work, also grabbed some coffee and sat at their desks. The shift commander, Sergeant Schwartz, spoke amicably with the other detectives, laughing and joking, as if it were any other day and then slowly idled over to me. He handed me an envelope without comment. I opened it, feeling apprehensive. Inside, were official chief's orders. The orders transferred Sergeant George Hempe *back* to the detective division and placed him in command of the Special Mission Unit. Now *my* current unit. I couldn't believe it. My mouth slowly fell open. This was the fucked-up sergeant I had chased at high speeds around the SE part of town and caught at a dead-end street, dead drunk. Because of me, he had been suspended from duty for thirty days and kicked out of the detectives division permanently. Now, they were going to bring him back and make him my boss? When I looked up, from reading the orders, with a dazed look on my face, the whole crew of about six men were staring at me tight lipped and silent. Then, one guy started to grin, and another started to chuckle, and pretty soon they were all roaring with laughter. I didn't get it. I looked around, confused. "What's the matter son? Don't you get it?" asked one of the sergeants, slapping me hard on the back and laughing. "It's a joke! A big fucking joke, DuPay! Welcome to the detectives!"

From Behind a Desk

SIX THOUSAND DOLLARS AND SOME CHECKS

After three weeks, most of the burglars we were looking for were in custody and things got back to normal. For me, that meant working the day shift with Tuesday and Wednesday off. Only the new guys worked weekends. I felt like I had rejoined civilization, going from night hawk to day person; an eight-to-four, suit-and-tie, go-to-work-in-the-daytime, kind of person. I marked off the thirtieth day on my desk calendar with a feeling of satisfaction. It had been a whole month since I'd seen a dead body. The burglary detail was a wonderful place to work. The detectives maintained a small crew on weekends; just myself, and Big Ned. Marlen W. Nedderman was a former motorcycle cop I'd known when I'd worked as a traffic cop. In our new environs, working in the detectives, there was just me, Big Ned and another new detective, named Archer, down the hall in robbery. Although we were assigned to burglary investigation, we were also required to work any case that needed immediate attention, from rape and robbery to auto theft and check fraud. Big Ned was my new partner. He'd been a motorcycle cop, for PPB, for many years. According to Ned, riding a motorcycle for fun was one thing, but *having* to do police work on a motorcycle was something else again.

Chasing speeders, running red lights and investigating accidents can be very dangerous on a bike. It took a special personality to do it, and Big Ned was that personality. Ned was a big, strong, jovial, man, about six feet four inches and 260 pounds. I can remember when Ned worked as a motorcycle cop, and he'd swing his leg over the bike, the back wheel would squash down, almost flat from his weight. Ned lived on a farm forty miles down the valley with real horses, cows and a tractor. As a cycle cop he'd been allowed to take the bike home at night. That meant free transportation to the farm and back every day. Only motorcycle cops and police captains got a free, city-owned vehicle to drive back and forth to work. But with the promotion, to detective, Ned had to give back the cycle and drive his own car. Sometimes he'd grump about the price of gas, this being 1967. Gas was around 36 cents a gallon and Ned often complained about it, and about the way the world was changing overall. He'd also complain about the price of hay, for his animals. It made me glad I was a city dweller and didn't have to worry about such things. Big Ned was fun to work with. He was laid back, confident and had a sense of humor. And because of his sheer size, nobody ever gave us any shit. When Big Ned said you were going to jail, there was no argument.

One of our first cases together involved a furnace manufacturing company, with a plant over on North Russell Street that had been burglarized over the weekend. When we came to work on Sunday morning we were told that a uniformed car was awaiting our arrival to investigate some kind of an explosion. When we arrived, it did look like an explosion had occurred. In the main office was an ancient, square-door safe. It had been turned on its back and the two burglars had chopped it open with an ax. After they had torn the safe apart, there were scattered bits and sections lying all over the floor. The insulating fire clay from the safe, also covered everything with a fine, white dusty powder.

The owners of the company were astonished that their big old safe, the one they had been keeping company payroll in for over twenty years had been broken into so easily. "They got the payroll checks and the check printer too! I thought that safe was *safe!*" said the owner indignantly.

From looking at the mess they made and the way they attacked the safe, it was easy to see that these burglars were strictly amateurs and probably employees or former employees of the company. Sadly, the safe was typical of hundreds of old safes built from the 1850s to the 1920s, and still in use by many companies at that time, in the middle 1960s. During the days of the Old West, the pioneer businessmen needed a safe place to keep money, gold and records. Many Eastern companies responded by building safes.

What they really built was a thin steel inner box surrounded by six inches of insulating fire clay. Fire clay is something like cement only softer. The fire clay is covered with another layer of sheet steel and a heavy cast iron door, also full of fire clay, and the door is then fitted on the front. The combination dial on the safe door activated the locking bars inside the door when the combination was worked. The safes were big, heavy and appeared formidable with their massive, thick, square doors. These old safes were actually nothing more than junk and could be easily opened in less than thirty minutes by someone who knew how. Far from being a secret, in terms of how to bust one open, many burglars specialized in opening these old boxes and made a career out of it.

The poor businessmen soon learned that his new safe afforded him no protection. Burglars opened them easily. There were three different ways. The easiest way was to break the dial off with a big hammer, hitting it cleanly so the spindle broke off flush. They then took a "punch" tool and hit the spindle hard, driving it back into the door and into the safe. With the spindle controlling the locking device gone, they could just turn the handle and the door would open. This was known as a punch job. Another way to bust open these safes, was to lay the safe on its back and hit the upper left hand corner of the door with a sledge hammer four or five times. That would cause the steel covering the door-face to curl back, allowing a crow bar to be inserted beneath it. The door-face plates on the safe were riveted to the cast-iron door frame, so by working the crow bar down the edge of the door, the face plate steel peeled back. Now all you had to do was dig the fire clay out and push back the locking bars. This was known as a safe peel.

The third way was the most crude but also effective. Turn the safe upside down. Then with an ax, you could chop through the outer sheet steel, dig out the fire clay there, and then chop your way through the thin inner steel. You were in, and it was simple. This was called a chop-job. The safe companies responded by making their products a little better. They changed the shape of the spindle from straight to tapered and added a re-locking

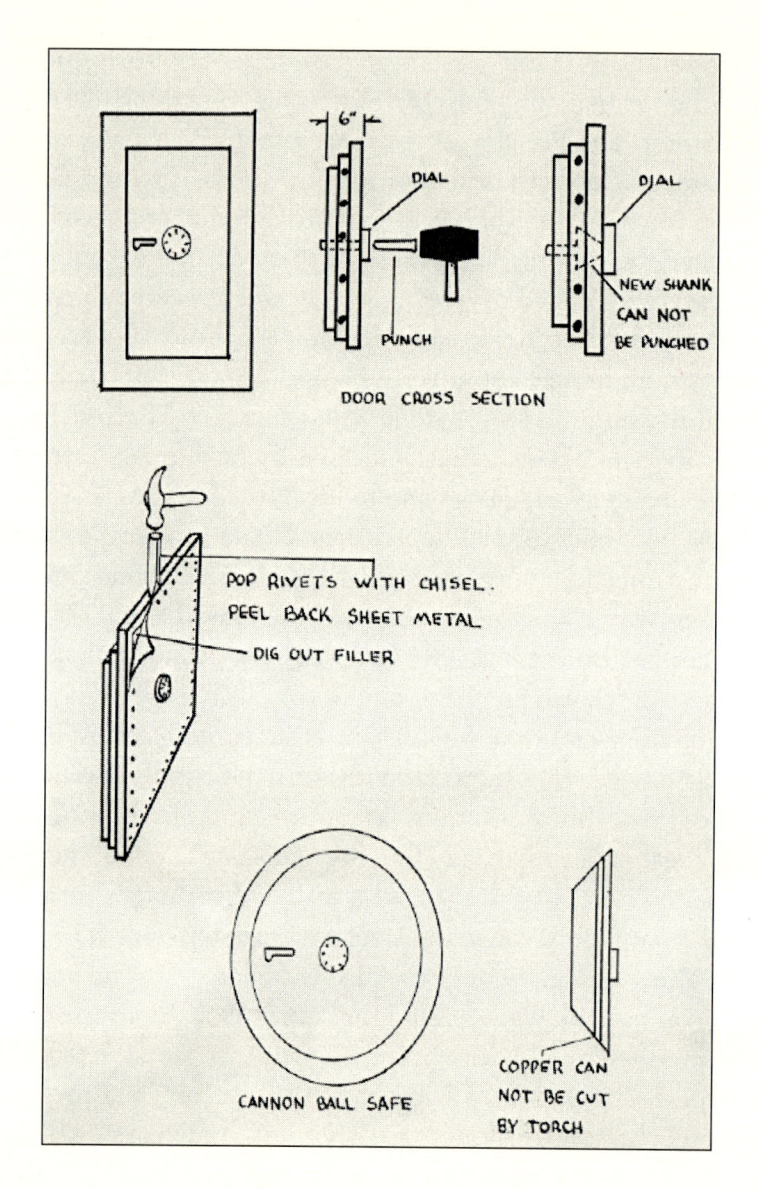

Diagram labels: DIAL; 6"; PUNCH; DOOR CROSS SECTION; DIAL; NEW SHANK CAN NOT BE PUNCHED; POP RIVETS WITH CHISEL; PEEL BACK SHEET METAL; DIG OUT FILLER; CANNON BALL SAFE; COPPER CAN NOT BE CUT BY TORCH

device. Now, when the burglar hit the dial spindle, the now tapered shape wedged the spindle even tighter and set off the re-locking device. This would freeze the door in the locked position. But it could still be peeled or hacked open. Somewhere along the line it dawned on the safe companies that there was no way to secure a square door safe and they began doing research and looked around for something better. The eventual answer to security was heavy metal. They called it the Cannon Ball Safe. It weighed over a thousand pounds and was made of very thick steel shaped like a huge cannon ball with a thick, steel, round door. It proved to be a formidable monster. No way to punch, peel, or chop it open. Still, as the use of oxygen and acetylene cutting torches became more and more common, more of these "round doors," as they were called, were forced to give up their booty. Once again the manufacturers retaliated by upgrading their product. They sandwiched a layer of copper into the round steel doors.

Copper is able to dissipate the heat of an ordinary cutting torch so fast that the steel can't be cut. The best quality round door safes are still made that way today. But thousands of these old square door safes were still in use, and as the furnace company realized, it was not a good place to keep $6,000 cash and the company check book. About a week went by and Ned and I received a teletype from the Las Vegas Nevada police. They had arrested the two Portland men trying to cash the checks stolen from the furnace company. In just a few short days the $6,000 in cash had been gambled away and the safe burglars had put the check printer to use trying to crank out more. Well, cheaters never prosper.

In order to prosecute these two guys, they had to be returned to Oregon for trial, and that was going to cost money, airfare, meals and lodging for two detectives, plus return airfare for the prisoners. Of course there was a budget for returning prisoners to Oregon. As long as the criminals didn't escape beyond the seven Western states, and that included Nevada, chances were good they could be extradited. The district attorney generally decided each case on its own merits and seriousness. The unofficial policy of the detective division allowed the case detectives the first chance to make extradition trips. And so the question was asked; would Ned and I like to fly to Vegas and bring them back? Hell yes we would!

The Stardust and the Strip

TWO BURGLARS AND A DINNER SHOW

AFTER JUST A FEW SHORT weeks as a detective, I was flying off to Vegas to bring back a couple of safe burglars. This was the big time for me. I had never been to Las Vegas, but Ned was an old hand there. We took a cab from the airport to the Stardust Hotel on the strip and checked into our room. Gambling is not in my nature, so I bought tickets to a good dinner show, and an after dinner show. Then I hit the casinos and started drinking and seeing as many entertainers and comedians as I could stuff into one night. It was a tough job, but somebody had to do it. It ended up being a damn tough job, the next morning, as I tried to clear the cobwebs away. We had a 9:00 a.m. appointment the next morning, with the Vegas detectives. When they arrived at our hotel, we chatted about the case and drank a lot of coffee. It didn't help; I had a bad headache. As we discussed the case, it came out I'd been right about the burglars, they were former employees who had worked in the plant. They knew the office didn't have a burglar alarm and they'd have the luxury of the entire weekend to work on the old safe.

We picked up the two yeggs at the Las Vegas county jail. The electric doors clanged open and we accepted custody. Each prisoner had a paper sack with their personal effects. I carefully searched both burglars. Ned and I didn't want any surprises on the plane trip home. I snaked the custody chain around the prisoner's waists, through the belt loops and locked the handcuffs tight. Two burglars in chains, and ready to go. The Las Vegas detectives took us to the airport and said goodbye. From here on, it was more dangerous. We contacted the ticket agent and were allowed to board first. Airline regulations, at that time, forbade guns on airplanes, even guns carried by policemen. Quietly, our guns were surrendered to the pilot without letting the prisoners know we weren't armed, and we sat down to await take off. It felt great to have a partner like Ned, simply because of his size. Ned was big enough to kick both burglars' asses in two seconds flat. And besides, I had a hangover. By the time the plane touched down in Portland, we had obtained signed, handwritten confessions from both criminals. They planned on hitting it rich in Vegas using the payroll money as a grub stake. Now, they were broke, busted, and bound for an Oregon jail. I often marveled at the criminal mentality. Sometimes because of their sick perversity, sometimes because of their rare ingenuity, and sometimes because they just didn't get it; that crime doesn't pay. You can't do bad and get good in return.

Working Morals

MY LEAST FAVORITE DETAIL

ONE WEEKEND MORNING, THE PHONE on my desk was ringing as I walked in the door. It was a uniformed officer at North Precinct. He had an elderly rape victim he was bringing into the office and it would be my job to interview her. Sex crimes, or what we referred to as *working morals*, were my least favorite crimes to investigate, and I'll share with you why. Women who are rape victims are not generally victims of greed, but victims of another person's desire for control, power and domination. Sex offenders are the lowest on the criminal totem pole. A convicted rapist once told me that rape is not really a sexual crime but a crime of female degradation. I remember sitting there and not really understanding the rage he felt toward women. "How could I degrade the bitch more than by sticking my slimy dick in her mouth and cunt?!" he asked me aggressively, with wide eyes and a perverse smile on his face. Another rapist once told me, "A rapist who rapes? It ain't somethin you just go out and do; a rapist is something ya *are*!" Having to hear these words and learn the details of violent acts of sexual degradation, against women, always made me feel extremely uncomfortable.

It was very difficult having to interview rape victims and it didn't come naturally to me. Hearing the male offenders say these terrible things, with not a twinge of remorse for their victims always left me feeling sickened and repulsed. I sometimes flashed back to the bizarre intensity I saw in the butcher Richard Marquette's eyes and thought about his inability to deal with females and his pathological hatred of women. On this day, an officer from the Women's Protective Division came to my office and together we sat down so I could interview the victim, who had been brought in. The female officer's role was simply to act as a buffer, a comforting presence and a witness to the interview.

The victim was white, elderly, in her middle seventies and had been raped by a young man in the neighborhood who ran errands and did odd jobs for her and other people. She had awakened to find him in her bedroom, nude from the waist down.

"What was he doing?" I asked.

"He was, you know, playing with himself, I call it," she said.

"What happened next?"

 I yelled at him to get out of my house."

"Did he go?"

"No, he just kept, you know…?"

"You mean he continued masturbating?"

"Yes, and then he…" her voice trailed off and she started to weep. "He slapped me and told me to shut up or he'd strangle me, and all the time he was…" The old lady continued to sob. "I'm *so* sorry Ma'am," I said, "but I have to ask these questions so we know what crime has been committed." I sighed, looking down and hating every minute of the interview. I glanced at the female officer and she seemed embarrassed too, looking down awkwardly. "What exactly was he doing?" I asked the victim. "He was slapping me and wiping his, you know, on my nightie and on my leg."

"And then he ripped my nightie with his hand, and he forced…" she broke off crying again. The lady cop offered her a box of tissues.

"He forced my legs apart and jumped on top of me."

"What did he do then?"

"He kept slapping me and demanded that I….that I…"

"What did he want you to do?" I asked gently.

"He wanted me to hold it open."

"He forced you to hold your vagina open?" I asked.

"Yes," she said, "He slapped me until I did it."

"What did he do then?" I continued.

"He had his way with me!" she cried.

"Did he force his penis in your vagina?"

"Yes," she whispered.

"And did he ejaculate?"

"Yes," she sobbed.

"Yes he did...and he *hurt* me!"

I took a deep breath before I spoke, feeling suddenly exhausted. "We should be able to make a good case of forcible rape," I told the victim, looking over at the female officer, who nodded her head grimly. I felt so sorry for this little old lady. She was an elderly woman in her seventies, had probably been a wife and mother and she had endured the worst kind of violation. The least I could offer her was an attempt at justice. "We have to take your nightie and the bed sheets from your bed for evidence. One of the officers will make sure that happens. And for now, you'll be taken to the hospital to see a doctor for an examination. The results of that examination should provide us with more evidence. Then we'll get a warrant for this creep and we'll get him arrested, okay?"

The victim continued to weep and didn't look up. I stood, bent over her and offered her my arm, helping her up from the chair. I looked down at her, as she stood bent over and still very upset, and told her once again how sorry I was. I assured her she would be taken care of and we would arrest the man who had done this to her. I walked her to the office door and an officer from North Precinct, who was waiting took the old lady gently by the arm and to the hospital. When they were out of earshot and walking down the hall, I asked the female officer to make sure the semen stained nightie and sheets were recovered and then taken to the lab to be processed as soon as possible. I could tell she didn't want to touch the disgusting things, let alone carry them to the lab. Fuck it, I thought, this is what equal employment is all about. If you're a cop, you do your job, even when it repulses you. As I mentioned earlier, morals crimes were my least favorite crime to investigate. I never could get used to talking to a woman about what had happened in her private parts. Having to question victims of sex crimes is not generally a comfortable endeavor, for any investigator male or female, and those interviews were certainly not comfortable for me.

Accidental Death

LEATHER BELTS AND SCARFERS

At some time during 1967, when I was still working weekends, I got a call while I was in my office. The uniformed cops at the scene thought the dead body they had was a suicide, but they weren't quite sure. The patrolmen were at a somewhat upscale apartment complex in the SE part of town, called the Wimbledon Apartments. There they found the lifeless body of a young man, hanging in a closet. Having gone through rigor mortis, he'd been dead several hours. Upon entering the unit, I saw a young man, about twenty-five-years old, in the hall closet of a studio apartment. His leather belt was looped around his neck and secured up over the wooden closet pole, where some of his clothing hung. His tongue was hanging out the side of his mouth and his pants were drooping down around his knees. A small, burnt down votive candle and some burned matches lay in a china dish at his feet. A cardboard box next to the body was full of porno magazines and an open, nearly empty container of Vaseline lay on its side. I had never seen anything quite like it. While I was waiting for the coroner's van to arrive, I searched the apartment looking for a suicide note but found nothing.

It was a typical bachelor pad; bean bag furniture, a stereo on a stand made of cement building blocks, and tattered posters on the wall. Not much in the fridge but a frozen pizza, a half consumed bottle of coke and an open package of hot dogs which was slowly growing mold. The bedroom had a small dresser containing the normal socks and t-shirts of any young man. There were clothes in the closet, but still, no suicide note. When the coroner arrived, I got behind the body and lifted it up about ten inches, so he could unfasten the belt around the victim's neck. As I did so, a sixteen ounce Coke bottle covered with feces and Vaseline slid out of the victim's rectum. It fell about six inches to the floor, with a dull thud.

The coroner looked up at me and we both shook our heads. The expression on his face was a combination of disapproval, sadness and disgust, and I'm sure my expression looked similar.

Partial strangulation, causing oxygen deprivation, is said to increase the intensity of a sexual climax. The coroner had a term for it: auto-erotic-asphyxiation. The belt cut off the blood in the young man's carotid arteries and in a few seconds he passed out. His unconscious body relaxed and he slowly asphyxiated to death. He had *accidentally* hung himself during his own private sex party. The next of kin was the young man's father, who eventually arrived at the apartment and identified the body for us, confirming the body was indeed his son. The father stood and stared at the small closet where his son had died. He saw what I had seen, the magazines, the Vaseline and the soiled Coke bottle. "What in God's name happened?" he asked me desperately, fighting back tears. I tried to explain that his son had died *accidentally*. "He certainly had no intention of losing consciousness," I said. There was an awkward silence as the father stared forlornly at the porno magazines. "Apparently, he's been collecting these magazines for a while," I said quietly. "And what's this?" his father asked, pointing to the Coke bottle in disbelief. "Only your son knows and he'll not tell us now," I said as gently as I could.

It had been a while since I'd seen a dead body and it was hard to write the report on this young man's death. It felt like I was a trespasser in a tragic sex fantasy gone wrong and I felt terrible for the father, who had just lost his young son from such an avoidable and bizarre form of accidental death.

Auto Theft in Portland

IT WASN'T REALLY A CRIME

THE AUTO THEFT CASES THAT came to us on weekends were a constant frustration. The pattern was always the same. If a stolen car wasn't found within a few hours, parked or wrecked some place, it probably *wouldn't* be found. Banks (and the companies that repossessed cars for them) always let the cops know about the *repos* that were in custody. For the other victims, if your car was found abandoned on the street that likely meant that juveniles had taken it for a joy ride and no one was going to go to jail over it. If the car wasn't found soon, it had probably been stolen by a gang who had already dismantled it for parts at a chop shop. Car parts, especially high performance parts are expensive and fetch a high value among the criminal element. Who hasn't heard about a good deal on car parts? Here's a tip: "The Midnight Auto Supply," isn't really a store. Look at it this way, if I found your stolen radiator and brought it to you, could you positively identify it in court? Probably not.

Car rental companies were the easiest target. If a person rented a car for the weekend but didn't bring it back on Monday, Tuesday or Wednesday, the car wasn't legally stolen. The renter had the car with permission and maybe he would bring it back in a few days.

Once I missed an extradition trip to Ft. Lauderdale Florida on an auto theft case. A young man rented a Cadillac for the weekend from the Hertz car rental agency. He drove off after paying $150 cash deposit upfront and never brought the car back. After it had been gone for three weeks, the district attorney felt that the thief probably intended to keep it and he issued an arrest warrant. Two months later, the car and driver were stopped in Ft. Lauderdale and the driver was arrested on the Hertz warrant. Even though he stole a Cadillac and was in jail in Florida, he didn't qualify for extradition. "Florida's way beyond the seven *western* states," said the district attorney, as I stood across from him, in his office. "We can't spend the money to return this guy to Oregon, but we'll keep the warrant on file, just in case he ever comes back," he said firmly. "Is that right?" I asked, trying hard not to lose my cool. "Just in case he ever comes back?" I continued, getting angry. The district attorney shrugged his shoulders. "Yeah, it's always about money. Sorry, DuPay."

So, now you know how to get across country cheaply. Rent a nice car and just don't come back. My problem with auto theft was that it wasn't really a crime, not really, but just *maybe* under certain circumstances. Perhaps it's the reason two of the old timer auto-theft detectives operated a repo service, working for the banks and car finance companies. During the time I was in uniform at North Precinct, the two repo dicks, often let us know what cars they were interested in and looking for. "This guy hasn't made a payment in three months," they would tell us, giving us a mug shot and telling us to keep an eye out. "If you see the car rolling, find a reason to stop it and tow it in. There will be twenty five bucks in it for you," I was told. It was easy to see, there was more incentive for cops to look for repos than stolen cars. Eventually the chief of police, Donald McNamara decided it might be a conflict of interest to let two auto theft detectives run a repo service. After all, it was hard to tell if they were out looking for stolen cars for the good of the citizens *or* for the good of their own bank accounts and wallets.

Around this time, I learned there were some city employees who were working more for *themselves* than for the good of the city. This became apparent to me by more than just the repo dicks conduct, after I learned that there were other city employees stealing from the city too. I recall one afternoon, I got a call while in the burglary office. Two downtown uniformed officers had arrested a parking meter employee, caught stealing money from parking meters. They watched him use a key to empty the coin boxes into an old bank bag. As the bank bags were filled, he threw them in the trunk of his car. The trouble was, he worked for the city parking meter division and was supposed to turn in the meter keys, each day after work. Here he was moonlighting by stealing money out of parking meters and he wasn't the only one doing it. Once he was caught, he snitched off his city co-workers after only a few minutes of me questioning him.

It helped that I recognized two of these guys. I was working at the dog track in Fairview as extra security, and I got to know the regulars. Two of the parking meter thieves would go to the track and gamble and eat, often making a lot of noise while they had fun. When I walked into the interrogation room, I recognized them immediately.

For over a year, some of these city employees, whose job it was to collect parking meter money, had been stealing thousands of dollars off the top each month. "We never woulda got caught, if that greedy bastard hadn't gone out on his own!" one of them told me bitterly. "We always split the money evenly between us. There was plenty for everybody." The extra cash was used to pay for vacation trips, cars, boats and gambling debts. This inner circle of meter thieves had a good thing going. They were even selling meter keys. For $500 you could buy one and cut yourself in on the city revenue. I felt a sense of betrayal the whole time I worked this case. These jerks weren't cops, but they *were* city employees, who should have known better. Who could you trust anymore?

A Sense of Violation

WHAT'S THAT THING IN THE TOILET?

M<small>ANY OF YOU HAVE KNOWN</small> the sick feeling of coming home and finding your house or apartment burglarized. The sense of intrusion to your privacy, your possessions ransacked and your personal treasures taken, can destroy your sense of security in the sacredness and safety of your home. I have investigated literally thousands of these burglaries and I can tell you this: the burglar who comes into your residence has come for one reason only and that is to steal. He already knows you're not home, because he's knocked on your front door and your back door, or has called your telephone number, (if it's listed publicly).

Entry is gained as quickly as possible in generally all cases. How can I keep someone out of my house, you may ask? You can't. As long as windows and patio sliding doors are made of glass, and door frames of wood, you can't protect your home all of the time. Doors are easily kicked open and deadbolt latches are of little consequence. An ordinary large screw driver can pry open a front door. A small pipe wrench can twist the doorknob open, and then getting inside is simple. Once inside, the burglar will always go to the bedroom—always—always! Why? Because that's where we keep our treasures. All the dresser drawers are dumped on top of the bed and quickly sorted through to find anything of value. Things to be stolen may be put in one of your pillowcases, as pillowcases make nice big sacks to carry your things away in. TVs, stereos and similar electronic items are also easily carried out. It's amazing how much of your stuff will fit into the trunk of a burglar's car.

Some people presume a barking dog will scare away a potential burglar. Don't depend on a dog. You may find Fido locked in a closet or a bathroom, or even shot and killed. I've seen house burglars neutralize male guard dogs, in upscale neighborhoods, by bringing in a female dog in heat. I've even seen a dead junkyard dog, a once beautiful German Shepard, with a broken off broom handle rammed down its throat. It was barking, with its mouth open, apparently too close to a chain link security fence, when it was killed by a burglar vicious enough to ram a broken off broom handle down its throat and let it slowly bleed to death. Big dogs and small dogs will cower if hit with an electric cattle prod or stun gun, and lots of burglars will just shoot a dog. Don't depend on a dog to protect your home.

Do you think your little home-safe will protect your treasures? We've already touched on the topic of safes. If you have a small "home" safe, it can be carried out of your house the same way it was carried in; in someone's arms. A hatchet and a half an hour is all it will take to open a small home-safe. If you have a safe at home, use it only for fire protection of your records. Shut the door, but don't lock it. Tape a note to the safe that reads: "This safe is not locked and contains only documents." It will save you buying a new one.

Well then, will a burglar alarm keep them out? Alarms *can* help but are expensive for most people. Besides, alarms are sold by salesmen who have never talked to a burglar. Salesmen get paid according to how much they can sell you in terms of hardware and services, not by how much they know about burglary. To make a point, have you driven by a business or house when the burglar alarm was ringing? Did you stop to call the police? Did you stop to check it out? I doubt it. Nobody does. So much for burglar alarms. The most effective burglar alarm, in my seasoned opinion, is a thin tripwire, stretched across the bedroom doorway, wired to a 6-inch fire alarm bell. Don't put the bell outside the house, or under the eaves for your neighbors to hear, he's probably not home either. Put the bell where the tripwire is located. As soon as the tripwire is hit, the bell goes off in the burglar's ear. He'll probably be *very* surprised, drop everything and go out the way he came in. Don't use the alarm bell to notify the neighbors, use it to scare the damned burglar away.

I used this type of alarm successfully in my mother's house on NE Oregon Street, because she was concerned about a rash of burglaries in her area. And after all, her son was a burglary detective. When a burglar crawled into the bedroom window from her backyard, several months later, he hit the tripwire on the way to the front room, looking for loot. He went right back out again and took nothing. It happened again several years later, at the same house. A burglar crawled in the kitchen window from her back yard, hit the bedroom tripwire and went back out again. This kind of alarm works and it's cheap. The bell, the wire and the trip switch should cost less than about one hundred and fifty dollars. If you really need a safe at home, spend the money and buy a good "in the floor," round door safe. It is built in the ground, covered with concrete and is generally safe ninety nine percent of the time. Anything else is a waste of money.

Modern commercial burglar alarm systems protect only the perimeter of a home or business, and when breached, the system does not contact the police directly. The system contacts the alarm company, and it is the alarm operator who then decides whether the police need to be contacted or not. This process can take up to five minutes. Meanwhile, the burglar is in and out, and he's taking your possessions with him. It is for this reason that I believe a simple trip wire is the best protection against burglary, as opposed to a fancy and expensive perimeter system of burglary protection that often simply does not work.

Here is an interesting side note about burglar psychology. Many burglary reports, after itemizing the list of stolen possessions, note that the burglar has *defecated* in the house, sometimes in a corner on the floor and sometimes in the bathroom and sometimes in the shrubbery outside, beneath the broken window. I remember one burglary victim telling me, "He took all the stereo equipment in the den, ransacked the bedroom and then took a shit in the bathroom but didn't flush. I came home and found a big turd floating in the toilet!" It almost seems to add insult to injury, doesn't it? Actually, there is a physical reason for this. Burglarizing a house causes the burglar to produce several stress hormones, like noradrenalin, cortisol and adrenalin. Often an extreme amount of stress hormones can be created while in the act of burglarizing a home. And some people react to stress by taking a shit. Not flushing the toilet, that's the insult part.

Getting Noticed

I DIDN'T KNOW WHO I COULD TRUST

As time went on, the good job I was doing caught the eye of the burglary detail lieutenant, Myron Warren. Myron was a man of considerable integrity who commanded a great deal of respect in the law enforcement community in Portland. He was thin, stood six feet tall, with a greying crew-cut. He had sharp features and a wonderfully charismatic, friendly demeanor. When he talked to me, he always had his hand on my arm or shoulder, demanding my attention and my focus. Myron was very supportive and encouraging, and acted almost like a father figure. He helped me find part time work at the race track, when he knew I needed the extra money to support my family, at a time when police officers didn't earn a living wage or even anything close to it. Myron was always there for me, with a sympathetic ear and a word of counsel or encouragement. He complimented me often, on my natural ability and *feel* for burglary investigation as he put it. In a performance evaluation report, written April 11, 1968, he noted that I was "interested, aggressive and determined," in my approach to police work. I was *all* of those things. Police work was my forte. Police work was my baby and I loved it.

However, a certain reputation for being "difficult," to work with had followed me to the dicks, largely because of my problems with Jim Purcell and my poorly disguised attitude of contempt toward those complacent officers who suffered from what I termed "the old-timer syndrome." But those officers with integrity such as Myron, (and several others I knew and worked with) understood my attitude and reserved judgment on me. I personally didn't give a fuck about the others; the shirkers, the drinkers, the sleepers and the repo men. All that mattered to me what that I did good police work and kept the citizens safe as well as I could, and as safe as I would want *my* own family members to be.

In an earlier performance evaluation report, dated December 4, 1967, Sergeant Schwartz, wrote: "Detective DuPay seems to be an interested, precise police officer who is willing to do anything asked of him. Although observed only a short time, he seems to be trying to grasp the procedure of his new duties as rapidly as possible. He does have difficulty with his personal relations with other police officers, and the public, due to a rather cool personality. He has been urged to try and "loosen up" and seems to be putting forth extra effort in this area." This was an accurate appraisal of me at the time. Part of the perception that I had a "cool personality," and needed to "loosen up," stemmed from my overall distrust of other officers. I knew too well, the level of corruption that existed among them. Would they actually go out and work, like me? Would they put in eight hours work for eight hours pay, or would they sleep half their shift away in preparation for their day job? Would they tell me to keep an eye out for cars they wanted to repossess, or engage in other forms of dishonesty?

It was hard for me to know whom I could trust. To me, police work meant doing what I was paid and trained to do, working for the citizens and not laying down on the job. The realization hit me early on, as a patrolman, that not everyone was there for the same reasons I was. There were many cops who had their own agenda for personal gain, with little regard for the demands of the job. I knew who they were, and I chose to keep my distance from them, when I could. That early realization was something I'd never forgotten, and it made it hard for me to either loosen up or naively trust the motives of other officers who were not as dedicated.

Every Christmas Eve, in the burglary office, beginning when I was a new detective, Myron Warren would bring three big bottles of booze and we'd all file into his office toward the end of the shift and start drinking. He'd bring in a bottle of whiskey, vodka and gin and place them on his desk, acting as generous host, with small water glasses and lots of ice in a big bucket. The first time he did this, inviting us in, I was nervous the captain would walk in and catch us in the act; drinking on duty. It was clearly against the rules but Myron didn't give a damn. He was a detective whose reputation was beyond reproach and this was something he felt he could justify and get away with. There would be six of us in burglary, along with a couple other guys from the check fraud detail, down the hall, whom we'd invite over. As we sat around Myron's office drinking, some of us sitting in chairs, others standing, we relaxed our tongues and enjoyed the camaraderie of our very special profession. Myron encouraged that kind of brotherhood among all those he led and it was good for us. He was all about teamwork and working well together. Not only were we proud to work for him but we knew there was no one with more integrity or more dedicated to doing good police work than Myron Warren.

There was one particular Christmas Eve I vividly recall. After all the other guys had left, Myron and I sat alone, feeling no pain and commiserating about the job. Once again, I told Myron, as I had in the past, of my secret desire to kill Jim Purcell Junior. There was no other person in the bureau I hated more than Diamond Jim Purcell. He had tried his best to destroy my career and discredit and humiliate me into the bargain. There was no one that I knew of who was more corrupt than Purcell, other than his close friend and associate, Lieutenant Carl Crisp, whom I had worked for in vice. That afternoon, I told Myron of how I fantasized of doing away with Purcell during that month when I had to direct traffic at the end of the St. Johns Bridge, right before I got promoted to detective. I was so furious that I'd been taken off the district and given that assignment *and* desk duty, that the fantasy preoccupied my mind. In the fantasy, I would call Purcell's office from a telephone at the precinct and ask to meet him late in the evening on a street corner in St. Johns to talk. After he picked me up in his car, I'd force him to drive up Germantown Road to Forest Park, at gunpoint, where I would then shoot him with his own gun, after getting it away from him. As I was 31-years-old and in great shape, and he was almost sixty, a boozer and a smoker, and in failing health, I knew it wouldn't be hard. And then, after I'd done the deed, I would just walk away, leaving him in the car, an apparent suicide. Myron listened thoughtfully to my story, nodding his head and agreeing that Purcell had been one corrupt bastard and he well understood. Then he said, "Well, lemme tell ya what they tried to do to me, Don." I learned forward, eager to hear Myron's story.

"You know you're not the only guy who's wanted to kill over this job. That fucker Carl Crisp and a couple of his cronies tried to set me up, years ago."

"They tried to set you up? How? On what?"

"They were gonna set me up on dope."

"Dope?! You?!

"Yeah. I was supposed to go meet them, late at night and I had a bad feeling about it."

"Whad ya do?"

"I got lucky when I made a phone call. That feeling I had, it prompted me to make a telephone call. That call paid off." Myron Warren told me an all too familiar tale. He was known for being a completely honest, hardworking cop. And he was known for not taking money or kickbacks of any kind. As there were lots of crooked cops in the bureau then, doing just that, he'd developed a reputation as one of the untouchables or what people in law enforcement had started calling The New Breed; Honest. Idealistic. Dedicated. I also considered myself one of The New Breed.

One afternoon, Myron got a call from Carl Crisp asking to meet him after hours, which to Myron was an unusual and out of the ordinary request. They were not friends and didn't associate in their off hours. Myron felt uneasy about the request, made a phone call to one of his closest friends in the bureau and asked him what he'd heard, if anything. What his friend told him was not good. His friend confirmed that he'd recently heard that Crisp had it out for Myron and wanted to get him out of the way. Crisp was going to try to set him up, to have him either arrested on dope or have him shot over it.

"I was so angry at that motherfucker, I decided I was gonna kill him," Myron said calmly.

"How were they gonna try to do it?" I asked.

"What I heard is they were gonna meet me, plant dope on me, and arrest *or* shoot me, saying I was crooked, dealin' dope, gettin' kids hooked." At this point, I whistled through my teeth. And I thought I'd been dealt a bad hand by Jim Purcell. What had happened to *me* seemed to pale in comparison to what Myron had been put through. "I don't know why that sleazy punk ever thought he could set me up," Myron said, disgusted.

"So, what happened?" I asked. "What happened in the long run?"

"I ignored our scheduled meeting and never showed up. Then I made sure to talk to a couple of my buddies and tell them what was up. Word got out quick and right back to Crisp. *He* knew that *I* knew what he'd tried to do. A couple weeks later, I drove by his house. I could see the lights on in the living room. I knew the cocksucker was home. I drove around the block several times, slowly, crawling down the street, with my headlights on. I wanted him to know it was me driving by his house. And I *did* wanna kill him. Then I thought I should go to my parish and pray about it first. To make a long story short, Don, I decided not to do it, just like *you* decided not to do it. But Crisp never tried to compromise me again. And the fact is, he was afraid of me. He never went out of his way to cross paths with me after that. And why would the cocksucker?"

The Heavy Squad

AND THE ELECTRIC COMPANY CAN KISS MY...

Soon after completing my probationary year as a detective, Lieutenant Warren handpicked me to join the safe detail. I was happy and very flattered that he'd chosen me personally, but damned surprised. Surprised because the four or five detectives who worked in that detail all had twenty or more years experience on the job. Not only was I one of the youngest ever promoted to detective in 1967, but I was the youngest then assigned to work in safe burglaries. Although these guys had been around a long time, there was no old-timer syndrome with these men. They were hardworking and dedicated law enforcement men. Sometimes they called me "the kid," because I was so young, but I had their respect. And because Myron had said I was okay, they accepted me as one of their own.

Actually, the safe detail did more than investigate safe burglaries. We were responsible for criminal intelligence. The seven western states cooperated in sharing intelligence information on these punchers and peelers, as they were called, and we detectives were generally the best informed on their movements. Two or three top notch *yeggs* lived in Portland, but normally operated only in other cities like, Los Angeles and Las Vegas. We conducted loose surveillance of their cribs, and photographed and reported the comings and goings of their criminal associates. As a result, we usually knew what gangs were responsible for safe crimes by the way they attacked the boxes and the types of boxes they chose. Catching them in the act, of course, was another matter.

Major burglary losses such as large thefts from jewelry stores, warehouses and public utilities were also our responsibility. The utility companies throughout Oregon were routinely reporting large losses of expensive copper wire. Cable reels of the heavy duty wire costing hundreds of dollars were being stolen from rural storage facilities. The state police were also getting reports of power and phone outages in rural areas and near mountain roads. These bastards were cutting the wire right off the poles, rolling it up and hauling it off. Hot sticks, used to cut the live wires down were often left leaning against the poles or laying, having been tossed in muddy ditches. Copper wire theft was close to the perfect crime. As long as the thieves didn't get caught in the act of stealing, they were home free. The rolls of wire were then tossed on a bonfire and the insulation burned off. Scrap copper, all that was left after burning off the insulation, was then ready to sell. With or without the insulation, copper wire is unidentifiable, and is sold by the pound. It's kind of like your car radiator, in a sense. No identification, no prosecution. Sweet deal, these criminals must have thought.

One of the most active of these insulation burners, was a black junk dealer named Roosevelt Jenkens. Roosevelt had a business card that read, Hauling and Cleanup; junk of all Kinds. He had an old house in the ghetto and when he first started stealing copper wire, he almost burned his house down trying to burn the insulation off a roll of copper wire in the living room fireplace. After that near disaster, he would regularly burn rolls of copper wire in his backyard fire pit. His neighbors constantly complained about how he kept smoking up the neighborhood and adding to the general stink. And just like with the pawn shops, the police department required scrap metal dealers to keep records of who they bought scrap metal from. The three main scrap metal buyers were buying between 500 and 1000 pounds of stripped copper wire a week from Roosevelt.

Roosevelt was a shrewd dude and knew well, the rules of the game he played. He feigned a kind of *step-n-fetch-it* act designed to fool the white man but I never bought into it. He once said to me, "Yes suh, Mr. Don, we steals da wire. Gotts ta make a livin' somehow. Sides, ya'll got's to catch me doin' it. Why ya'll so uptight about it anyways? Its jus the motherfuckin' electric company. Nobody likes dem bitches no how! Do you?" he asked me, laughing. "Well, I'm never too happy about paying my electric bill either," I confessed, "but you *know* stealing is wrong, so cut the jive."

"Stealin' from the white man ain't wrong," he said. "I'll steal from ya'll if ya got somethin' I can get," he said laughing harder and slapping his thigh. "Besides, I'm good for the economy. I makes a few dollars, the syn-a-gog man that buys it, he make a dollar or two and the electric company can kiss my black motherfuckin' ass!" I had to admire one thing about Roosevelt Jenkens: he was honest about his dishonesty and his cheerful nature made it hard to dislike him.

That was more than I could say about the scrap metal buyers. I knew of two prominent Jewish families from the Portland area who were regular buyers of Roosevelt Jenkens scrap metal. They knew damned well the rolls of burned copper wire weren't his, but they didn't give a shit about that. They bought them anyway. Roosevelt would run over the rolls of wire with his truck, grinding them into the dirt, making the used copper look really used. Perhaps the synagogue man put a few extra dollars in the offering plate on their particular Sabbath day to make up for the crimes they were committing by buying stolen copper wire.

The Homemade Surveillance Truck

PISSIN IN THE STREET

AFTER WORKING BURGLARY FOR THREE years, I came to realize that I had two distinct advantages over other detectives. I had an intuitive *feel* for the burglar, which was a sense of insight into the burglar's thinking, and lots of patience. I had the patience to sit hour after hour in the surveillance van photographing their comings and goings, and I had the patience to wait for something to happen, which is a must for any good cop. To match my photographic skills to my patience, I enrolled in a photography class, in 1971, at the Mount Hood community college and specialized in surveillance photography. The bureau paid for it.

Using a long distance telephoto lens, similar to that used by sports photographers at football games, I was able to get clear, crisp, easily recognizable facial photos from our surveillance van parked two or three blocks away. For night photography I used a night vision scope. The surveillance van was an old converted bread truck that had been fitted with the necessary communications equipment. This included a radio, so I could talk to the dispatcher, if I needed help, and a periscope in the top, which allowed me to see in all directions. Toilet facilities were crude for this surveillance truck. You pissed into a plastic funnel that was stuck into a six foot length of garden hose, which then drained onto the ground, under the truck, by the back right tire.

Never mind that it was against the law to urinate in the street, but nobody seemed to notice the puddle from *this* detective, urinating in the street, via a plastic funnel, hooked up to a garden hose. To take a dump you had to leave and find a service station, which was often inconvenient and troublesome. This meant hurrying several blocks away and then once the deed was done, having to make sure no one saw you as you got back into the van. To do this, I had to stand by the van for several minutes, look at my watch, run my hand through my hair, look around as if I were perhaps waiting for someone, and then as casually as I could, reenter the vehicle, with hopefully, no one noticing. The van was equipped with a $2,000-plus night-scope camera but not a $100 Mini-Porta Potty that could have been placed in the back. That never made any sense to me.

As well as night-scopes, other technology was coming into play in police work. For instance, the bureau had purchased a number of silent burglar alarms, which was, at that time, a new form of cutting edge technology for police work. We immediately saw the advantage to silent alarms. After all, the best way to trap a burglar is to catch him inside, while he's in the act. Using the silent snitch, the burglar himself unwittingly told us when he was breaking in. The alarms were actually radio transmitters in a metal box the size of a brief case. They could be set off in several ways. A simple tripwire, could do it, but there were also infrared devices, also commonly known as heat sensors, that detected the burglars' body heat. We also used pressure pads that activated the transmitter when they were stepped on. As the smarter burglars were starting to use police scanners, to monitor our radio calls, we had to devise a way to let our cops know that a silent alarm had been set off without actually broadcasting a message over the radio. For instance, "Car 72, cover a silent alarm at the ABC grocery," would now no longer work because of crooks being able to monitor police radios themselves.

The alarms were designed to be absolutely noiseless. When tripped, they silently transmitted a two digit number like twenty nine. The number would print out on a special alarm receiver located in the police radio room. The call was then dispatched as, "Car 72, call extension 29." Car 72 already knew where alarm number 29 was located. If everything worked out right, the burglar was caught inside, in the act, and never aware that we'd pegged him. In the meantime, we were being plagued by some safe burglars operating out of SE Portland. Three guys were peeling and chopping open every old safe they could find that wasn't protected by a burglar alarm. They weren't very smart but they *were* getting to be a nuisance. The first of their attacks was at a large tire store on 82nd and Holgate Street that had an old, square door safe in the back office. The building was constructed of concrete blocks and the burglars had loosened the mortar around three of them.

Working in the dark in the back of the building, they scraped the mortar loose until they could remove the blocks and crawl inside. We could see they had jockeyed the old safe around until they could push it over and lay it on its back. The dial was knocked off and heavy pry bars were used to peel the safe open and remove the money. We saved pieces of the safe door for evidence; the pieces that had the best identifying marks from the prying tools used. The suspects weren't very smart because they used the same tools repeatedly. They didn't understand they could be identified later, by the crime lab, through the tools they'd used, and the specific marks left on the safe door fragments.

Next, they picked an isolated tavern on 72nd and SE Woodstock, for their target. It was an old rundown building that had probably been built in the 1920s. They chopped a hole through the roof, and then using ropes, climbed down inside and fixed themselves a few beers. After all, wrestling a five hundred pound safe was going to be thirsty work. Judging from the quantity of beer they drank and the mess they made peeling the old safe open, the job had taken them most of the night. As usual, we saved the safe door parts that had the best pry marks and again, the crooks took their tools with them. Trying to figure where they might hit next, I set about doing some research. I decided on the busy George Morlan plumbing company located in the same general area on SE Foster Road. The company was housed in a large old building that would be easy to break into. There was no burglar alarm, and the office safe was another old, heavy, square-door.

But most importantly, the store had the right *feeling* as I wandered around inside, trying to think like a burglar might think. To think like a burglar you have to ask yourself some simple questions; how and where would I break in? What door or window is the most concealed and easily broken into? What tools might I use? Will I need help and bring someone along? Will I need a van or maybe only a car? Will I work alone? And once inside, where's the score? Where's the jewelry, the TVs, the stereos, or the guns, and how quickly can I get in and then out? Morlan's Plumbing had the right feel. It was easy to break into, and the safe was big and full of money. Along with that, there was no alarm installed in the store. A burglar would think he'd have all night to work in such a place. I asked the owner if I might install a silent radio alarm for a few days, to see what might happen. The owner seemed amenable to the idea, and so I set to work. I hid the briefcase sized alarm box high on a shelf out of sight, behind some plumbing parts, and positioned the trip switch on one side of an aisle about sixty feet from the office. For a trip-wire, I used a length of thin nylon fishing leader. It was invisible in the dark, and I attached it to a plastic spacer. The spacer held the switch contact points open and would pull out easily when someone walked toward the office safe, after closing time. The trip-wire was at ankle height and would do the job. That right feeling that I had, about Morlan's turned out to be correct. The plumbing company looked just as good to the burglars as it did to me and within only a few nights they hit it. Two of them broke in through the back door dragging their tools with them and inched slowly up the aisle toward the safe.

"Car 18," cracked the radio."
"Go ahead radio,"
"Would you call extension # 29?"
"Extension # 29, right away."

That's how easy it was when it worked right. It was pure pleasure for me, coming to work the next morning and finding that two of the three men had been caught inside, with all their tools and then arrested. "Hey DuPay!" Myron Warren told me, slapping me on the back in the burglary office, "You got two burglars out of Morlan's last night. Good job with the bug!" We were both very pleased that two potentially dangerous criminals had been arrested and were now off the street.

I loved it when I was right about where burglars might hit next, and working the silent alarms made working the burglary detail a lot of fun. It felt a little like winning the lottery when I got it right and gave me a sense of job satisfaction that working the streets had never given me. Burglars can be incredibly stupid sometimes and these burglars were no exception. They had pulled six or seven safe burglaries and I'd caught them red handed, with my six feet of fishing leader. I chuckled later, after questioning one of the culprits; a thin, unshaven white man, with bad teeth, named Marvin.

"I knew I screwed up when I felt that wire tangle around my feet," he complained to me. "Why didn't you just leave *then* Marv?" I asked him, trying to conceal a smile. "Because the cops were already there, man! They were all around the building. There was nowhere to go to." Marvin told me that as they were trying to jockey the safe around and lay it on its back, the uniformed cops surrounded the building and took them into custody. I was able to take their bag of pry tools along with the safe parts we'd saved from the tavern and tire store jobs and then go to the crime lab with them. In less than three days, the technicians were able to make a definitive match. The tools were positively identified as the same tools used to pry open *all* of the other safe doors. Now we had these guys cold on three safe jobs, tools and all. We learned that the third member of the group was hiding out at home and we went out to arrest him. When we broke through his front door, we found three people inside, including his wife. The stereo was blasting *Gimme a Little Sign*, by Brenton Woods and they were all more than a little surprised when we broke in. The house itself was full of stolen merchandise, boxes full and overflowing, stacked against the walls. So much stolen stuff, there was barely enough room to walk around. The guy we wanted to arrest, a man named Homer, was standing beside a rickety, wooden cabinet in the dining area.

I noticed his right hand slowly moving toward the inside of his jacket, near his waist, and I quickly approached him head-on. I jammed my cocked gun up against Homer's crotch without a word, as I got right up in his face, glowering at him with big eyes. Then as I reached inside his jacket, he stiffened and leaned back against the wall, throwing up his hands. I removed a loaded .38 automatic from his belt. The fucker had intended to shoot someone with his belly-gun! But not today, and not me. I had gotten the jump on him. He was going to jail and I was going home.

There wouldn't be any legal wheeling and dealing or plea bargaining on this one. These guys were going straight to the state penitentiary and they knew it. One went to the pen, the other two jumped bail and split. They were able to hide out for four months before being arrested in Dallas Texas. We extradited them back to Oregon and while they did go to jail, they got to see Texas first.

The Professionals

ALL IN A DAY'S WORK

There were many groups of safe burglars besides the previous three guys roaming the western states, knocking off old, easy-to-open safes. There were so many in fact, that you seldom see an old safe around anymore; they've all been broken into, destroyed and then discarded. If you're a business man and you're still using one of these old square-doors, do yourself a favor, donate it to a museum. Marv and Homer were amateurs and they paid the price for their stupidity by going to prison. The next level up in traveling burglar circles was what I called the Journeyman level of skill. These guys knew how to do one thing and they did it well. Their targets were usually large chain grocery stores. If the chain had sixty stores, for example, a Safeway store, then it also usually had sixty of the same brands of safe. Learn how to open one, and you could open them all.

The grocery store owners had to keep large amounts of cash on hand and they bought large heavy round-door safes to keep it in. The steel in these safes was at least one inch thick and the round-doors were a sandwich of hardened steel and copper. Remember that copper dissipates heat quicker than the torch can melt the steel. Technology has a way of advancing with the times, and it certainly did with these gangs at the journeyman skill level. Although this kind of safe was almost immune from the cutting torch, it could be drilled open using high speed diamond drills.

Using a pre-made jig they brought into the stores with them, which was designed for just this brand of safe, they'd bolt it securely to the front of the safe door. Next, they'd bolt a high speed, heavy duty diamond drill onto the jig. The idea was to drill through the door and hit the locking bars dead center, cutting through them. This was an efficient operation but it took two to four hours to complete and a lot of equipment to boot. If nothing went wrong, the store manager would find the safe door open and empty with nothing left behind except a pile of drill shavings sitting in a pool of cutting oil.

Grocery chains lost thousands of dollars to these traveling journeymen professionals, and these losses, of course, were passed onto the consumer in the form of higher priced merchandise. Portland stores didn't get hit that often, but stores in rural parts of Oregon were regular targets and suffered large losses of money, cigarettes and alcohol. These journeymen professionals didn't hit very often. They were the kind of sophisticated criminal who worked a regular job as a front, in order to have a stable income, respectability and the invisibility that was essential to remaining under the radar of law enforcement. Two or three of these guys carefully picked scores at about three hits per year. That was all they needed to remain active and in money.

One of the very best in the business lived in Portland and his name was Billy Lewis. Lewis was about forty-five-years old. He was a slender white man, and stood five feet seven inches tall. He had patrician features, pale skin and short, black hair and was completely unassuming in appearance and manner. As Lewis was understated, intelligent and well-spoken, he seemed like the last person who would become a safe burglar and a skilled one at that. Lewis worked around town in some of the night clubs as a bartender, such as the White Elephant in Beaverton on 115th and Canyon Road, and Bill's Gold Coin on West Burnside Street in Portland. But Lewis was shrewd enough to do his important capering in other cities, outside of Portland and Beaverton. It was a good criminal policy, but did not insure complete anonymity. Work a day job and don't do burglaries where you live, also known as "not shitting in your own back yard," was a good plan but not a fool proof one. Still, we knew Billy Lewis pretty well, better than he ever realized.

We kept track of him, first having heard about him from Myron Warren, who had been informed of his capers, by other law enforcement men, from various burglary conferences he'd attended. We knew where Lewis lived and where he worked. We knew what cars he drove and where he parked them, and we knew his skill level. Lewis had studied locksmithing by correspondence course and had passed several of these classes with perfect marks. He could pick a lock with a set of picks or make a key by *impression*, which only a skilled locksmith can do. Lewis was particularly good at making his own burglar alarm keys. These keys were used by merchants and also maintenance men, in order to turn off the blaring alarm that might be keeping people awake at night, from a recently burglarized industrial building, for example. Lewis would use these burglar alarm keys to turn off an alarm during one of his jobs, if the need ever arose.

Lewis was also a journeyman safe mechanic and had manuals and written specifications for most safe brands. He was an expert at using an acetylene cutting torch and could cut through steel an inch thick. The man was a super-talent and a hell of a challenge to law enforcement, mainly because he was able to break into so many safes, and get away with it, taking all the money with him. Only when he broke his own rule of not capering in Portland, were we finally able to catch him. Lewis decided to hit the business office of the Portland Zoo and he studied the logistics carefully for several months. He figured the office safe would contain a large sum of money after the busy fourth of July weekend, this being the early 1970s when the zoo was still a prime place to be on such a date. Money from zoo admissions plus restaurant and gift shop receipts would be in the same safe. Lewis knew he would need a key to the business office and made one for the front door. Once he had a door key, he could let himself in at night and study the safe and the office layout.

To get his equipment in and out he needed to use a back access road that came into the zoo from Washington Park. The road was closed every night with a heavy chain and padlock. Not a problem for Lewis, he just made a key for the padlock. He studied his safe manuals and knew that to break into the zoo safe, he'd need a hammer and chisel, a high speed drill and a cutting torch and acetylene tanks. Black plastic garbage bags would be needed to cover the windows and a couple of rolls of scotch tape to secure the plastic. That and a little luck. The Fourth of July weekend came and went. Attendance at the zoo had been heavy and all the money was put away in the safe. Everything was going according to plan. In the middle of the night, the tools, tanks and torches were brought up the back road, probably in a truck. Stopping at the chain barrier, Lewis unlocked the padlock with his key and drove through leaving the chain unlocked. Driving to the business office, he parked and unlocked the front door. Making sure no one was around, he brought in a duffel bag containing the tools. Next came the cutting torch and the two tanks. Black plastic was brought in and with everything safely inside, the door was relocked. The plastic was taped over the windows and the job begun.

The safe was a large round-door *Gary* brand and fairly new. Lewis attacked through the top. With the chisel and hammer, he cut through the thin top metal and removed about six inches of insulating concrete. This exposed the one inch thick steel inner body. Next he cranked up the high speed drill and drilled a half inch pilot hole clear down through. He got a bucket of water from the rest room and poured it into the pilot hole until the safe was as full of water as he could get it. This would soak the legal tender but keep the money from burning. It could always be dried out later. The cracks around the safe door were covered with scotch tape to keep the water from seeping out too fast. He fired up his cutting torch and using the pilot hole as his starting place, cut a hole in the one inch thick steel plate, big enough to later stick his hand in and pull the bank bags out. As soon as the cut was completed, the steel plug was removed and all the money taken from the safe. There was nothing to do then but pack up and take everything home. It must have been a sight to see, the heat and fire of the cutting torch and the hot steam pouring from the safe. We could tell that Lewis had done the zoo job, from his modus operandi, or 'signature' style of busting into safes, even before we had definitive proof. Lewis was the only yegg we knew who could make a key to the front door of the zoo business office and then cut a hole so cleanly into a safe like he had done, but we were damned surprised that he was capering in Portland, and we knew Lewis would have to be dealt with.

Knowing something and *proving* something are two different things though and we had no evidence to go on. A week or so later, a longshoreman loading a ship in St. Johns noticed a green duffel bag floating in the river, bumping up against the pier, and he fished it out of the water. Had Billy Lewis's luck run out? When the longshoreman saw what was in the duffel bag he called police. We took the wet duffel bag up to the detective office and laid everything out on a table to dry. We found gloves, a pair of crepe sole shoes, money receipts from the zoo, a hundred or so dollars in partially burned money and a check stub with Billy's name on it. Worse, the back of the check stub had been used to calculate the take, in Lewis's own hand writing, no less. An amount was noted as "burned money" and deducted from the total. Using what we had, we obtained a search warrant and went to see Billy Lewis in person. He wasn't home, but with our warrant, we broke into his place anyway. We found more zoo receipts in the garbage sack under the kitchen sink. Well thumbed through safe specifications were carelessly tossed in a chest of drawers, along with his grades from locksmith school. We had Lewis cold on this job and we knew he'd go to prison.

Around the same time, Portland's biggest pawn shop, the H & B, located in downtown Portland, on Fourth Avenue, was burglarized. The burglar made a key for the alarm and shut it off, while still outside. With another key he opened the front door and relocked it. With no alarm to protect it, the big, square-double-door safe was burned open and over $200,000 dollars' worth of jewelry, gems and gold coins were stolen. After questioning the pawn shop owner and showing him photos of Lewis, he told us he recognized Lewis as someone who'd been in the shop several weeks before and had been seen lingering around the front door, looking, apparently, at the window displays. He had to have been casing the place and we well knew it. Although it was one of the biggest losses in the history of the state, we could never prove who did it. We heard through the underworld grapevine that within hours, the jewelry was on a plane to Honolulu, and from there wound up in Singapore. It was never recovered. I could never prove it, but the only person I knew of who could make both an alarm key and a door key so efficiently, was Billy Lewis.

Boreascope Benny

PRACTICE MAKES PERFECT

Another safe man of the time who probably deserves some mention is *Benny*. He was an excellent motorcycle mechanic, but looked and talked like a mild-mannered grade school teacher. Benny was a middle-aged white man, in his early fifties. He wasn't very tall, and had a paunch and a noticeable double chin. He wore dark horn-rimmed glasses, which he was always looking over the top of, giving him the appearance of a patient high school math teacher. With no criminal background Benny was an anomaly among safe burglars. It was clear to me Benny lacked any street-wise understanding of crime or danger, and as a result he only pulled off a few jobs before we caught and arrested him. Benny used a boreascope in all his capers, and so I nicknamed him "Boreascope Benny." A boreascope is a thin steel rod with a light and viewing device, used by motorcycle mechanics to examine the cylinder walls of a cycle's engine without actually taking it apart. Boreascope Benny reasoned that if he could drill a hole in a safe door, in just the right spot, he could insert the boreascope in the hole and turn the dial, while watching with the scope. By rotating the dial, he could watch the combination wheels line up and open the safe door without having to know the combination beforehand. But he had to drill in exactly the right spot and that could be a challenge.

We were tipped off about Benny after he bought several safe doors, over a period of time, from a local safe company called Allied Safe, located on the corner of NE Union and Weidler. A representative from their company called us out of the blue one day, to inform us that they knew of a man who was regularly buying "only safe doors," and they were concerned as to his motives. The company manager was concerned that this man might be a potential burglar, buying the doors to practice the art of safe burgling on. Practice makes perfect and before long Benny was as good at opening safes as he was at fixing motorcycles. For several months Benny hit various merchant safes in Oregon, Washington and Idaho, and made a lot of money. When we saw the actual burglaries, all we found was a safe door with a very small hole drilled in it and it was opened and the money gone. We were amazed at the ingenuity of using a boreascope to open up a safe. We'd never seen that done before. But eventually we caught up with Benny and put him in jail. Benny's lack of street wise smarts led to his arrest. He had used his own name and address to order and purchase the safe doors. When we arrested him, we found six safe doors in his garage with just the right holes and identifying tool marks on them to connect him to the other actual burglaries. That's how we knew he'd been practicing his art. His later confession sealed the deal. With no appeal, Boreascope Benny went off to prison for a while.

As the early 1970s wore on, safe burglary was becoming a thing of the past. Burglar alarm technology was becoming more sophisticated and modern. Even the best of the safe men needed forty-five minutes to an hour to do the job, and alarms didn't give them that much time anymore. Grocery store chains were beginning to stay open twenty-four hours a day, so there was no way to burglarize a store that didn't close. You couldn't get the money out of a safe anymore with a torch or a drill, you had to come in with a gun. But burglars are burglars; they're not hold up men or armed robbers. Stick-ups are a completely different mindset and always will be for the criminal who does them. Eventually, by the early 1970s, the safe detail at the Portland Police Bureau was dissolved. It represented the end of an era for many of us who had worked that detail. Crime was evolving in a multitude of different and complex ways, and safe cracking had become a lost art among yeggs. The Safe Detail had been one of the elite squad's and I'd felt privileged, as the youngest detective there, to be hand-picked by Myron Warren to work with such competent investigators. I felt disappointed that my team would no longer work together. We'd been a good team and had been involved in putting away the very best safe crackers in the state of Oregon. I would miss working this detail with the likes of, Myron Warren, Ladd Hunt, Al Vigna, John Wayne Wesson and Bob Chappel. They were all great men and all honest men, and all hand picked by Myron Warren, of course, just as I had been.

The Little Old Plumbing Store

THE STING AND THE SMASH AND GRAB

Although the safe burglaries were declining, burglaries of homes and businesses were becoming more prevalent. The drug influence was driving up the stealing of items that could be easily fenced and the smash and grab style of theft was becoming popular. A few lines of cocaine, a six-pack of beer and the smashers were ready to go caper. Business offices were common victims, losing electric typewriters, computers and printers. A business can't operate without its office equipment and in a few days the insurance company would replace the stolen machines. Often the drugged up smashers would go back and hit the same company again knowing there would be the fresh new replacements for the taking. Jewelry store windows were smashed and display items taken right out through the broken glass. Trucks were backed up through store windows and TV's, stereos and guns were loaded up quickly.

The new breed of smash and grab burglars knew they would be inside the store less than thirty seconds. It didn't make any difference if a store had a burglar alarm or not. Speed was the key to not getting caught. Hit-it-get-it-and-go! Large fencing operations were springing up and truckloads of hot TV's and office equipment were moving in and out of Oregon. Boats and motors were being stolen in Seattle and trucked to Portland in covered eighteen and twenty-two wheelers. So much property was being stolen that the burglars and thieves were always on the lookout for a new fence to buy up the stolen goodies.

The burglary detail decided to get into the fencing business too. We needed a better idea of who was stealing things and we needed to recover more stolen goods. The smash and grabbers were forcing us to change the way we were investigating these crimes. So, several of us detectives rented a not-too-reputable appearing storefront on NE Broadway and 25th and set up our own fencing operation. It didn't take long to attract customers, once we put the word out on the street. Any stolen property that came in would be videotaped from the moment it came through the front door. The entire transaction (including the money changing hands) would be captured on video, taped in full color and sound. One of our shaggy haired, criminal type undercover officers posed as the fence and worked the store. The thieves would steal the stuff and bring it right to us. Most of the time we had the items before the owners even knew they were gone. We checked the items we purchased against the lists of things stolen each day. We looked at the video tapes every night, in the burglary office, and tried to identify the thieves.

When we were able to identify the thieves, we obtained warrants for their arrest and saved them up, for later service. We operated our first store for six or seven weeks before we closed down and arrested all the crooks in one big sweep. I'll never forget how fun and exciting it was rounding up the thieves and arresting them, which took several hours. It was very possible, Joe Public might see his friendly neighbor or old school chum on the six o'clock news, because of our sting operations, which were ongoing in different locations, over several months. Maybe that little shoe repair shop that doesn't really seem to repair shoes, or that plumbing supply shop that doesn't really seem to sell plumbing supplies is the cops next sting operation. So, you can see how busy these detectives were. You just never knew where the police would set up another sting next. These were complex operations that required video cameras at a time when video surveillance was not entirely sophisticated or reliable, and also extremely expensive.

Luncheon Appointments Before Police Work

I DECIDED TO WRITE A LETTER

Because of the heavy workload, the bureau decided that splitting up partners was one way to be more efficient and that's what we were forced to do. Now each detective worked his cases alone. Splitting up partners was okay with me, but it created a shortage of detective cars, which in time became a serious and problematic issue. Before, while working, my partner and I drove together in one car and after the changes were instituted, we each needed our own car. More work to do, and no way to get there, which caused pressure because the sergeants did not stop assigning cases, nor could they have ever done so. Several days a week I sat at a desk with a stack of cases to work, while waiting for another detective to come back to the office with a car so I could actually get out into the field to work those cases. It was impossible to keep appointments or go out and talk to witnesses or victims or even look for suspects, because I didn't know if I'd have a police car to provide the transportation necessary to do so.

One day, with a tall stack of cases to work, that I could barely see over the top of and once again, no wheels, I walked down to the basement parking lot area to see if there was a detective car I might use. The detective captain's car was parked in its regular parking spot, so I returned to the office and talked to the working sergeant. "Hey sergeant, could I use the captain's car for a couple of hours to work on these cases I've got?" I pointed to the stack of cases on my desk, in frustration. "Nah, the captain has to have his car. He's gonna go to lunch pretty soon," he said, distractedly. "That's bullshit! How the hell am I supposed to work, then?" I snapped, as I walked back to my desk to sit and wait. The sergeant ignored my comment, and glared at me. I glared right back as I sat at my desk, with nothing to do. The citizens sure were getting screwed, I thought to myself, once again. Something was wrong with this scenario. If the captain's lunch appointment was more important than the criminal cases I was assigned to investigate, something was very wrong. Somehow, down the line, the priorities had gotten all screwed up. We sure could have used another eight or ten unmarked cars for the dicks and I knew exactly where to get them. Since the time I started as a probationary street cop, each police captain was given a new unmarked car to drive back and forth to work with. As it was explained to me, captains were *in-charge* of everything. So, in case of a police emergency, they needed that new car, so they could get to the scene and be *in-charge*.

Each new model year, the old captain's car would go back into service as a detective car and the captains would then get a shiny new one. Well, maybe this was okay before there was a police car shortage, but it was clear mismanagement of the taxpayers' money now. So, I typed and mailed a long letter, through channels, to the Chief of Police at the time, Chief Donald McNamara, explaining my views on the issue. I suggested that the captains might be better advised to "assist police work rather than impede it," by having "more cars available to the working detectives who need them." Here again, captains were hindering my police work and I found it frustrating. I told the chief that captains could facilitate police work by driving their own personal cars to work like the rest of us and make the police cars available for *police* work. Besides, the Portland bus company gave free tickets to any cop who wanted or needed them. All they had to do was go down to the records department and ask for a book of free tickets. The captains could still get to work free, just give them some bus tickets. Was this a new concept or what?

My letter was met with stony silence. The chief's office never formally acknowledged it. They read it, though, because I heard through the police grapevine that the captains were damned mad about it and my perceived insolence in writing it. My friend, the police chaplain, Ed Stelle, who also drove an unmarked city car, personally told me they were angry. One afternoon, we sat drinking coffee and discussing the bureau's shortcomings.

"Why are they pissed off at me for? I'm only trying to make things better," I told Ed.

"Because you're right," he answered.

"So, why won't they do anything about it?"

"Rank has its privileges, Don, but you *have* made your point."

"Nothing's gonna change around here," I remarked.

"Yeah, change is slow."

"Can I use *your* car then?" I joked, "I've got some burglaries in your area?" Ed laughed and took another sip of his coffee. The only thing that *did* change, after my letter, must have come about from the captains own personal embarrassment. And that was that the bureau began charging the captains a small monthly fee to help out with the cost of gas. I always felt that change was a paltry slap in the face to the citizens. To hell with the citizens, who were *they* anyway, other than our bosses? The citizens usually get to see the patrolmen on the streets, at work, and sometimes maybe even a sergeant, if there's a particularly hairy situation going on, but they never get to see a captain at work, unless he's out making a speech at some public or private function with a personal or professional agenda in mind.

A police captain in Portland is the same as a company vice president. At that time, they earned over $50,000 dollars a year, and were equipped with a private office and a staff of sergeants and lieutenants to assist them in their work. A secretarial staff was also available to manage their correspondence. The captain was furnished a city car with maintenance, gas and insurance. A free parking space went along with that. As a member of top management, captains had their own private supplemental retirement plan in addition to what the lower ranks received. When I worked with the bureau, in the 1960s and 1970s, the command structure of the department consisted of eleven captains, including the chief, and the assistant chief, who were all ranked as captain's, despite their titles as chief or assistant chief. This included Ed Stelle who was also ranked as a captain, given his position as police chaplain.

If the average cost of a new car was $10,000 and the radio and siren package another $2,000 that was a total of $132,000, investment of the taxpayers money. And with over seven hundred sworn officers to supervise, the taxpayer should have decided if they actually needed eleven, $50,000 dollar a year captains to do the job.

The moral of this story is that Portland is not unique. Big city police departments operate much the same way everywhere. Watch your local news stations. When talk comes around about hard times and budget cuts in city government, they always talk about cutting *patrolmen* first! They never talk about eliminating captains or the administrators losing pay or getting salary cuts. Maybe the priorities are messed up in other cities too. Maybe, just maybe, the war on crime needs one more fighter and one less $50,000 a year Captain. If you can, open up your police department, and take a good look at its guts. It's okay, they work for *you* after all. The Portland Police bureau conducts regular studies on crime statistics and offers information on budget decisions. This information is available to the public and can be obtained.

The Instructor at the Academy

INNOCENCE AND IDEALISM VS. REALITY AND DISILLUSION

ONCE A YEAR, THE POLICE bureau held an academy for new recruits, similar to the academy I had attended in 1961, in which I had graduated first in my class. For several years I helped out by teaching burglary investigation and the basics of search and seizure law to the new recruits. I enjoyed teaching at the school because it gave me an up-close look at the quality of the newbies who wanted to be police officers and I felt it was important work. The equal employment lawsuits filed a few years earlier had been successful and minority hiring was now encouraged. The faces and bodies before me in the classroom were changing in appearance, compared to when I'd been a recruit. In 1961, recruits were all tall, white, male and athletic. Now they were male and female, tall and short, black, white and Hispanic.

For the most part, I think the changes that were enacted by the lawsuits were good changes, except for one: Women in police work. Call me old fashioned, and I know that people will, but my views about women in police work are not entirely progressive or modern. And I am the first to admit this. I have several pragmatic reasons for having this viewpoint, based on my experience as a street cop and my understanding of the physical differences between most men and women. While I was a street cop and a detective, I always felt that women should not have been denied advancement opportunities, while working in The Women's Protective Division. They should have been allowed to take the detectives test and be promoted to detective, because we had some really capable women working in the (WPD) who were also exceptional and skilled investigators. But I do believe, and I believed then too, that women should be spared working the streets as uniformed street cops. That part of police work is still a man's job. This is my opinion. I base this on my understanding of physical agility, speed, strength and endurance. Most woman cannot complete with a man who is opposing them with violence. Most women will eventually be overcome and when a female cop is fighting a male offender, she is almost always at a physical disadvantage, particularly if she's working alone. This means she is likely to rely more on the use of tools like stun-guns, Chemical Mace or beanbag rounds to resolve a violent altercation, than she is in using physical hand-to-hand combat. And sometimes hand-to-hand combat is the best way to resolve a violent altercation.

Stun guns and Chemical Mace are not always reliable, and beanbag rounds can be and often are fatal, when used indiscriminately. In my opinion, a police officer should be tall enough and strong enough to subdue a suspect without relying exclusively or primarily on the use of imperfect law enforcement "tools" that may or may not work. Police officers have to be able to wrestle and *fight*, and most female officers lack the strength, force and aggression that a male officer will naturally possess and demonstrate. It is for these reasons that I do not believe women should be working the streets as patrol officers. This is what most male police officers feel in their heart of hearts, but will rarely admit to. I know this because I've spoken to several male police officers about this very issue over the years. But I'm pragmatic about women in police work. In the current world, they're here to stay.

When I worked as an instructor at the academy, I set up a mock burglary of a service station for the recruits to investigate, at the Kelly Butte training area. This was located in a building we often used, which was made to look like a service station, rather similar to a movie set and it was always a lot of fun for both me, as the instructor, and the eager recruits, trying to out smart each other. Enough clues were provided at the burglary scene to obtain a warrant for the burglars' arrest, like a fingerprint on a broken glass or some kind of plastic ID card dropped in the shrubs outside. If the students did a thorough job, they completed the exercise with a suspect in custody. If not, they knew they had missed important clues and had to go back. They learned that a thorough investigation was all that was acceptable, and nothing less. "Remember who you work for," I always told the young recruits I taught. "The guy who called the police; you work for him. You work for the *citizen*."

Also helping out at the police academy, and deserving of special mention, was one of the FBI's finest agents, assigned to the Portland office. His name was Leo App and we became friends. Leo was a firearms expert, who assisted with firearms training for our new officers when I was teaching at the academy. Leo was Mr. FBI, in both appearance and demeanor. He stood about five feet eleven and appeared slight and thin in the dapper suits he always wore, but no one could have been more confident. Leo had a shock of thick salt and pepper hair and a gravelly voice and he always struck me as someone who had been born to be an investigator. He was well qualified in his specialty, professional, confident and a crack pistol shot. He was famously rumored, in the bureau, to have shot and disabled a fleeing bank robber from almost two blocks away during the early 1970s.

Although the police bureau wanted its officers to practice their shooting proficiency, there was never enough target ammunition to go around. The lack of ammunition for officers practice needs was blamed, of course, on a budget shortage. "There's just not enough money for practice ammunition," we were routinely told. "You'll need to buy your own extras," they said, "If you want to get any practice in." Leo thought that was a lot of crap and often said so. "Ammo's cheap," he told me one afternoon. "Pennies don't count when your life's at stake. Any time you want some ammo to practice with, DuPay, you just let me know. The Federal Bureau will be happy to provide it." That's the way I felt about it, too, and I took him up on his offer several times. Leo App was one of two FBI agents who I came to admire as real professionals. He was generous and always kept his word, often giving me one hundred rounds of ammunition at a time. This enabled me to go to the range and practice and get "my eye trued-up" as I used to say, when referencing my need to practice at the range.

The other FBI agent I came to know and admire, was Ralph Himmelsbach. Ralph was taller than me, a bit over six feet. He had a quick smile and intense brown eyes that seemed to become lost in thought whenever he spoke of the DB Cooper case. DB Cooper was the elusive man who stole a large sum of money, well over $200,000 from an airline and bailed out over Oregon with it in 1971, by parachuting out of a plane. That case became Ralph's life project and some might even say an obsession. He eventually wrote a book about it, providing pertinent details of his investigation and his various theories.

You have to give credit to J. Edgar Hoover, though. Not only did he hire some talented people, most of his agents looked like FBI agents, according to the common stereotype. Leo and Ralph both looked like FBI recruiting posters, with their dark suits, skinny ties, shiny black shoes and square jaws.

These two FBI men were a couple of the good guys, in a profession that got a lot of flak from regular patrol officers. A lot of police officers felt FBI men were too insulated from the reality of street patrol and street problems. They would often actually sabotage good police work, because they didn't have the same kind of experience on the street, as a regular cop and didn't understand street crooks in quite the same way as a street cop. A lot of cops felt FBI agents could be a little full of themselves and unwilling to listen or admit when they'd screwed up. Leo and Ralph were not like that though. And they supported me, in my capacity in law enforcement, and made me feel good about the work they were doing, to keep Portland safe. They were capable and dedicated agents and I admired them both very much for their role in law enforcement.

An Avalanche

TROUBLE IN LEGIONS

IT'S FUNNY HOW EVERYTHING BAD in your life seems to save itself up so it can engulf you all at the same time. A few months after my thirty-fifth birthday, in 1971, I suddenly became very ill and wound up in my family doctor's office. After a bunch of tests, he told me that the ringing in my ears was high blood pressure and the pain in my gut was a serious bleeding ulcer. The good doctor himself had been a victim of both and well understood the pain I was experiencing. He also understood *why* I was in pain. The stress of the job was showing up in my body. After years of internalizing the constant frustration, danger and stress of police work, the job was starting to kill me. It didn't help that the only thing that could help me sleep was slamming a glass of whiskey before bedtime. Some changes would have to be made. After so many years on the job, I'd become increasingly burnt-out and convinced that there was no way to get ahead of crime. Crime never gets better, it just seems to get worse, as society breaks down, in one form or another. Too often there is no sense of job satisfaction for a police officer. At some point, a cop comes to realize he's wasting his time and endless effort. What happens when your life's work turns out to be the ultimate exercise in futility? What happens when the general public seem to hate you and the authority you represent? And your body revolts against the constant negativity and relentless stress? What then?

It seemed also, that by 1971, a shift had taken place from the innocence of the 1950s, when police were well regarded and respected in Portland, to a time when they slowly became more and more hated by criminals, the vocal minority and others in society. When I was a cop, we had no support groups or Traumatic Incident Committees, as many agencies do today. Those groups help officers deal with the inevitable burn-out and disillusionment the profession creates after so many years on the job. In these therapeutic groups, people can talk about things. Officers can also receive private counseling if they need it, something that was *never* encouraged when I was a police officer and later a detective. For me, the stress, the anxiety, the crushing depression and sense of futility that sometimes hit could seem insurmountable, and I had no one I could share those feelings with, other than the very busy Ed Stelle who was sometimes not available to talk. We were expected to contend with these issues alone. The feelings of depression and hopelessness often led me and countless other officers I worked with, to question why we had chosen a career in law enforcement in the first place. Back in the 1960s and 1970s you were expected to "be a man" and just deal with it. When your health suffered, it was much the same. Just deal with it. Suck it up and keep it to yourself.

"What can I do about this doc?" I finally asked my doctor.

"Well, we can change your diet and treat your ulcer, and we can medicate your blood pressure, but ultimately, that's just treating symptoms of the underlying problems. And the problems are from the stress of your line of work. Sooner or later, Don, you'll have to decide between your health or your job," my doctor told me solemnly. I tried for over four years to deal with my health concerns in the way my doctor wanted. I began eating bland food and drinking less coffee, as directed. It was always a challenge, addressing these issues, particularly my periodic episodes of secret depression, which I could not formally accept, even to myself.

Then, in 1975, after yet another appointment with my family doctor, he told me many of the same things, regarding how I would have to choose between my health and my career. While I was thinking about the implications of what the good doctor told me, my father, with whom I was very close, died suddenly of a heart attack in March of 1975 at the age of 70. I needed some time to think about my father's death and to grieve. The Bureau gave me a leave of absence so I could get away and arrange for the burial and funeral. For two weeks, I rested and took care of myself, and followed the doctor's orders. After all, if you pay a professional for his advice, but don't take it, then who's the fool? The one bit of advice I couldn't yet take from my doctor, was leaving the force. Once I felt better, I rejoined my fellow detectives and again tried to take up police work with a renewed sense of hope and enthusiasm. Dredging up that hope and enthusiasm was becoming more and more difficult.

Sitting in the Van

SAGNER GOES DOWN

After the teaching gig at the academy was over, in early 1972, I was back in the surveillance van taking photos of the front door of a car lot on 82nd Avenue, called Sagners Used Cars. The van was parked three blocks from the lot and with my telephoto lens, I could count the moles on the faces of anyone coming in or out of the premises. We were pretty sure that Max Sagner, who owned the lot, was operating a rent-a-car for crooks. Sagner had been in the used car business for several years and had built up a large clientèle of eager customers. Sagner thought he was Joe Cool. He was white, in his late thirties, with dark, slicked back hair and fairly good looking. He wore expensive clothes, black leather jackets, lots of gold chains, bracelets and rings, and I never once saw him when he wasn't wearing dark, stylish sunglasses. He leased a ranch-style house, with a brick front. The house had a big double garage and was located in the suburbs on NE Halsey Street, across from a golf course called Glendevere. Sagner drove a slick looking, black, 1969 Cadillac Eldorado, with blacked-out windows and black leather upholstery. It looked good parked in his driveway and always reminded me of the Bat Mobile from the original television Batman series of the 1960s.

Sagner's wife drove a shiny, red Corvette. She was a young, attractive, bleach blond, trophy wife, with a jaunty step who liked to strut her stuff. Sagner thought he had the inside track on life, kind of a criminal yuppie, but in reality he was just a common thief. As it turned out, he was running a pawnshop without a license and thought he was untouchable. From the van parked three blocks away, I got to watch what was going on from my telephoto lens. After only a few hours of watching I could spot the difference between the real customers and the thugs. The real customers looked at the cars and kicked the tires, opened the doors and looked inside. They asked questions of the sales people. The thugs would pull up in one car and park alongside the office. After spending a few minutes inside, they would drive off in one of the cars from the lot. There was no regular customer interaction. That became the red flag. An hour or so later, the thugs would return and hurriedly transfer items like TVs and guns back into their first car and take off. The burglary car was then put back in its place on the line.

I always photographed the thugs face-on as they came out the office door, and I took close up photos of the license plates on the cars they used. Day after day, the same thing happened. Sagner was doing a hell of a business in stolen loot. He was providing a rent-a-car service for burglars and business was booming. Gradually, as our file of photos grew, we identified most of the thieves he was doing business with. Some of the cars off the lot were showing up on the crime reports as suspect vehicles. We recognized one of the dudes in the surveillance photos as a bad guy named Jeff who owed us a favor. Jeff was a burglar that one of our detectives had gone easy on. Because the detective had felt sorry for his family members, Jeff had never been prosecuted. As a result, this bad guy owed us a favor, and he finally had the chance to pay up. Soon we knew for sure, based on Jeff's information that Sagner stored the stolen goods in his ranch house across from the golf course. That's what it took for us to catch these creeps; spending countless hours in a boring, stuffy van, taking hundreds of photographs.

A good detective already knows the answers to most of the questions he asks anyway, when he's conducting an investigation, but it's the little details that are often the most important. A little information gathered here and there and pretty soon the cops will have a damned good idea what's actually going on. Armed with a search warrant, we broke into Max's house. It took five detectives, along with a deputy district attorney several hours to catalog and load all the stolen items. There were so many stolen items that two large rental trucks were needed to haul all the stolen merchandise to the police property room. Many people got their possessions returned, and what couldn't be returned to the previous owners was sold at the city auction or donated to the Sunshine Division police charity.

Max was arrested and prosecuted for receiving and concealing stolen property. But we got him best by turning the IRS loose on him. The IRS did him in, with their own sound case against him. They examined everything he had, assessed his net worth and then taxed him on it. Our case against Sagner later went clear to the Oregon Court of Appeals. In August of 1974, it became a well-known search and seizure case, called Sagner vs Oregon. In that case, the finer points of search without a warrant and its various ramifications were examined by the court in detail.

Losing Another Cop

A BRILLIANT FUTURE AHEAD

Tears came to my eyes after I got a telephone call from a PPB associate and friend. He had sad news to share. Yet another of my cop friends had killed himself. Leo Miller was considered one of our bright new cops when he came to work for the city, but July 23, 1975, he committed suicide. After a first failed attempt with pills June 10, 1975, one of his buddies rushed him to the hospital where he was revived and then apparently released. After the June 10 episode, Leo *should* have been arrested and taken to a hospital, perhaps even if it meant going against his will. On more than one occasion, I had arrested people for attempting suicide. The charge of course was *disorderly conduct*. If a person was considered a danger to themselves or others, they were arrested and taken to a mental health facility for evaluation. Had this happened with Leo, he could have been evaluated by a mental health professional and set on a course of rehabilitation. Instead he was let go, after that first suicide attempt and he killed himself a few weeks later.

Leo was a slightly built man with a dark crew cut and clean cut features who had a natural and easy command presence. He inspired confidence in all those he led, and was an ambitious over-achiever and a natural peace maker. I worked for Leo when he was a traffic sergeant and again when he was a captain. Leo was a very supportive leader when I worked with him. He was a man of considerable integrity, and did everything by the book. Some cops might bend the rules, but not Leo. His integrity was untouchable and he was someone I felt I could completely trust. Talk around the police bureau had it that Leo would probably be the chief one day. But not now. I came to find out later, Leo had been seriously depressed about the command structure, feeling he could no longer fight the frustration of the never ending politics and his difficulties with then Mayor Goldschmidt and chief of police Bruce Baker.

Leo wanted to be chief but was concerned that it would mean having to defer to Mayor Goldschmidt about police issues, and he was not willing to do that. He was not willing to allow a man with no experience, training or background in law enforcement tell him how the police bureau should be managed. In 1973 Leo resigned from PPB and I remember his resignation was a shock to many because captains don't generally quit. He had also been so well-liked and so very competent in his role within the bureau. Leo had accomplished a great deal and had been an absolute asset to the bureau in every way for almost twenty years.

Why had my friends given up on life and killed themselves? Frank, and then Leo, they'd both done the same thing. Frank had blown his brains out with his service revolver and Leo had taken pills to end his life. I never knew the more intimate details of *why* they killed themselves until much later, but the shock of losing two such great law enforcement men was heartbreaking for me. And Leo, specifically, had so much going for him. He'd already made detective captain, which was a prestigious position and he would have had a brilliant future ahead of him, had he not given up. The end result of Frank's suicide and then Leo's suicide, years later, is that I felt heartsick and began to lose hope for the profession and for my role in the profession. Was this the kind of burn-out that I had to look forward to?

While doing some general research for this memoir, as I looked over various documents at the city archives, pertaining to Leo's 1975 suicide, I learned that he'd been drinking heavily for quite a while before his death and that he was also extremely depressed. Along with that, I learned of a very disturbing article that had been published in the September 1975 issue of The Rap Sheet regarding Leo's suicide that I'd never seen before. The quote came from his sometime girlfriend, Penny Orzaetti, who later became Penny Harrington and the first female police chief of PPB. She was quoted as saying, "My main concern is that people understand that there was nothing wrong with Leo's mind. It was just that he had taken all of the frustration that he could take and couldn't go on any longer. He told me once that when a person is no longer a contributor to this society, he has no right to live. He felt that the bureau was his life, as his note said, and that with the way things were on the bureau, he was prevented from contributing. You can't just take a man who was always a contributor and say 'you're not needed' anymore. That's what they did and that's why he's not here anymore." (The Rap Sheet, 1975).

The quote comes across as ludicrous, simplistic and completely lacking in any insight into the human condition. How can a man not have anything wrong with his mind and then later commit suicide? How can a man first attempt suicide, only to have that attempt ignored so that he could then finish the job a few weeks later? Where were Leo's friends? Where were the people who claimed to care about him? It seems to me that Leo had little or no support and was not taken seriously after that first suicide attempt in June of 1975. What he *was* suffering from was typical police burn-out. The quote from Harrington defies common sense logic and seems steeped in denial. The truth of the matter was that there *was* something *very* wrong in and with Leo's mind. He was depressed, alcoholic and so isolated and bereft, he felt he no longer *wanted* to continue living. For any person to feel that way, there has to be much more than just job difficulties they are contending with.

I lost touch with Leo a couple of years before his resignation and never knew to what extent his depression and troubles brewed. Had I known, I would have made an effort to help him. Losing Leo Miller to suicide was a huge blow to law enforcement in Portland, Oregon. And I consider it a personal tragedy that his friends and family did not make more of an effort to get him the help he desperately needed.

The Crook

NEW LICENSE PLATES

AS FATE WOULD HAVE IT, a few months after my own father died, my wife's father Wesley also passed away. Wes was a good guy, always smiling, always friendly and always drunk. He had been a cable splicer for the Bell Telephone Company during most of his working life. That meant he spent his working hours down in a man hole re-routing and fixing broken phone cables. Wes was good at what he did but never obtained a promotion because of his daily drinking; he was a vodka man and when he finally retired, he drank a fifth of vodka a day, until his death a year or so later. When my mother-in-law could no longer tolerate the drinking, she divorced him. After that Wes lived alone in a small apartment in Gresham and continued to drink.

My wife and I visited him on our weekly support-visits to bring him food and check on his welfare, and we always found him sitting in his favorite, tan, beat-up recliner, watching television and happily surrounded by numerous bottles of vodka. The bottles collected at his feet and on a nearby coffee table, some empty and some full. Wes drank straight from the bottle and spurned any kind of a mixer, saying jokingly, "Mixers are for sissies." His doctor had long ago given up trying to dry Wes out, and he told my wife and I that it was "too late," to hope for anything different and we might as well "Let him die happy." My wife and I had also given up trying to convince Wes to drink less. He would never listen. When Wes could no longer walk the short distance to the liquor store and back, he found he could have his vodka delivered by Radio Cab, and they were more than happy to oblige him, for the expected fee and maybe even a tip. So it was not a surprise when on one of our visits we found Wesley dead, slumped over in his recliner with an open vodka bottle between his legs and a paper bag from the liquor store containing two more fifths, on the coffee table.

I tried, as I stood there, looking down at Wesley's body to figure out how many dead bodies I'd already seen in my life but could not remember the number or even guess at a rough estimate. I knew I was jaded, numbed really, by both my father's death and all the dead bodies I'd seen as a patrolman and a detective, but the truth was it made me very sad to lose Wes to the bottle. He had been a good guy and might have lived much longer, had he not also been a hopeless alcoholic. I could only hope Wes died happy, feeling no pain, and perhaps even unconscious. It now fell upon my wife and I to arrange his funeral and settle his affairs. As had been his wish, Wes was cremated and his ashes were placed in a small urn. The urn was then secured in a nitch in a mausoleum in the Sellwood district of Portland, next to the urn's containing the remains of his father and his brother Milo. Pragmatically though, the saying goes "It is an ill wind that blows no good." Wes left my wife nearly $9,000 in insurance money. We now had the means to, temporarily at least, get away from the job that was driving me nuts and affecting my health so adversely. I knew I had at least thirty days' vacation time coming on the books and I applied for another thirty days unpaid leave of absence.

After some discussion, my wife and I decided, since coming into the unexpected inheritance money, we would take a trip to Hawaii. I needed a vacation and she needed a vacation. There, we would be able to get some much needed rest and I could decompress from the stress of the job. With cash in hand and two months of freedom ahead of me, we decided to buy a good car before flying to Honolulu. I wanted a Cadillac, and was lucky enough to find a 1974 Sedan Deville in a good car dealership in Lake Oswego. It had an all-black leather interior and a gleaming black paint job, with sparkling factory wire wheels. It was a boat! And looked a bit like a gangster's car. Parked at the curb you half expected to see Al Capone in the back seat, with a gun in his hand. After we purchased the car, we drove it about as fast as it would go down the Baldock freeway (now Interstate 5) to Salem and back. The car liked to go 80 mph best. It seemed like its favorite speed; it floated and it purred and people looked at us in envy. I was beginning to feel better already. I had a fancy car, a pocket full of money and the knowledge that I didn't have to go back to work on Monday.

Instead on Monday, my wife and I woke up in a nice room at the Ilikai hotel in Honolulu to love making and champagne drinking. Walking around Waikiki, I inhaled the smells of the tropical paradise I was now enjoying. The sultriness of the heavy air, the fragrance from the plumeria flower lei around my neck was intoxicating. I wanted to look like a tourist, so I bought two pairs of tropical white slacks and three or four colorful Aloha shirts, white shoes, white socks and blue tinted sun glasses. I was a tourist and I wanted to look like a tourist. I hoped no one would suspect I was a cop.

After about a week of sleeping in, eating well and sunbathing I could feel the stress and anger beginning to drain from my body. I was beginning to feel human again. We spent the next seven weeks hotel hopping, staying in the best; the Hilton, the Sheraton, and the Royal Hawaiian, until our money started getting low, and then we stayed in cheaper hotels, which were clean but off the main drag. After spending a lot of time laying in the sun we were getting a good tan and I noticed while sitting at the bar drinking Blue Hawaiians and eating Pu-pu's (bite sized appetizers) that we were treated a little better by the bartenders. They seemed to treat us more like regulars and less like haoles, pronounced "howlies" which is a contemptuous phrase used solely for white tourists who have just hopped off the plane.

As I became more of a regular at my favorite Tiki bar, the Hawaiian bartender began to talk more about how things were run in Waikiki. All the tourists walked around the torch lined streets at any time of the day or night in complete safety. The police drove a few blue and white marked cars but most of the officers were allowed to buy and use any car they wanted with no exterior markings. The Honolulu cops drove Pontiac Trans Ams, Plymouth Barracudas, and Chevelles, all muscle cars. It looked like they were having a lot of fun driving fast in hot cars and dressed in their spiffy police uniforms. Why couldn't we do that at home, I wondered? It would be great I thought, to use my long black Cadillac as my detective car and have the city pay for it. I ordered another drink and thought more about having my black caddy as my detective car, smiling to myself. Eventually, I shared with the bartender how safe my wife and I felt when we were out at night. I felt confident enough to leave my gun in the hotel room, although I kept that to myself. He leaned forward in a confidential manner and told me that crime was not allowed in Waikiki, because "the Samoans run things here."

"Around here nothing is more important economically than the tourist business," he confided. "We keep the tourists safe. We protect the haoles," he said with a smile. "So, what happens to your criminals?" I asked. "You know, your problem people?" He considered the question for a moment. "Sometimes problem people go fishing with the Samoans, off the Molokai Channel. And sometimes? They just don't come home again." I laughed, swallowed another pu-pu, finished my drink and paid the tab. A few days later, The Honolulu Advertiser, reported that two black men from the mainland had been found dead, floating in the nearby Ala Wai canal, which was a manmade waterway. This waterway constituted the north boundary of Waikiki. The paper speculated the men were doing a little free-lance hustling on their own. I remembered what the bartender told me about the Samoans running things. I guess the two black guys hadn't checked in first, to get permission.

 Crime was everywhere I realized and nothing could stop it. Except maybe a few 300-pound Samoans. I was beginning to wish we had a Molokai Channel at home where I could take some murderers and rapists fishing, and make *them* disappear. I casually mentioned this fantasy to my wife one afternoon. "You're not supposed to be thinking about going back to work, yet," she said. "Remember what the doctor told you about your blood pressure. Think about our shiny black Cadillac instead that's waiting at home." A few days later we were on a jet headed for Portland, almost broke, but with what I thought were spectacular tans. I had gone from a pale Portlander to a deep nut brown. When I looked in a mirror, my face was so tanned, that my teeth looked extra white when I smiled, and my blue eyes stood out more. But I was nervous. I could just *feel* my blood pressure beginning to rise at the thought of going back to the grinding job at home; the job of being a police detective and all that that entailed. Getting off the plane in Portland, reality overcame me. It was cold. It was raining too, a chilly rain, not like the warm tropical rain I'd become so accustomed to. I was shivering. We hadn't taken our coats to Hawaii. Huddled against the rain, I waved at a Radio Cab parked outside the baggage return and we headed home. "Turn on the heater," I told the cabbie. "We're freezing."

The following Monday morning, my wife pulled our newly purchased Caddy up to the Pine Street side of the police station in downtown Portland and dropped me off for work. As I got out, I heard catcall whistles coming from the corner burglary office on the second floor. I looked up and could see a couple detectives, with their heads sticking out the windows, staring down. I walked up the stairs to the second floor and down the long hall toward the detective division offices. I waved and smiled at our office clerk, Emma Jozaitis, as she pushed the electric lock-button that allowed me to enter. All the typists behind the counter stopped their work and stared at me. "Nice tan! Wow! Nice tan, Don!" was all I heard, along with a couple more whistles. I must have looked better than I thought. In the burglary office I also had to run the gauntlet of admiring stares and whistles from the guys. "Look at this guy!" said Sergeant Fred Brock to the other six detectives in the room. "Pulls up in a long black Cadillac, lookin' like a movie star." Brock was grinning as he handed me a stack of burglary cases six inches high. Good naturedly, he said, "Get back to work, DuPay. The vacation's over!" And it was over. Between the new cases I'd been assigned, and a pile of old files still sitting on my desk top, I could hardly see over the mountain of work that I now had before me.

That first day back at work went faster than I thought it would. But as the day came to an end, I heard one of the dicks say, "Geez, some gangster's car just pulled up out front." Again, several of the guys jumped up, and hurried over to look out the window. They saw my wife sitting in the Cad, which sat idling at the curb. The unmistakable timbre of envy was in their tone as they continued to make comments and remarks about the appearance of the bright Cadillac. I guess it was just too much for them, super tanned as I was and with my ride waiting. "It *is* a nice car," I said flatly, offering no further explanation. "I hope she brought me a whiskey on ice today, I need it," I further remarked, in a teasing tone, as I strolled out the door.

The working routine had resumed again and as the days went by, my beautiful, nut brown tan faded. Eventually I began to hear rumors about the Cadillac my wife and I had purchased. Whispers were circulating, shared with me by a couple of my closest cop buddies who liked me, were loyal and talked openly with me about all the bureau bullshit and how frustrating it could be. I felt these were not good rumors to be circulating about a dedicated police detective. It became apparent that people were wondering how I was able to afford the car and also take an entire month off work without pay, for a two month vacation in Hawaii. Since I had always considered my private business private, as I'd always been a very discreet person, I never told anyone at the police department of my father-in-laws death or the insurance money we had recently inherited. Because of this, the whispers continued over the next few weeks growing more insistent each day. It finally dawned on me, from the information gleaned from my buddies, that some of these cops were wondering if I was doing something illegal to earn extra money, on the side. The well-oiled rumor mill that *was* the Portland police department infuriated me, as it always had.

If some of these guys had wanted to know where I'd gotten the money from, all they had to do was *ask* me. But no, they would rather snoop and speculate, wondering if I was engaging in blatant criminal activity, rather than ask a direct question, for fear of losing face. Had they forgotten the corruption of people like Captain Jim Purcell or Carl Crisp? Or the fact that I'd had to work for Purcell and that we'd famously clashed because of that? I had worked for the worst of the corrupt, in my time at PPB, but that wasn't me. That was not how I operated. For more than two weeks, I stewed over the insult of anyone thinking I'd do anything illegal to make extra money. And I plotted my revenge. It would be sweet if it worked out right. On a whim I applied for an Oregon personalized license plate that read, CROOK. Just that and nothing more. CROOK was what I wanted it to say. It would be a sarcastic "Fuck you!" to all those who would suspect the worst about me, simply because I was able to buy a new *used* car and go on a vacation for eight weeks. I honestly didn't think the Department of Motor Vehicles would issue the plate to me, so my second choice was "BAAD." I thought they might issue the second choice, and so I was very surprised and pleased when my first choice was accepted.

When the new license plates arrived at the DMV office, I got a telephone call from the DMV, informing me that I had to return the old ones. After dropping off the old plates, I finally got my hands on the new ones. I unwrapped the shiny, new yellow plates and saw the word "CROOK," in equally shiny black letters. I was astounded and ecstatic. I really didn't think my request for a CROOK license plate would be accepted. I set to work to install the new plates and then later stood back to admire them smugly. With the new plates installed, the car looked even *more* like a gangster's car. My oldest son, borrowed the car one evening and when he returned it, he had installed pull down black-out curtains over the back seat windows and several decal bullet holes dotting up the trunk toward the rear window. Now it was perfect. We stood together laughing at his great work. "Wow! It looks great son!" I told him proudly. It looked like a movie car from the set of a gangster flick. Driving around town, people stared at it. Some honked their horns, others just waved. But the best reactions were at work, when my colleagues got to see it.

While my wife waited for me on Pine Street, to take me home after work, I would regularly look out the office window and see the beast freshly washed and waxed and gleaming like a cut diamond in the sun. I would dilly-dally, in no hurry to go downstairs, secretly enjoying the unspoken angst and flagrant envy of the insufferable grapevine in which I worked. It didn't take long now for it to become known that the conspicuous looking gangster car was owned by a Portland detective. *Oregon Journal*, columnist Doug Baker, wrote in his daily column, "A Bakers Dozen," about the "Portland Gendarme," who was now driving about town in a black Cadillac with license plates that read "CROOK." I knew the bureau would not be happy about the column when it appeared in the newspaper, but I didn't give a shit either and I never heard anything more about it.

All anyone needed to have done, was just *ask* me how I was able to buy my new *used* car, but instead, they chose to speculate foolishly as to my character and integrity. That pissed me off and made me want to even the score. And I did. There was absolutely nothing anyone could do about it. I had successfully rubbed their collective noses in the poop of their own curiosity, envy and shallowness. My wife continued to pick me up after work on the Pine Street side of the precinct, and I'd always slide into the back seat with a sense of smug pride. Sometimes I'd wave out the curtained open window of the Cadillac, at the snoopy on-lookers I knew were watching from the second floor burglary office. I'd pour myself a glass of whiskey from a gold flask I kept in the rear console, lean back and rejoice that the working day was over. The smoky brown glass was always there, with ice clinking in it, brought from home by my wife. No one ever did ask me about the car or the vacation and I never mentioned it either. No questions, no answers. I had scored a victory. Crook indeed!

The Secret Snitch

AN ATTRACTIVE NUISANCE

I WAS DOWN ON MY HANDS and knees in a local service station, fastening an infrared silent alarm sensor underneath a cigarette vending machine and humming the phone company ditty. The one about letting your "fingers do the walking," through the yellow pages. Only I was humming, "Let your ankles do the talking to the police dispatcher." The sensor I was installing would detect the heat from the feet and ankles of the next guy who tried to break into this particular service station. The cigarette vending machine sat in the service bay area of a small neighborhood gas station, on SE Powell Boulevard. The owner had been burglarized twice in the previous month and the cigarette machine had been pried open both times. I hid the transmitter box behind a stack of oil filters and flipped the switch for a test. The sensor picked up the heat from my ankles as I walked toward it. At about six feet away it triggered the silent alarm transmitter. If the burglar came back again, we'd be the first to know.

I was back to work doing surveillance photography, installing the silent alarms, coaching new detectives as they came through, and teaching at the police academy again. The teaching and the burglar alarm work freed me up from working traditional burglary cases in the office. I was able to concentrate on catching burglars and teaching instead of pushing so much paper around. Besides, the alarm job had a car permanently assigned to it, which I considered a huge bonus. The tools, rolls of wire and sensors were locked in one car, and I didn't have to wait around for a set of wheels. With the car, the surveillance van and my tools and equipment, I set out to catch some more thieves. I read every burglary report that came into the office, to see if I could figure out where a burglar might have the right *feeling* about a place and where he might hit next. After I picked out several locations that might be possible, I checked on each one to see if an alarm would be feasible for that location.

Was the owner interested in having one of our alarms for a while? And could the owners be relied on to properly set up the alarm each night, for maximum effectiveness? And most important, did the location have the right *feel* to me? Once I had installed a silent alarm, I always spoke with the officers who might cover the call, to make certain they knew where the alarm was positioned in the building and how best to cover it, to prevent the burglar's escape. Each installation took a lot of thought, study and preparation. It was strictly a game of percentages, a mental chess game, if you will. If I didn't score with an alarm in two or three weeks, I'd pull it out and set it up in a new location.

We owned about seventy of the silent transmitters and I kept them moving all the time, putting them to good use consistently. I bugged doctors' offices and drug stores that had been hit a time or two, and we were able to catch the druggies breaking in. I caught lots of burglars returning to businesses for the replacement machines that had been stolen earlier; typewriters, computers and cash registers, among others. The robbery detail, which handled armed robbery, often asked me to set up the silent machine as a hold-up alarm in small grocery stores that had been plagued with stick-ups. Sometimes the homicide detectives needed to protect a witness and I'd wire their pad with a similar panic button. Boxcars loaded with tires were being broken into while sitting on train tracks, so I wired the sliding doors with a trip wire and we caught those thieves too. I never really cared how they broke in, I concentrated on what they were going for and tried to put a trap in their way.

There was one cherry patch that caught two or three burglars a week. It was the Jacob Kamm house, located at 1425 SW 20th, which was an historic residence sitting on a dead-end street in SW Portland, just south of Jefferson Street, across from the current location of the popular Goose Hollow Tavern. The Kamm house was privately owned by the same good citizen who saved the historic Pittock mansion from demolition. The gentleman had purchased this piece of Portland history and was trying to preserve the Kamm house intact until it too could be placed on the historic registry and then eventually restored. But so many break-ins had occurred that soon there would be no artifacts left to salvage. Burglars were walking off with old light fixtures, plumbing fixtures, marble from the fire places, and anything else they could pry up or pull down.

In an effort to protect the old mansion, I decided to put a pressure pad under some tattered carpeting at the foot of the huge wooden staircase. Anyone wandering around inside the old mansion would either go up the stairs or come down and the cops would be the first to know of their presence. The empty mansion, on a lonely street couldn't help but be a kind of "Attractive Nuisance," as it was called. Were it not for my well placed pressure pads, it would have been dismantled and hauled away piece by piece or set fire to, over time. Over a two-year period, my Kamm house alarm caught more than thirty-two people. The old mansion attracted all kinds of trespassers. Some were antique thieves who knew precisely what they were looking for; we prosecuted those individuals for burglary. And many of the trespassers were merely schoolboys attracted to the old house out of curiosity; we prosecuted the kids for simple trespassing.

These trespassers were never quite sure just why the police showed up so promptly, and I never told them during the interviews the following day. "God damned rotten luck getting caught!" one of them said to me, as he sat at the interview table. Luck had nothing to do with it, I thought, smiling to myself. During the time I installed these types of silent alarms for the police, I achieved a 68% hit rate. That means that in 68% of the places I installed an alarm, the burglar actually did show up and hit the trip. No other cop ever had that ratio before. It was the *feeling* that I had for burglary. Working in the Burglary detail had always been my forte and where I experienced the highest level of job satisfaction, while working for the Portland Police Bureau.

Homicide Detail, summer of 1975

STAB 'EM AND SLAB 'EM

THE CRIMES THAT DETECTIVES INVESTIGATE are divided into two groups; crimes against property and crimes against persons. I had been working property crimes for a long time. I knew everything there was to know about burglars and thieves, robbers and vandals, and I had proved it through my successes and numerous commendations, while working in that detail. For the most part, burglars don't really get caught, so much as *they* catch themselves, by doing stupid, self-sabotaging things while in the commission of a crime. Like the safe burglars who kept using the same tools, the kid that dropped his wallet in the service station in St. Johns or the zoo burglar who threw the incriminating duffel bag in the river. I seldom felt like it was a fair catch, because they were so careless and basically, I always felt *they* caught themselves. As a uniformed cop, when I nabbed a guy in an alley with a trunk full of TVs, I felt like I had caught him fair and square using my skill and alertness. When a burglar hit one of my tripwires, I felt I had caught him fair and square with my cunning. But other than that, these criminals caught themselves.

My career seemed to boil down to the silent alarm catches and the guys who happened to be in the alley. Not very much to look back on. I felt I needed a change. The thief mentality was no longer a challenge for me and I was becoming bored with the burglary detail. I knew it inside and out. But a change to what? Working morals crimes was not an option for me because I couldn't deal with the rape victim's anguish and I couldn't stand being around the neurotic creeps who committed sex crimes. That left homicide. I knew I would be pursuing a different kind of criminal there, not a thief, but a murderer. Murderers were an entirely different breed of criminal. Homicide might be that challenge I felt I needed. The homicide detail was just down the hallway from burglary and occupied an equally large squad room. A separate sound-proof room housed the polygraph machine and the small office space for our two polygraph examiners, Robert Bertalot and Rudy Bouwman.

A large chalkboard on the back wall acted as a status board for active homicide cases. As the cases were solved, the victims' names were erased from the board. I came to work one morning, to find seven active homicide cases, and showing on the board, the detectives assigned to each case. Since homicide was also responsible for investigating armed robberies, there was a separate pin-map on another wall listing the active hold-up cases, which more often than not turned out to be convenience and jewelry store stick-ups. The homicide office had a different atmosphere than burglary. It was less raucous and had a more somber tone. There was less joking around and the atmosphere was far more serious. Homicide detectives had more prestige than those working burglary, auto theft or check fraud. And because they were more experienced detectives, they were considered the elite investigators within the Portland Police Bureau. I already knew most of the detectives in homicide, and they were, for the most part, all capable men I'd worked with before, either as a patrolman or as a detective.

The sergeant hadn't been a sergeant very long, and I remembered him from when he was a patrolman. Sergeant Bonaventure was just a "face in the crowd," type of guy, unaggressive and certainly not a leader. He stayed out of the way, sat at his desk and did his paper work. He didn't want to make waves and always seemed a little lost working the homicide detail. Rickie, the homicide lieutenant was just the opposite. He had always been a leader. He was tall, quite young to be a lieutenant, (in his thirties) and wore his prematurely gray hair cropped short. Even wearing a dress shirt, tie and slacks, Rickie had an unmistakable military air about him. He had worked as a motorcycle cop earlier in his career, but his attitude never got over it. Rickie exuded command presence and had an air of arrogance and entitlement that many of us found annoying and tedious. I would never try to influence the reader's impression about this lieutenant, and the fact is, there is a world of information I cannot include about him here, but considering my subsequent personal experiences with him, I soon learned he was a racist, amoral asshole.

The detectives on the crew seemed to have a lot of things on their minds besides police work, which was not uncommon. One of the guys was in the middle of a messy divorce. Nothing else was on his mind. I knew him from my patrolman days at North Precinct. He'd been one of the sleeping beauties. Another guy who I worked with on and off at East Precinct was now a detective in homicide and he still had the serious drinking problem that he'd had as a patrolman. At least twice a week this man would arrive staggering into work completely blotto and his buddies would have to hide him from the sergeant. They'd stuff him in a detective's car and get him out of the office and drive him around, feeding him strong coffee for a while, until he could sober up enough to work. He, too, was going through yet another divorce, and seemed troubled, disappointed and sad whenever I bumped into him. You'll remember him, *he* was the East Precinct patrolman on top of the Lampus department store roof shooting magnum loads at the fleeing burglar.

A third detective I'll call Joe was already divorced. His main interest in life was limited to finding his next female conquest. When I rode with him, doing cases together, police work waited until he'd checked in on his newest sweetie. She was a pretty, blond, cocktail waitress who worked at the Original Taco House on SE Powell Boulevard. Joe's *other* sweetie was a female attorney who worked in the district attorney's office, who later became a judge. Joe was having a hell of a time deciding which of these two ladies was his favorite. I knew both women but didn't offer Joe any advice about them, even after he'd asked me. I had no desire to get involved in any way. I'd just smile when he'd ask me what I thought, saying nothing. I'm not saying these guys were not competent investigators, because they were, when they were sober, had put their libido aside for a moment and were paying attention to police work. But their personal problems did seem to take first priority in their lives and this impacted their ability to do good, investigative police work.

Working the homicide detail required the close assistance of our polygraph examiners, Robert and Rudy. They were both in and out of the squad room a lot because the lie-detector room was there and they did a lot of the exams on homicide cases there also. The examiners were detectives first and received polygraph training at city expense sometime later. I had always been fascinated with the lie-detector machine, and eventually took a polygraph course at Portland State College to learn more about it. My fascination existed because if the test worked and was reliable, it could be a wonderful way to find out if someone was being deceptive and trying to cover up a crime. Just wire them up to the machine and ask them questions. It seemed so simple. The machine was located in a small sound-proof room in the homicide office. There was a one way mirror so cops could watch the test subject without their knowledge and observe body language and eye movements that might indicate deception. Polygraph means *many graphs*. Calling it a lie-detector machine is bad advertising at worst, and wishful thinking at most.

The suspect taking the test would sit comfortably in a special chair. The machine measured blood pressure, pulse, breathing rate, and the perspiration in fingertips all at the same time and displayed that information on a moving graph. The machine didn't actually detect lies, it simply measured things that were happening in the body when it might be under stress. The real skill lay strictly with the examiner. It was his job to convince the suspect that there was no possible way to lie to the machine, because the machine would *know*. The suspect could save a lot of time if they confessed to the crime and we were always encouraged as investigators, (and some might say even pressured) to get those signed confessions. If that tactic didn't work, the suspect would be hooked up to the machine and a few simple tests would be run.

In those scenarios, the suspect may be asked to pick a number between one and five and get it securely in their mind. "Now sit back and relax," the administrator of the test would say. "Just say no to every question, okay?"

"Did you pick number one?"

"No."

"Did you pick number two?"

"No."

"Did you pick number three?"

"No."

"Did you pick number four?"

"No."

"Did you pick number five?"

"No."

One of these responses will naturally be a lie. The examiner will tear off the graph paper and show you your lie in black and white. *Now* you're convinced! It's all part of the psychological maneuvering. The real test comes next with questions the suspect doesn't want to answer, like "Did you kill her?" and "Do you know where the gun is?" or "Do you know where the body is buried?" The examiners got a lot of confessions this way but very little of it had to do with the machine. It's the psychology of a guilty conscience and thinking someone else already knows the truth of what happened, and in this case a machine that can't be lied to.

I recall a homicide case, shortly after I'd been accepted into the homicide detail, where there was no real evidence to go on. The suspect was tested by Rudy Bouwman, our most experienced examiner. He proclaimed the man guilty. Guilty as sin. Not convinced, and wanting a second opinion, I arranged for a test with an Oregon State Police polygraph examiner, on SE Mcloughlin Boulevard. This state police examiner proclaimed the suspect innocent, without any knowledge of the guilty determination from Rudy Bouwman. Here were two examiners in which I had equal faith who had come up with opposite opinions. The truth is, so called lie-detectors don't detect lies, they detect stress in the body. The tests are not reliable and that's why the results are not permitted in court. If you are forced into taking a lie detector test, you can easily invalidate the results by putting a tack in your shoe. When the examiner asks a question, press your toe down on the tack until you feel pain. It will make the needle jump off the graph. Holding your breath, or breathing irregularly will do the same thing. The test won't come out, and will be deemed inconclusive. A skilled investigator shouldn't need a machine. Adults generally know when they're being lied to and I've been lied to by some expert offenders, many of whom were sociopathic, narcissistic and in some cases unconscionable people.

Once, when I was a detective, I gave a Personal polygraph exam to a suspect from the North End. He was not a well-educated man, and some might say even a little simple. As I held his left wrist and felt his pulse, my right hand guided a sharp pencil on a clean piece of white paper. I asked him if he had committed the burglary. He said "No." I told him I could "tell," by feeling his pulse that he was lying to me. I asked him another simple yes and no question and he said "No," at which point, my right hand made a sharp spike on the paper to convince him. At that point, he looked at the paper and then at my hand, fearfully, and seemed convinced. He leaned back in the chair, sighed and then confessed, admitting to the crime. I let go of his arm and put down the pencil and though I didn't feel smug about the ploy, tricking him into a confession, I also knew he was guilty of the crime. He had been caught by several patrolmen in the act, with multiple witnesses, also present, who had seen him break into the house and he had a history of previous burglaries. Looking back on it now, I can see how people will find fault with what I did to this potentially illiterate man. But the fact was, this ploy had been taught to me by an older detective I'd worked with named John Skoko. Detective Skoko claimed to have used it himself on more than one occasion, and that it was a useful ploy, when he knew someone was guilty, not very bright and backed up, of course, by other evidence.

I only went after a confession when I had other hard evidence to support the offender's guilt. This could be ascertained if they were caught in the act, or if there were more than one witness, both corroborating important facts of a crime having been committed, when and where. In this case, I knew the guy was guilty, stupid, violent and dangerous and that he needed to be locked up. I still chuckle though, when I think about it sometimes.

Murder on the Riverbank 1975

I JUST POKED HIM A LITTLE

THE WILLAMETTE RIVER CUTS THROUGH the heart of the city, dividing east Portland from the west side. On the east riverbank was a freeway with an active hobo camp situated just beneath the ramp, currently the site of the east bank Esplanade. The dead body of a transient was found by another member of the hobo camp, who then called police from a pay phone. Bits of torn, ragged cloth and splattered blood dotted the rocks, providing a clear trail to where the body lay, face down about three feet from the waterline on some jagged rocks. The deceased had been dragged from the camp to the edge of the river and abandoned. The body was cold, in rigor and had probably lain on the rocks since at least the night before. I turned the body over and could see a large blood stain on the dirty blue shirt, just under the deceased man's heart. The eyes were open and dry, and crusty blood came from a cut at the mouth. The blood ran down into the beard stubble and disappeared into the folds of skin at the neck. From the looks of the deceased, he had been living on the streets for years, perhaps even decades. Although the body was dressed, it was barefoot. Now, I wanted to know who had his shoes.

I looked up and saw the hobo camp. Walking east, about fifty feet up the bank, I found another transient rolled up in a dirty sleeping bag snoring. He was an old wino, probably in his late fifties, though he looked much older. Near him was a new pair of brown Army boots with numerous flecks of blood dotted on the laces. An empty green wine jug was also nearby, with blood stains and a bloody palm print on the neck of the bottle. I nudged the guy with my foot. "Wake up! I wanna talk to you!" I told him. He woke up startled and crawled out of the sleeping bag, rubbing his face and looking for all the world like a deer in the headlights. He had shit his pants from the wine, probably the night before and he smelled like it. My colleagues and I referred to this as "The wine shits," that transients were often afflicted with. I moved so that I was up wind from him, took out my police ID badge and flashed it at him, identifying myself as a homicide detective with the Portland Police Bureau.

When the guy stood up I could see blood on his clothes and he was wearing only socks on his feet. He was so dirty I hated to touch him, but patted him down quickly to check for weapons. In his jacket pocket, all I found was a small folding pen knife, with dried blood on the handle. There was no identification on him other than a tattered Social Security card with his name on it.

"Who's the dead guy down by the riverbank?" I asked point blank.

"I don't remember his name. We were pretty drunk." he offered.

"How'd you get blood all over you?"

"We musta had an argument, but is he *really* dead?"

"Yeah, he's really very dead. Let me read you your rights."

I read the man his rights and put him in handcuffs. He offered no resistance and hung his head. Two men from the coroner's office had arrived at the scene sometime after me, to put the body in the meat wagon and take it to the morgue. They had the deceased strapped to a gurney and were struggling to get it up the hill and over the rocks to the van parked at the edge of the freeway. One man was pulling, one was pushing as the gurney rocked from side to side and kept getting stuck in the jagged rocks. Progress was slow. And as I stood silently, with my hands in my pockets, watching and listening to their huffing and puffing and intermittent cussing, I couldn't help feeling grateful that I didn't have to help.

As I'd refused to drive the suspect downtown in my detective car, because of his deplorable condition and overwhelming stench, an unlucky black and white showed up and the patrolman took the prisoner downtown for me. "See that he gets cleaned up and save the bloody clothes for evidence," I told the officer, who nodded glumly. After the jail had given my killer a good hot shower and dressed him in clean coveralls, I went up to the city jail to talk to him. He said his name was Henry and he agreed to talk to me about the crime without a lawyer butting in. He wanted to come clean, he said. According to his story, all he could remember was that he and his pal had shared a big bottle of cheap red wine under the freeway ramp and had gotten drunk. They had argued, but Henry was too drunk to remember what it was about. He admitted to "poking him a little," with the small knife, but didn't think he'd hurt the guy until he fell down and wouldn't get up. Henry said he remembered dragging the body down by the river, but was too exhausted to lift it up and throw it in. He took the boots because they were better than the ones he had. That was the sum total of it. A drunken argument over God knows what, one man dead, and one man in jail.

All I had to do now was go to the autopsy. The morgue was located in an old facility in the ghetto on NE Knott Street. It had always been there and the ghetto had kind of developed around it. The front entrance looked like a funeral parlor with a loading area around the side. Just inside the front door was a small waiting room and an information counter. A door marked *Morgue* was just to the right and opened into a hallway. Down the hall was a large sterile looking room with a big stainless steel cutting table. Above the table, on an adjustable arm, was a microphone hooked up to a dictation machine. On the tile floor were three stainless steel buckets with tools in them.

A deceased body lay on the cold steel table; it was the naked body of the transient I had last seen down by the riverbank. Attached to his right big toe was a tag listing his name and the morgue file number. The smell in the room was a terrible combination of strong cleaning alcohol, disinfectant soap, and the underlying smell of death. Feeling apprehensive and queasy, I wanted to leave the room but knew I couldn't. Although I had been a cop for many years and had a vague idea what the medical examiner was going to do, this was the first actual autopsy I'd ever attended. Homicide detectives are expected to attend all autopsies of the cases they investigate, in order to be better able to testify in court as to the manner of death. As a result, I was required to be there.

Dr. William Brady, the medical examiner, was a tall, thin man with gray hair, pale skin and even features. He had the demeanor of an eager and interested investigator and it always surprised me, in my dealings with Dr. Brady, how much he seemed to enjoy his line of work. I sometimes wondered how a person could become interested in forensic pathology. I wondered how they could make a career out of dissecting the deceased. But Dr. Brady was a consummate professional and always struck me as competent, engaged and hardworking.

When I walked into the autopsy room, the tape recorder was turned on and the procedure begun. Dr. Brady was checking the body closely and talking into the Dictaphone, describing what he saw. The head and mouth were closely checked and all wounds, bruises and abrasions were noted in detail. When Dr. Brady got down to the chest, we could see a small half-inch stab wound just under the left nipple. The cut was fairly small and didn't appear significant by itself, but it went clear into the chest cavity.

"How deep is it?" I asked.

"Can't tell until we get inside," he said.

Standing as close to the exit as I could, while still watching the procedure, I felt myself getting queasy. Shit! That's what I was afraid might happen; that I would start feeling sick. I knew Dr. Brady was going to cut the guy open, but there was no way to prepare myself for what came next. The medical examiner took a curved linoleum knife and plunged it in the throat just above the breast bone. With one swift stroke he cut the body wide open from the neck clear down to the pubic bone. Involuntarily, my jaw dropped and I sucked air, staggering back a little. Several things flashed through my mind. I half expected the guy to jump up off the table from the pain, but remembered he was already dead. It felt like the bottom had dropped out of my stomach and involuntarily I had to turn away. Where in hell was the door? I felt faint and sick and embarrassed all at the same time. A cold sweat broke out on my forehead. I was a big, strong man, but seeing a human body cut open with a linoleum knife was like seeing something out of a horror movie. It was undeniably chilling to witness.

Before I could steel myself for what came next, the medical examiner picked up a bone saw and jammed it down into the incision in the throat. He sawed and crunched his way down through the breastbone until the chest cavity was open and exposed. When he had a hard time getting through some area of the ribs, he picked up a lopper, much like something one would use to trim a tree with, and he cut through the individual ribs that way. I had never before heard the sound of a human bone being snapped by a pair of long loppers. The crunching sound was gruesome, like fingernails on a blackboard. I expected to see blood spurting from this kind of slaughter but reality slammed back and I remembered dead people don't bleed. With the bones cut open and the chest ribs showing, the dead man was starting to look less human and more like a side of beef. Finished with the bone saw and linoleum knife, Dr. Brady placed them in the stainless steel buckets on the floor and picked up a scalpel. Holy shit, there was no end to it, I thought. "Now we can get a look at the fatal stab wound," he said simply, as he cut out the man's heart.

He held the heart in his hand and washed the blood off by dipping it in a bucket of water. "Come here detective," he said casually. "We can see what killed him now." This was too much for me. I felt like passing out. I edged closer, not wanting to see, but knowing that I had to look at it, to satisfy police procedure. With the heart removed from the body and laying on the table, Dr. Brady pointed to a very small cut with the point of the scalpel. He had sliced the heart open and then stuck his finger behind the cut. As he held the heart, I could see his finger wiggle through the small hole. "Not a big hole, but big enough to kill the guy," he said philosophically.

Dr. Brady put the heart in a plastic bag and tossed it into one of the buckets on the floor. With the scalpel, he made a few more cuts and pulled the lungs out of the body. He examined them thoroughly and added them to the plastic bag. I could *feel* every cut he made and it made my skin crawl. I wished he might take a break but he didn't. Next he cut out the liver and brought it up on the table top, slicing it open. "From looking at the liver, he would have died of cirrhosis anyway," he said and went on to describe its condition into the Dictaphone. The cut open liver was tossed into the bag in the bucket. The stomach and all the intestines were cut out next and hoisted on the table, next to the body. When Dr. Brady cut into the stomach and intestines, the stench of bowels and partially digested food erupted into the room like a vapor and I turned and rushed to the door, gagging. Dr. Brady looked over at me as I fled, smiling. I had to have some fresh air and find my own stomach again. When I was able to return to the slaughter house, the medical examiner had everything out of the body cavity and was suctioning the blood and other muck through a plastic tube.

With all the organs in a plastic sack, and dropped in a bucket, the corpse was looking more and more like the side of meat you might see hanging from a hook in your local butcher shop. I didn't see how anyone could keep up this intense level of cutting without a break. It was too much, for me anyhow, but Dr. Brady didn't stop. Next he propped the head up on a wooden block. The block had a place scooped out for the neck to rest in. Before I realized what he was doing, he sliced around the scalp cutting down to the skull bone. With his fingers, he peeled back the scalp and pulled the hair flap down over the face. It was awesome looking, but not in a good way. The slick skull looked like a bloody peeled orange and the hair flap covering the face, folded over as it was, looked like a diseased vagina with a nose. A small, high-speed bone saw that looked like an Exacto tool cut through the skull. It looked and sounded like he was cutting a coconut shell in half. When he was done with the surgical saw, he lifted the top off the skull exposing the brain. Bending over, Dr. Brady looked closely at the brain and commented on its appearance, using technical medical jargon I would never understand or remember. The brain was removed from the skull, with a delicate touch and he examined it more closely, turning it over in the light, so he could view it better, then placing it in the plastic bag.

There is no way to describe the inside of a skull with the brain removed except, *empty*. I thought he would put the brain back in, but he didn't. It went into a plastic bag and into the bucket with the rest of the organs. The top of the skull was put back on and the hair flap pulled down into place. The plastic bag full of human giblets was then tied off and put back into the body cavity. A large curved carpet needle and heavy stitching cord were used to sew up the three-foot long incision. When Dr. Brady was finished, the body was rolled onto a gurney and pushed to the rear of the building near the cold storage lockers. *Thank God it's over*, I remember thinking. The autopsy report would be on my desk the next day.

Later, sitting in the homicide office, reading the medically matter-of-fact language of the autopsy report gave my stomach a turn. I tried to focus on the important details. The report indicated that the deceased, in advanced stages of cirrhosis of the liver, was fatally stabbed in the heart. "The size and shape of the stab wound is consistent with the pen-knife in police custody and is probably the murder weapon," the report read. "Blood tests show the victim was intoxicated at the time of his death." The body could now be released to the funeral home for burial. It was all over with. I erased the case from the homicide status board the next day. The transient was now just another statistic to be counted in the annual report. Stab 'em and slab'em, as we detectives called it.

Pals No More

A LITTLE MISUNDERSTANDING

UNIFORMED OFFICERS WERE STANDING NEAR a homicide scene in SE Portland. They had a dead body in the bedroom of a house. Three days it had lain there, they told me. *Oh no!* I thought to myself. It was summertime and had been hot all week. There were just two of us detectives in the office when the call came in on the homicide, me and one of the old sleepers from North Precinct, a guy I'll call Detective Bales. Bales had been an occasional sleeper but was also a pretty good cop who worked and was dedicated to arresting bad guys. The trouble that day was that, once again, neither one of us had a car.

Working that afternoon, was Sergeant Bonaventure. I liked to call him "Sergeant Wussy," because he always hid behind his desk and didn't really seem to enjoy doing police work. That afternoon, he asked if we could take the murder call. "Of course we can." I told him, "We're the only one's here. But you need to find us a God damned car!" We were always short of detective cars and it was a pain in the ass sitting around waiting for one. And he knew I damned well didn't like it. I offered, with some sarcasm, "Do I have to take the bus to a murder?" But Sergeant Bonaventure didn't seem to appreciate my humor or impatience at having to wait, yet again, for a set of wheels. Still, he hurriedly borrowed a car from the check fraud detail and a few minutes later, Bales and I took off for Sellwood in SE Portland. On the way to the call, while I drove, Bales and I talked about old times at North Precinct, when we were both young, idealistic patrolmen who thought we could change the world and make it a better place. He'd heard through the grapevine that I'd wanted to be a pallbearer at Captain Purcell's funeral, in 1968, and wanted to know if the rumor was based on fact.

"Is it true you wanted to be a fucking pallbearer at the Captain's funeral, Don?"

"Yeah, I applied for it, but they turned me down. I guess they knew I hated him."

"He wasn't that bad was he?" asked Bales, laughing and trying to get a rise out of me.

"He was just a pimp with a badge. You know that as well as I do."

"I guess you were the only cop that didn't put up with his bullshit."

"I didn't like being told who I could arrest and who I couldn't. That goes against my grain."

"Okay, Don," Bales said with a smile.

They all knew I had hated Diamond Jim Purcell. I hated him for sending me memo's telling me to report to his office, so he could then tell me to leave Fat Mary alone. I hated him for telling me I couldn't arrest Fat Mary for flagrantly running a house of prostitution. I hated him for claiming there were bogus complaints about me, when there weren't. And I also hated him for making me direct traffic on the St. Johns Bridge, as punishment for defying him, and then driving by and tipping his gray fedora at me, with that smug smirk on his face.

As Bales and I ended our trip down memory lane, laughing at how young and green we both had been, we approached the task at hand. The murder scene was a modest bungalow on a quiet street in the Sellwood district. The uniformed car was parked in front, so we pulled into the driveway. Two cops were standing on the porch with the front door open and some of the neighbors were standing around curiously watching and talking among themselves. According to the officers, his closest neighbor hadn't seen any activity at the house for three days and the guy's car was missing. From the open front door I caught a whiff of something rotten, like a dead cat, only much worse. The uniformed guys nodded to us and told us the body was on the floor in a back bedroom.

As I walked into the house, I could see that some of the furniture had been tipped over and the lamps had been knocked down. It was clear, as I walked through the first floor, that a scuffle had taken place in the front room and then later in the kitchen. A drawer that contained kitchen knives had been pulled out. We found the man's body on the floor in the bedroom. He was lying on his side with both arms outstretched. His trouser pockets had been turned inside out. The body was bloated and the rotting flesh was starting to turn green and oozy, particularly where the hot sun hit it, coming in through the bedroom window. I had to jog back outside to fill my lungs with fresh air. The stench was making it difficult to breathe. "We knew you wouldn't be in there too long," said one of the cops on the porch with a morbid chuckle. I took a deep breath and went back inside. In the bathroom I found a clean wash cloth and held it over my nose, but it didn't do much good. Returning to the bedroom, I opened one of the windows for ventilation and rushed back outside. Eventually, after about thirty minutes of waiting, the stench of putrefaction had cleared out enough for us to return to the bedroom for more than just a couple of seconds.

Without blue protective gloves, which were not issued to patrolmen or detectives at that time, we turned the body over with our bare hands, trying to tug on the clothing, as opposed to touching or gripping any fragile, rotting flesh. After turning the body over, we found the deceased to be an obese, middle-aged, white man. There were several visible stab wounds in the chest but it was difficult to discern if there was any bruising because the body was in such a state of quick decomposition due to the heat. Looking around the room, I could see a framed photo of the deceased man on the night stand, smiling and wearing a dapper looking suit, but it sure didn't look like him now. He was so bloated and rotten his mother wouldn't know him. The bed was messed up and it was obvious the struggle had ended in that room.

Since we could find no sign of forced entry to the house, the dead guy probably knew his killer or let him in willingly. Neighbors said the man lived alone but would sometimes bring home male friends and they gave us a description of his missing car. The dead guy had been murdered, robbed with his trouser pockets turned inside out: no wallet, no money, no car, and no keys. We broadcast a description of the car and prepared to have the body removed.

Sometime later, as the morgue guys moved the body out to the meat wagon, I noticed they were trying to hold their breath, too. The curious neighbors backed away when the body was brought out on the gurney. Absolutely no one wanted a second whiff of this guy. I wondered how anyone would ever be able to get the lingering stench out of the house. It had seeped into the bedroom carpet and the wood flooring, and probably the sheet-rock of the walls as well. It would take a lot of money, time and effort to de-stink the house. But then that was someone else's worry, I thought randomly. As the doors closed on the coroner's van, I silently hoped that when we found the victim's car, we'd find the killer too. This was a particularly vicious murder and someone needed to go to prison. But I also decided, despite protocol, that there was just no way I was going to watch *this* autopsy. I wondered if Dr. Brady used a gas mask for these rotten ones.

Two days later a motorcycle cop was called to a minor accident on skid row near 3rd and Davis in downtown Portland. The officer arrested an undocumented Mexican man driving the stolen car. The Mexican had the car keys and the dead man's wallet, but he spoke very little English. Using one of our Spanish speaking cops as an interpreter, we got the story straight. Apparently the fat man was gay. He had picked up the Mexican while cruising the streets of the red-light district, near downtown Burnside. They drank some red wine in his car and then decided to go to the fat man's house in Sellwood and party a little more. The Mexican said the fat man made sexual advances at him while in the living room and attempted to force him to perform oral sex, by grabbing his head and shoving it into his groin, as they sat on the sofa. He told the interpreter that the man had wanted him to "suck his dick," telling us that the dead man was a "loco hombre," and he was not gay and preferred women.

"Me gustan las mujeres! Me gustan las mujeres!"

The Mexican man was evidently not gay and while partying with a little red wine was one thing, sucking dicks was something else again. The Mexican didn't go for it, became angry and killed the fat man, and robbed him out of anger and a desire for revenge. "Malo, hombre loco," he kept saying to the interpreter. It was a bad situation all around with one man dead, and another man on his way to prison. Sex sure gets a lot of people into trouble. You never know what you're going to get when you're out looking for a fuck. We booked the Mexican man into jail for murder and placed a hold on him for the immigration people. When he did get out of jail, he'd be deported back to Mexico. Didn't we have enough murderers of our own?

The Roof Top Assassin

EVERYBODY HATED HIM

SO FAR THE MENTALITY LEVEL of many of the killers I had dealt with had been low. Really low. The hobo, Henry, had left his victim in plain sight on the riverbank and never got more than about one hundred feet from the crime scene. "No place to go," he had told me in a matter-of-fact way, when I asked why he hadn't left the scene. Then there was the messed up Mexican man who killed and robbed the obese white man and kept the stolen car to drive around town in, never thinking anyone would notice. They both fit into my category of dummies that really caught themselves after committing their crimes. It seemed like murderers were just as dumb as some burglars.

One memorable case I was assigned was different though. It was an act of premeditated cold-blooded murder. And more than that, it was a pick-the-right-weapon, hide-and-wait-assassination-in-the-ghetto type of murder. The victim was shot and killed September 10, 1975. He was a black man named Ronald Lee Holbert, aged forty-three. The people who knew Holbert in the community referred to him as a player, meaning, he was more than a pimp, more than just a dope dealer, and more than a gambler. The truth was that Holbert was of an all-around dink.

We had no idea who had killed Holbert but it seemed that everyone who knew him had a good reason to want him dead. His girlfriends, past and present, described him as "A bad-ass mother fucker," and "An ill-tempered asshole." Another girl we interviewed spat out, "I'm glad the motherfucker's dead! He had it coming!" And still another man said "About time somebody offed that piece-a-shit!" We talked to about fifteen people who admitted knowing Ronald Holbert and not one of them had a good word to say about him. When we told them we were investigating his murder and were looking for information, they tended to break out into applause. "Right on!" and "Righteous!" was about all we heard. "I don't know who did him," said one black man I interviewed, "but if you find the guy, give the dude a medal!" This was unusual.

We tracked down his ex-wife, a white woman living on welfare in the SE part of town. She had been divorced from him for two or three years, but had a couple of his children. She described Holbert as worthless and a violent man who beat her and physically abused their children until she had to take her kids and run away and hide. She hadn't seen him for a long time either, but was glad to hear he was dead. "He won't be able to hurt anyone else now. That's the best part," she confided solemnly. There was no shortage of murder suspects. Everybody who knew Holbert either wanted to kill him or was glad to learn he was dead. Some people may have felt Holbert's murder was deserved but it was still against the law to kill another person, even when that person was reputed to be a cruel, asshole predator.

After interviewing several witnesses, we were able to ascertain what happened and how Holbert had died. The killer had to have known his victim well, or at least to have known off him. He had to have known Holbert's habits and where his hangouts were located. The shooter had probably been a victim of the man's violence or had been double-crossed by him, as had happened to so many others in the community. He arranged to murder Holbert without a confrontation. The killer picked the time, the location and the weapon and then waited quietly in the darkness for his chance.

Mr. Mean was a regular customer at one of the busiest black taverns in the ghetto. The Baron Tavern, located at 2211 NE Alberta Street was generally always jumping. The only available parking was on the street in front of the tavern. Customers would park there and walk right in the front door. Inside, there were three pool tables and a shuffleboard table. A juke-box had all the latest jams. Behind the tavern was a big dumpster for trash and near it was a stack of neatly piled wooden pallets. A small hand-lettered sign indicated that the pallets were for sale but it was summer and no one was buying.

Someone had stacked up the pallets and they were so high, the top came nearly even with the roof. From there, the killer climbed up on top of them. From the top of the pile he could reach the roof of the tavern and pull himself up. He climbed onto the roof to the front of the building and from there he'd have a clear view of the street. Anyone entering or leaving the Baron Tavern was in full view. It was a perfect ambush, a perfect setup. He could hide there without anyone knowing, see without being seen, shoot without warning, and then escape into the darkness, undetected. Now all he had to do was wait, check his weapon and hope that Holbert showed up. The killer had done all his homework and the murder was a perfect illustration of pure textbook premeditation. I often wondered what thoughts were going through his mind as the killer hid on top of the tavern, waiting quietly in the summer darkness to kill a man. Was it revenge for a beating, a fight over a woman, or maybe a dope shooting? Whatever it was, it was payback time and payback would be a motherfucker.

When asshole finally showed up, he didn't go directly into the tavern. Instead, Holbert stood on the sidewalk shuckin and jivin and talking to some people, according to witnesses we interviewed later. At one point, a pretty black girl in her early twenties came out of the tavern. She was someone Holbert apparently knew well. They began to make out leaning against the front of the building. As it was a warm night and the front door of the tavern was open, they would have been able to hear the juke box playing music while they were standing outside. One of the witnesses I interviewed remembered that "Baby Workout" by Jackie Wilson was blasting from the Juke box.

While Holbert was making out with the young girl, he turned around and leaned his back up against the side of the building facing the street, about ten feet away from the open tavern door. It was perfect. This would be show time. The killer leaned down over the edge of the roof and extended his arm straight out. Holbert was directly below him, still with the pretty black girl. There was about twelve feet from the end of the gun barrel to the top of Holbert's head. Twelve feet; that's almost point blank range.

When the killer squeezed the trigger, the gun pulled just slightly to the left, missing the top of Holbert's head. The .357 magnum slug tore down just alongside Holbert's skull and clipped his left ear. The bullet then smashed into the top of his left shoulder, shattering bone. It continued its downward path and struck the heart, tearing it completely apart. It tore through the heart and crashed through part of the stomach, and the bullet finally came to a stop somewhere in the upper intestines. Fragments tore off and damaged the liver. Did asshole fall down and die? No, he didn't. He turned and walked down the sidewalk ten feet and into the front door of the tavern. Once inside, Holbert made his way past two pool tables and the juke box. He staggered past the shuffleboard table and back toward the rest rooms and finally collapsed on the floor bleeding heavily. As one can imagine, after a loud gunshot, a screaming young girl who had only moments before been in Holbert's arms, (and could have been killed) and then a wounded man staggering inside spurting blood and flopping down dead on the floor—well the tavern was thrown into complete chaos. The scenario at the Baron Tavern must have been closely similar to the bedlam at the Doodle Bug when the two guys were shot off their bar stools and I'd been the first responder. While at the Doodle Bug, I'd had to contend with over two dozen hysterical people all screaming, yelling, crying, with some trying to leave the scene, as material witnesses to a double homicide. It was one of the worst scenes I was ever called out to. I can imagine that the situation at the Baron Tavern on that September night in 1975 was basically the same.

The end result of this crime was that Mr. Mean was dead and his assassin had disappeared into the night without a trace. As you sow, so shall ye reap, goes the old expression, or as one of Holbert's ex-ladies said, "What goes around, comes around!" Damn! I thought to myself, this meant I had another autopsy to attend and I had to go to this one because I had bowed out of the last autopsy I was expected to attend on yet another murder. The Holbert autopsy was scheduled for early afternoon, the day after the homicide had occurred, September 11th. All the other detectives were out of the office working their cases and once again, there was no fucking car to drive. I trudged downstairs to the records division where they issued free bus tickets to those officer's who wanted them.

"Why do ya need bus tickets?" the guy asked.

"Not enough detective cars, why else?"

I signed out a book and took a city bus over to the morgue. It took about forty five minutes with one transfer stop. I was late for the autopsy. So far so good. When I got there the body of Ronald Holbert was already on the stainless steel table and the pathologist, Dr. Larry Lewman, had begun his examination of the entry wound into the shoulder. The three stainless steel buckets were on the floor along with the plastic giblet bag for various organs. It flashed through my mind that Mr. Mean, AKA, Ronald Holbert, a man everybody hated, was even in death about to suffer a few more indignities at the hands of the current pathologist. The scene in the autopsy room was just as I remembered it. The table, the body, the tools, the smell. It was like being trapped in the same horror movie again.

But this time I knew when to shut my eyes. When the pathologist finished the recorded description of the exterior of the body and its single wound, he turned and picked up the curved linoleum knife. That's when I shut my eyes and turned away while the big long cut was made. I didn't turn around again until all the sawing and crunching was over. I didn't have to look, to know what the doctor was doing, as I recognized the stench of stomach and bowels erupt into the air, like a gaseous vapor. But this was the first time I'd ever seen the damage that a .357 slug could do to the inside of a man's body. The bullet's path was easy to see, as it tore into flesh and bone, making its downward spiral. After destroying the shoulder and sending bone fragments deep inside, it hit the heart dead center causing it to explode. Pieces of the heart were everywhere inside the chest cavity. Stomach, liver and intestines were all torn up and somewhere in all that bloody mess was what remained of the bullet. It had gone in but hadn't come out.

My stomach told me it was time for some fresh air and I walked outside. At least I walked outside this time. I was able to maintain some of my dignity, instead of jogging out, as I had before. When I returned to the house of horrors a few minutes later, the pathologist had recovered the bullet and set it aside. Maybe there was enough left to send to ballistics. I hoped so, because the killer had taken the gun with him when he fled. With a bullet maybe we could catch the shooter.

The pathologist had cut out the damaged liver and was examining it on the steel table. Dr. Lewman knew I was extremely uncomfortable in this environment and I think he relished that. "All this liver and no onions!" he said in a sing-song voice. He turned and grinned as he looked up at me from the chopping block, obviously enjoying my acute discomfort. The look on my face must have been a combination of annoyance, pleading and disgust. I've always wondered what it is about medical examiners that makes them want to do that. Why do they enjoy tormenting cops at an autopsy? Cops who are about to puke from the gore and the awful stink?

Soon Dr. Lewman was finished examining the body cavity and was positioning the head on the wooden block. I knew what would be coming next. When he picked up the scalpel, I shut my eyes again and turned away. I heard the buzz of the high speed surgical saw as it cut off the top of Holbert's skull. When I opened my eyes again, the pathologist was holding the brain in his hand and talking into the Dictaphone. I couldn't help wondering what the brain would have looked like if the slug had hit it first. Too bad the killer couldn't see the results of his handiwork. Ronald Holbert, the man everyone wanted dead was just an empty shell with all his parts sewed up inside him in a plastic bag and would soon be buried six feet under.

I fished around in my pockets and found the bus tickets that would get me back to my office. On the bus ride back to the precinct, as the bus drove over the Burnside Bridge, I looked out the window and couldn't help thinking about Ronald Lee Holbert's life and sudden, unexpected death. I thought about what a bad guy he'd been, and all the people he'd hurt in his life. Payback was a motherfucker; a motherfucker indeed. Forty five minutes and one transfer stop later, I was back in the homicide office with more work to do.

Mr. Mean's killer was eventually arrested some time later. A young 25-year-old Portland State University student, Torrence Williams, of 3530 North Mississippi Avenue, was sentenced September 12, 1976. Williams was a young African American man, trying to better himself and taking classes at PSU and trying to get away from the ghetto of NE Portland. Williams was sentenced by Multnomah County Circuit Judge, James Ellis, to eighteen years for manslaughter. The judge heard more than a half dozen witnesses testify to the defendant's good character, as a "nonviolent" person who had been pushed over the edge by Holberts violence and abuse of others. The judge was troubled by the case and explained that the murder of Ronald Holbert presented him with "as difficult a problem as I can imagine." He was referring of course to sentencing. Ellis went on to add, "I simply cannot put you on probation. I can't think of a quicker way to cheapen human life … I have no doubt what you did was premeditated murder." Defense attorney Micheal Bailey asked for probation or work release, saying Williams was "torn between what he knew to be right and his own background" of growing up on the dangerous streets of north Portland and the "atmosphere of violence and associations he was trying to put behind him." (Oregonian, 1976). The truth was, the crime was textbook premeditation. It was only because of mitigating circumstances that Judge Ellis didn't sentence Williams to life in prison. Everyone knew, including the judge, that Holbert had been a dangerous, and abusive predator who didn't discriminate when he preyed on those weaker than himself.

It turns out that Ronald Holbert had allegedly assaulted one of Torrence Williams cousins and the murder was revenge for a particularly vicious assault. Karma had caught up with Ronald Holbert and he lost his life in the long run. By the time Williams was sentenced to the manslaughter charge, for killing Holbert, I had already been kicked out of the homicide detail by a particular lieutenant, but I'm getting ahead of my story, so you'll have to wait for those details.

The Convenience Store Murder

INCREASING BURNOUT

When I arrived, the yellow crime-scene tape was already blocking access to the entrance of the Plaid Pantry store, so I had to duck under it to get inside. The store was located at 5920 East Burnside Street, the day Sunday, September 14, 1975. It was one of the worst months I could remember, in a long time, for violent and bizarre homicide deaths in Portland. Two uniformed officers were standing guard speaking quietly with the store manager, a bald man in his late fifties. The man's blue work apron was stained at the pocket from blue and black pens that had leaked at one time or another and he seemed exhausted and distraught. He was showing the officers a sheet of paper that read "Employment Application," at the top and referencing a name, Barbara Jean Carrico, when he wiped his eyes with the back of one of his hands, which were shaking. "She's inside," said one of the officers quietly, nodding back to the cooler area with a somber expression. "We haven't touched anything. ID is on the way for pictures." I nodded, saying nothing. It was another one of those days when we were shorthanded in the homicide detail and I had this one alone. The store manager had arrived to work in the early morning, to relieve the night clerk, and found the woman, Barbara Carrico, dead. He'd rushed out of the store, terrified, and called police from the phone booth on the corner. He told radio that his store clerk had been murdered and the cash register emptied of all money.

I wasn't looking forward to seeing the body. A murdered woman was just about the last thing I wanted to see that day. As I stood inside the front door, I took a deep breath and moved cautiously through the store, unconsciously nudging my gun with my right elbow, making sure it was there. I looked around, making certain the back area was empty. I found myself walking softly, almost tip-toeing. Somehow the silence of the store seemed like a tomb. The sound of a compressor motor turning on suddenly, back in the cooler area, startled me. I was jumpy. The deceased woman, Barbara Carrico, was lying on her back in the crowded aisle behind the cooler area where they restock soda and beer. She was white, looked to have been about thirty five, perhaps older. The hair was shoulder length, straight and dark brown. It fell past the shoulders and was now saturated with blood. The eyes were open. They were brown, but now glazed over. Black work slacks had been removed and lay at the feet and were soaked in blood. Pink panties had been pulled down and hung around the right ankle, covering a black tennis shoe. The legs were spread. She had been raped. Both arms were in a defensive pose, lying limply over the chest, as she had been trying to protect her face. The arms showed several slash-mark defensive wounds that had bled onto her body.

Her throat had been cut below her right jawbone and the slash continued through the jugular vein on through to the left side of her neck. To borrow an old but effective cliché, her throat had been cut *from ear to ear*. Her white work blouse was torn open down the front. Her breasts were exposed and covered in blood, both from the defensive wounds on her arms and from her throat bleeding out. There was blood everywhere. It pooled several inches around her shoulders and above her head in a large, arcing semi-circle. The blood was beginning to turn black. I shook my head and turned away. This was horrible.

Later, when I interviewed the manager he told me Carrico had worked only part-time, about two days a week on the graveyard shift, alone. He thought she had kids, but wasn't sure how many. She had been a working mom; that much he did know. Barbara Jean Carrico had been a wife, with a husband, Leo Carrico and had young children. It was obvious she was just trying to make a few extra bucks working at the Plaid Pantry. And for a few extra dollars, working at a minimum wage job, she died a horrible death: raped, slashed and murdered.

While making some basic sketches in my notebook for my

report, I noted there were no surveillance cameras in the store, so there would be no help there. If other customers had entered the store, found no clerk available and just left, we'd never know that either. The manager was the first to find Carrico dead. I felt sorry for him, that he had to witness finding such a horror. It was clear he was just a regular working guy and not used to seeing such things. He'd been frightened and horrified to see such a bloody sight. I felt sorry for the ID technician who would have to take photos of the gory mess and dust for fingerprints. And I felt bad for the two men who would arrive from the coroner's office to place the body of Barbara Jean Carrico in a black zip-up body bag for loading into the wagon.

Ninety minutes or so later, when everybody had gone and the crime scene tape was removed, the manager still seemed dazed and confused and uncertain what to do next. "You need to close the store. At least for the day," I suggested mildly. "Yes," he murmured, barely audible. "The district manager told me to close the store. I guess I should close the store and leave a sign on the door?" he asked. "That's right. Just leave a sign on the door." The manager still seemed confused and didn't move. I could tell he was in shock and still traumatized from seeing the woman on the floor. *Blood simple*, as the expression goes; when a person sees something violent, bloody and traumatic and can't process it.

"Go ahead, lock it up," I urged him again, "I'll wait. And then I suggest you go home and do what I'm gonna do when I get home." He stood there for a moment, not comprehending. "What's that?" he asked blandly, still not looking at me. "Get drunk," I said evenly as I walked out the door to my car. The rest of my day was spent in the homicide office writing reports and trying to get the image of Barbara Carrico, with her throat slashed, out of my mind. Follow-up detectives would do the next of kin notifications and perhaps dig up some more information. Maybe someone had seen a car in the store parking lot. Maybe someone might know something.

When I finally got home the image of the murdered clerk, Barbara Carrico, was still stuck in my mind and I couldn't stop thinking about how awful her last moments must have been. I walked into the living room and stood quietly, so drained it took me a moment to collect myself. I walked over to the stereo phonograph and put an old record on, letting the needle down carefully. The melancholy tones of the old classic *Deep Purple* by Peter DeRose began to echo through the empty room. My wife was gone and I knew I'd be alone for the next several hours. I could feel that sinking feeling in my gut that told me a new bout of depression was coming on. I poured a tall, water glass half full of Black Velvet whiskey and added a dash of soda, as a matter of form. Walking into the kitchen, I opened the freezer. There was only one cube left in the ice cube tray and I tossed it in my drink. I swirled the amber colored liquid around in the glass and walked back into the living room. Grateful that I was now home and away from the office, I set the glass down on the nearby coffee table. Easing out of my jacket, I removed my handcuffs, gun and extra ammunition pouch from my belt and melted into the LA-Z-Boy recliner. As the whiskey in the glass slowly disappeared down my throat, the wonderful burn mercifully blurred the image of the dead girl and I fell into a tense silent sleep for a few hours, waking up exhausted with a headache.

    This homicide bothered me more than I cared to admit. I had seen many homicides in my career and lots of dead bodies, but this atrocity seemed to bother me a lot more. Barbara Carrico had been so young, only thirty-nine it turned out, and it was apparent she'd fought for her life and suffered horribly. She'd been a struggling, low income mother and ultimately invisible. She had lived at 5321 NE Couch, only blocks from the Plaid Pantry store where she would end up murdered.

    I found I couldn't drive by the store without the image of Barbara Carrico's slashed body passing through my mind, with the large black pool of blood arced around her head and shoulders. For years afterward I avoided the intersection on 60th and Burnside Street. And for a long time I couldn't go into any convenience store without spontaneously thinking of her. I learned later that her killer was a man named Donald Ray Rister, aged thirty-six, living off SE 65th Avenue in Portland. He had been apprehended sometime after robbing the store and shot in the neck by police. He was taken to University Hospital North and given medical treatment for the gunshot wound. He survived. Rister was later charged with first degree murder in the murder/rape of Barbra Jean Carrico. I hoped the worthless loser would spend the rest of his life in prison for such a pointless and brutal crime.

I knew not too long after this, that the job was wearing on me and contributing to a deep sense of futility. The truth was I was depressed and had been for a long time. I didn't know how much longer I could continue to do police work, particularly working the homicide detail, which was quite different from the burglary detail and far more depressing. My sense of exhaustion, depression and futility was now a crushing daily reality. No matter how many people I arrested or how many crimes I might solve, I knew in my heart I could not and would not change the world or make much of a lasting difference. I was one person trying to stop an avalanche of crime and there was no way I could do it. I was becoming an entirely different person from the idealistic young recruit of 1961.

Another Dead Body

THE SWAN DIVE 1975

THAT SAME SUMMER, LATE ONE afternoon, I'd been out working a murder case. When I arrived back at the homicide office, I found a group of five detectives looking out the north facing window at a commotion going on outside. Directly across Pine Street from the detective office was the David Hooper Sobering Station and Detoxification Center, at 132 SW third that had recently opened in 1973. Around that time, the city of Portland had stopped arresting chronic alcoholics for violating the ordinance against being drunk on the street. The police now allowed them to sober up and go home without the social stigma of having been arrested for drunkenness. The Hooper Center was named after David P. Hooper, the unfortunate man who was the last to die, March 6, 1971, of alcohol poisoning while in the drunk-tank at the city jail at police Headquarters.

On that particular afternoon, I walked over and joined the guys looking out the window and after peering over a few shoulders, I could see the deceased body of a man being covered with a white sheet. "What happened?" I asked, curious. "One of Hooper's drunks took a header out the second floor window," one of the detectives casually murmured. "The guy just took a swan dive out the fuckin' window!" said another detective with an amused chuckle.

Among the detectives watching, was Mike O'Leary, one of the grey haired, cigar chomping old-timers, and a really great, all around cop. Mike O'Leary shook his head and took another puff on his ever present, smelly cigar, moving aside so I could get a better look. "Looks like Hooper cured another drunk!" he said, matter-of-factly, turning around and exiting the homicide office, leaving a trail of smoke in his wake. O'Leary's attitude was testimony to how jaded he felt at seeing yet another dead body, but we were all jaded at that point. In that respect, we were all pretty much the same. When the coroner's wagon arrived and began removing the deceased from the sidewalk, all the detectives slowly meandered back to their desks to attend to their endless paperwork and phone calls. In a matter of only a few minutes the momentary drama of the suicide was forgotten. I lingered, staring blankly out the window, until there was nothing more to see. I felt nothing, and feeling nothing bothered me.

I walked to my desk, and sat down to make a few phone calls, and poured myself another cup of coffee. The suicide across the street meant no more to these old cops than slowing down to view a minor accident on a busy freeway. The original location of the Hooper Center at SW third and Pine Street is now an upscale restaurant, with rented office space on the second floor. Those second floor windows look out at the same concrete sidewalk, where a desperate and hopeless old man in his sixties chose to end his life.

I've always been confused by what motivates a person to commit suicide. Suicide, by its very nature involves great self-loathing. The transitory feelings of despair and hurt cannot provide those who engage in suicidal ideation the perspective to see even a moment further into their futures. But the devastation suicide victims leave behind can be awesome and is always irrevocable for the survivors, as I soon learned during the several suicides I was called to investigate during my career. One suicide that comes to mind happened when I was working in St. Johns as a street cop. While still in my late twenties, I took a call from a distraught ten-year-old boy who had come home to find his father dead in the garage. The boy had just come home from school. As he was trying to open the garage and put his bike away, he found that it was locked. He walked around and entered the house via the unlocked front door, walking into the garage from the area just off the kitchen. After walking into the garage, he found his father dead in the front seat of the family car, with a green water hose running from the exhaust pipe directly into the driver's side window. Because the car was still running, the exhaust fumes were overpowering and the little boy quickly shut the door and ran to the telephone, calling police. I'll never forget the look on the boy's face as he looked up at me, weeping, to tell me he couldn't get the garage door unlocked. It was an expression of confusion, dismay and grief.

"I tried but it wouldn't open, so I had to..."
"Go around?" I asked.
"Yeah—I went around and opened the door."
"Uh huh?"
"And that's when I saw Daddy! The fumes were awful!"
"I'm so sorry, son." I said quietly.

I placed my hand on the boy's shoulder feeling completely useless. There was nothing I could do to adequately comfort this boy whose father had just killed himself. I was on the scene of that suicide for about two hours, waiting for the coroner to remove the body, and also waiting about that long for the mother to finally arrive home from work. It was an awful scene and one that I never forgot. What a horrible thing for a boy of ten to see. The father must have known his wife and son would find him when they arrived home. To me, it seemed like a clear cut case of premeditated revenge suicide. I had called dispatch and asked them to send out one of our best officers from the Women's Protective Division, so someone could sit with the boy and comfort him. The female officer sat with him in my patrol car, talking to him and trying to figure out where his mother worked, which allowed me the time to do other things like air out the garage, contact the coroner's office and help with the removal of the body. I can remember vividly, standing in the garage and looking at the body of the man who had just taken his own life. He was slumped over on his right side, having been seated in the driver's seat and his face and exposed hands and arms were flushed a deep and unsightly red. I wondered how a man could be so thoughtless as to kill himself when his own son was soon to arrive home from school. As I stood looking at the dead body of the man, I felt angry at him for what he'd done. I knew this would be something the boy would carry with him his entire life.

Sometime later, I was called to investigate another suicide. This involved a man in his middle sixties who lived alone in the Columbia Villa projects. He'd sat down on a wooden kitchen chair, barefoot, which he'd placed in the living room and put a shotgun barrel in his mouth. He had pulled the trigger with his toe. The .00 buckshot splattered his skull and brains all over the ceiling. But his head didn't slow down the buckshot, as it went right through the ceiling and portions of the roof. He left a hell of a mess for his neighbor friend to discover several hours later.

Suicide for law enforcement officers is a regular occurrence and has been for decades. A popular misconception that is often bandied about, is that around three to four hundred police officers, mainly men, commit suicide each year in America. This is not true. The real numbers fluctuate between about one hundred and forty, to one hundred and fifty persons each year. The average age of a police officer who commits suicide is forty two to forty five years old, and the average time for length of service is sixteen to seventeen years, and it is true, it is primarily male officers who do this. I experienced the loss of two personal friends in law enforcement and was aware of several other colleagues from nearby departments who also killed themselves, over the years. These were men I might not have known personally very well, but they had been good police officers with good reputations who were highly respected. Ultimately, I am confused by the desire to kill oneself. There are too many suicides in the profession of longtime law enforcement officers and frankly, I've always felt dismayed by it.

Bessie Staley and the Canary

THE PERFECT CRIME

THERE IS A POPULAR MISCONCEPTION that there's no such thing as the *perfect crime*. The idea is that if enough effort and time are put forth, any case can be solved. That's not true. Many burglars commit the perfect crime every day and hundreds of homicides go unsolved each year. But I will admit that some cases are more complex and more difficult to solve than others. This next case, which occurred in early September of 1975, was the most bizarre case I ever investigated. Bessie Mae Staley had been a respected member of her neighborhood. She was a restaurant owner and a staunch Catholic. She owned and operated Staleys, a small restaurant located in the Sanctuary of Our Sorrowful Mother. The Sanctuary, commonly referred to as The Grotto, is a beautiful Catholic sanctuary on NE Sandy Boulevard and is open to the public.

Bessie Staley's little restaurant did well there. She had lived with her husband in a house they owned in SE Portland, on 34th Street just south of Hawthorne, until his death some years later. Built in the 1920s, it was an old, wood frame, two bedroom house with a large kitchen, separate dining room, a bathroom, and a large front room with a fire place. Always the business woman, after her husband died, Bessie converted the second floor of the home into an apartment. She installed an outside stairway up to the rooms and rented the unit to two elderly gentlemen. People in the neighborhood knew and talked to Bessie and would stop and chat when they met her on the street, but she was a busy lady and was always on the go. There had been no children in her life and she was managing by herself nicely. So, the neighbors were surprised when they began to see Bessie socializing with a new man, Charles Lewis, who sometimes came to the house.

Charlie was a bookkeeper by trade and took care of the bookkeeping duties at her restaurant. When they first met, Charlie was in his early fifties. Although Bessie was fourteen years older than Charlie, they apparently fell in love and in spite of the fact that Bessie was a good Catholic, she and Charlie lived together but never actually married. For the next fifteen years they were inseparable companions, living in the old house, running the little restaurant and collecting the rent on the upstairs apartment. Bessie made out a will leaving everything to Charlie and Charlie did the same, leaving everything to Bessie. But other than a few personal possessions, he didn't have much to leave her, whereas Bessie had a nice bundle of savings, the property and the restaurant. However, as Bessie got older, her health began to deteriorate and she became senile. Gradually, dementia took hold of Bessie's mind and she and Charlie were forced to close the restaurant and quietly retire at home.

As Bessie came into her late seventies, the dementia altered her personality as well as destroyed her short-term memory. According to a distant relative, Bessie had gone completely crazy, with Alzheimer's rage and was impossible to be around. She had become caustic, aggressive and verbally abusive to Charlie, and distant family or friends who might drop by for an occasional visit slowly stopped coming around. Charlie acted not only as Bessie's caregiver during this time, but also as her bookkeeper, collecting the rent money from the upstairs tenants and paying the utility bills. He also cashed both of their social security checks, when they arrived in the mail. Charlie would walk the five blocks to the bank on 39th and Hawthorne Street and cash the checks. Even though Charlie never had power of attorney, the people in the bank knew that Bessie was an invalid and couldn't take care of herself. They were happy to ignore standard policy and allow Charlie to cash her check, giving the money to him directly. Charlie would then hurry home because he couldn't leave Bessie alone for any length of time, or so he claimed.

He might say a quick hello to the neighbors who spoke to him on the street, but he was always in a hurry to get back home. "Yes, Bessie's still at home but not in good health. Thank you for asking, though," he sometimes said to a curious neighbor, never lingering in conversation. One neighbor I interviewed, remarked that in the past three years, he had seen Charlie only about six times. Charlie had groceries delivered by an errand boy, which were always left at the back door, and did all his laundry at home. He didn't go out much, but just stayed at home and took care of Bessie. Such a nice man, everyone thought. He must love Bessie dearly, they thought. One day, when the rent was due, the upstairs tenants knocked on Charlie and Bessie's back door with the rent money, as they usually did. Charlie was normally very prompt in answering the door, but not that day. Through the back door window, they could see Charlie lying on his back, on the dining room floor inside the house. Since he was down on the floor and didn't move when the tenants knocked, they decided to call the police for help. When the uniformed officers arrived, they couldn't rouse Charlie either, so they broke in to see what was wrong. They found him lying on his back, with his eyes open and still breathing, but he couldn't speak and he couldn't move.

It was obvious that Charlie had suffered a serious medical problem, like a stroke or heart attack and that he'd been lying on the floor for hours, perhaps even days. The cops called for an ambulance and Charlie was taken to one of Oregon's best medical facilities, at Oregon Health and Science University Hospital in SW Portland, also called Pill Hill by the locals. When the ambulance left the house with Charlie, the officers secured the back door and were ready to leave. "You're leaving?" asked one of the upstairs tenants, as he walked down the stairwell. "Yeah, he's been sent to the hospital," the officer said. "There's nothing more we can do here except lock up."

"But what about Bessie," the tenant asked, concerned, "What shall we do with the rent money?"

"There was no one else in the house," said the cop, confused. "Who's Bessie?"

Although no one had seen Bessie for three years, everyone knew she was an invalid, requiring constant care and attention and Charlie had always claimed he was taking care of her. The tenants insisted that the police officers go back in and make sure Bessie was not alone. The cops were fairly certain there wasn't another person in the house, as they hadn't heard any unusual sounds or calls for help. Charlie had collapsed on the floor in the dining room and no one had made any sound while the emergency personnel were taking him away, so the officers just presumed there was no one else present in the house.

Maybe Bessie had gone visiting, one of the officers suggested to the tenants, but the tenant's just shook their head, in confusion and concern. One of the police officers finally agreed to double check. He and his partner searched the house again, including the basement and Charlie's bedroom. They found no one. There was another door, however, the doorknob covered in a telltale dust that indicated the door hadn't been opened in a long time. An old bath towel was stuffed into the crack between the bottom of the door and the hard wood floor. The officer removed the towel, and became aware of a faint musty odor. When he opened the dusty door, he saw that it led into a small bedroom. He looked inside. Quickly, he closed the door again, and walked out to his patrol car to put in a call for detectives.

When I arrived, about an hour later, I reopened the squeaky, old, wooden bedroom door. I had opened the door of Bessie Staley's tomb. A thick dust covered everything. The blinds were pulled tightly shut and the window curtains had yellowed and were frayed and disintegrating. Very little daylight came into the bedroom. Bath towels, like the one under the door, were stuffed in the window cracks. At least thirty dead flies lay on the window sill. There were two heating vents in the bedroom. Both were blocked, with numerous rags stuffed into them. In the corner, on a metal stand, was an empty bird cage. At least it looked empty from the doorway. As I walked up to it, I could see the remains of a small yellow canary lying dead on the bottom of the cage, its water and seed containers completely empty. My footsteps into the room had left visible tracks on the dusty floor, as I looked behind me. The dust was velvety and thick, as if someone had sprinkled talcum powder all over the room in an equal distribution. When I took a step, the dust around my feet swirled up in small eddies, which stopped me in my tracks several times. As I stood there, I observed several personal items. A hair brush and comb, lay on the dresser top untouched and so dusty that the edges appeared indistinct. Photos of people I didn't know were on a night stand. Near them was an old wind-up alarm clock that had stopped ticking.

On the antique metal bed frame lay a skeleton lying face up. Dead maggots lay in the empty eye sockets and open jaw bone. Shoulder length gray hair covered the skull and part of the neck bones. Red cloth fragments of what had once been a robe or house dress were on the bed under the skeleton. The skeleton lay uncovered by either blanket or sheet. An arm bone protruded from a sleeve fragment. Both arms were laying at the side. Among the bones on the bed, and especially where the stomach had been, was a large pile of more dead maggots, at least several hundred of them, and maybe even a thousand. Looped around the pelvic bone was a garter belt. The fasteners were still connected to the shredded remains of two frayed nylon stockings. The stockings still contained the leg bones. Feet and toe bones poked through holes in the nylon. The bedding on which the skeleton lay was stiff and darkened from the dried blood and ooze that had seeped into it while the body slowly decomposed.

I looked around the room slowly. The thick dust, the maggots, the skeleton on the bed with long gray hair, the rags stuffed into the window cracks and the dead canary in the cage. It looked *exactly* like a set from a horror movie. But it wasn't a set. It was real. We had found Bessie Staley. Records showed that Bessie was eighty two-years-old. The coroner, however, would say that she had probably died when she was seventy nine-years-old. Charlie had taken good care of Bessie; very good care indeed. I later discovered that a concerned neighbor had filed a missing person's report in 1974, worried because he no longer saw Bessie go in or out of the house and he wondered what had happened to her.

Police came to the home and questioned Charlie on the front porch, but with his mild and respectful demeanor, he easily convinced them that he knew nothing about her disappearance. The police then spoke to the neighbor, telling him that Bessie had either "Changed residences or gone on a trip." The police had believed Charlie and made no attempts to search the home or press the issue in any way. I was anxious to talk to the medical examiner about this case. What could we learn from the autopsy? What was the cause of death? And Charlie, now that we knew where he had been keeping Bessie, I had a few questions for him too.

When I entered Charlie's hospital room, I saw that the nurses had him hooked up to drip tubes and monitors. He was lying on his side, eyes open, breathing slowly. I told him I was a detective with the Portland Police Bureau and that I wanted to ask him some questions about Bessie Staley. His steady gaze didn't change. His eyes didn't flicker and he didn't move or respond. Charlie didn't answer any of my questions or the doctor's questions either. In fact, he never spoke again. The doctor told me Charlie was dying. Tests showed that he had terminal cancer, pneumonia, diabetes, and fatal heart disease. I tried to find some of the answers by looking into his eyes, but poor Charlie, he wasn't there. Seventy-two-hours after the ambulance removed him from the house, he died in the hospital.

In an Oregonian Newspaper article, dated September 3, 1975, written while Charlie Lewis was still alive in the hospital, the journalist wrote that police had been able to communicate with him by asking him to nod his head. The article claims that he told police that he loved Bessie Staley and would never have harmed her. However, when I went to the hospital to interview Charlie, he was unable to respond and did not nod his head or acknowledge my presence in any way. He probably wasn't even conscious at that point. It is possible that the patrolman who were the first responders at the scene may have communicated with him, but I was unable to get any information from him.

The article also stated that the skeleton had been covered with a blanket, but I dispute this because when I went into the room, there was no blanket covering the remains. The medical examiner, Dr. William Brady, was no help either. After arriving at the morgue and being led into the autopsy room, the day after Charlie Lewis was sent to the hospital, the skeletal remains of Bessie Staley lay grotesquely on the stainless steel autopsy table in front of me. But there were no plastic bags this time and no cutting tools either. There were no buckets on the floor to put the organs in, because there were no organs to dispose of. With nothing left but a dried-up, dusty skeleton remaining, there was little to examine. The maggots and a lot of time had done their work.

"I can tell you how she *didn't* die," said Dr. Brady.

"She didn't die of a beating. There is not one broken bone, no broken jaw, no cracked skull, no crushed vertebrae in the throat indicating she may have been strangled, and no bullet holes anywhere."

"What do you think happened then?"

"She probably died of natural causes," he said, "Perhaps a heart attack?"

"But remember, she went crazy years before she died," I reminded him.

"Maybe Charlie couldn't stand her anymore," I persisted.

"I dunno Don—there's no indication of homicidal violence."

"Could he have put a pillow over her face and smothered her while she was lying down?"

"Yes, she could have died that way."

"Poison? Could he have poisoned a crazy, old lady who he was tired of taking care of?"

"Yep, she could have died that way too," he said.

"Could he have starved her to death?"

"Yes, she could have died that way."

"Why are you asking all these questions, Don?"

"Because she didn't just die in her sleep. Ladies don't sleep with their garter belt and nylons on."

"But maybe she was taking a nap?"

"Maybe. Or she could have been smothered in another room and carried into the bedroom."

"Why do you think he killed her?"

"Because Charlie knew he didn't need her anymore. Once he cashed her first Social Security check at the bank, without her beside him, he realized he was home free. Remember, Doc, Charlie was fourteen years younger than Bessie, and they'd never gotten married. I think he decided to kill her rather than take care of her sometime after he cashed that first check. She was crazy, and she verbally abused him, I heard this from three sources, including some of the neighbors. She got to be so bad, he couldn't take her outside or to visit friends anymore."

"He kept cashing those checks for three years after she died. He embezzled $18,000 dollars from the government. That's what liars and thieves do. And killers."

"Remember the canary?" I asked Dr. Brady

"Yes, you did mention a canary."

"I think the canary's the key to this mystery. I think Charlie had a ruthless streak in him. Otherwise, why didn't he feed and water the bird? What would have been so hard about taking care of a small canary? No, I think he said goodbye to Bessie and the bird at the same time. He killed them both. He killed Bessie in *some* way, perhaps through neglect and then he killed the canary by shutting the bedroom door and letting the bird die of hunger and thirst."

"We'll never know, now," said Dr. Brady.

"Yeah, I know. That's the hard part."

I believe to this day, that Charlie Lewis committed the perfect crime. Embezzlement for sure and maybe even murder. The old embezzling bookkeeper died with his lips sealed. He got away with it. But what must have gone through the man's mind? Didn't Charlie realize that when he shut that bedroom door he'd created his own prison too? With Bessie's body in the bedroom, Charlie could never again let anyone into the house. He could only go out to cash the Social Security checks and then hurry back home.

No wonder he didn't stop to chat with the neighbors, as he used to do. Charlie had a secret. What kind of man could live with a dead body in the next room for three years? Although Bessie Staley never got on the homicide status board and was never listed as a homicide, I *know* what happened to her. A little bird told me.

The Zebedee Manning Death

A SUICIDE IT WAS NOT

Sometimes a guy like Charlie Lewis can pull off the perfect crime in spite of the best efforts of the police. And sometimes killers can get away with murder *because* of the police. September, 4, 1975, I was called to investigate a possible suicide of a young boy on NE Hancock Street, over in the North End. Zebedee Allen Manning was a fifteen-year-old black youth, who struggled with poverty and addiction. He lived in a ramshackle house at 233 NE Hancock Street in the ghetto with his mother, Annie Mae. Annie Mae was a single parent, trying to keep things together and keep "Zeb," in school. But Manning wasn't into school; he didn't participate much and you won't find his picture in any of the Benson High school yearbooks. What Manning was secretly into was drugs.

If the Bloods and the Crips had been around in Portland then, it's likely that Manning would have been wearing the colors. He was born October 9, 1959, in Texas. But Zebedee lived in a different world than his mother and he did a good job of keeping the truth from her. Drugs seemed to be the extended families business and his mother was the only one who didn't appear to be involved or have any knowledge of the particulars. Manning's older sister Marcella had married Henry Johnson, who was a well-known drug dealer in north Portland at the time and drove around town in a Rolls Royce. Manning sold heroin for Johnson, and then later became a secret addict who kept his growing addiction from his mother, probably because he didn't want to disappoint her.

When I entered the house that day in September of 1975, I walked through the living room and into the large old kitchen, which was on the main floor with a door leading to the backyard. The kitchen table was in the middle of the room and on the table sat four empty drinking glasses and a half empty bottle of whiskey. The boy's mother had just arrived home from work, and after calling for her son and receiving no answer, had found her son's body upstairs in his bedroom, lying deceased on his bed. Crying and confused, Annie Mae had called police for help. After the first responders arrived, I was called to the house to investigate. I briefly consoled the mother, then walked up the very narrow staircase to the bedroom and went into Manning's room. The bedroom was small and crowded. The walls of the small room were covered with colorful psychedelic posters. Jimi Hendrix wailed silently from a poster looking down over the bed.

On the bed a young boy's body was laid out, with his arms and hands folded across a rifle that lay on his chest. The eyes were shut and I could see the boy had been shot at point blank range directly through the center of the forehead. My immediate question was: how do you shoot yourself in the head, then fold your arms and lay the gun on top of you? I've seen enough dead bodies and murder victims in my police career to know they don't have time, after being shot, to shut their eyes, let alone fold their arms peacefully over their chest. Most suicide victim's arms are splayed in an outward fashion, wide open, laying where they fall after having been shot.

What I saw is called *staging*, which happens when one or more killers or witnesses, attempts to cover up a crime by making it look like a suicide, instead of a homicide. Staging also happens in homicide cases where the killer feels a certain level of personal remorse for his or her actions. The killer may fold the arms of the deceased or place a blanket over the body. Sometimes certain rapist/killers will cover the face of their victim with a blanket or sheet, so they don't have to look at it. Staging also occurs when witnesses to a violent crime, or even police officers feel sorry for the victim and inadvertently alter the pose of the victim's body, after death, thereby contaminating the death scene. Whether because of remorse or simple carelessness, I know that someone staged the body of Zebedee Manning. I am certain of that. Maybe it was one of the three men who were likely present. I deduced that three men *were* present because of the number of drinking glasses on the kitchen table. There were four, one for Manning and three for his killers.

After looking at the scene, and the obvious staging of the body, it was then that I knew, this boy had been murdered. As I had stood in his bedroom, I tried to recreate the likely scenario in my mind. His killers had probably forced him to sit or kneel on the bed in the second floor bedroom and then had shot him dead center through the forehead, just above the eyes, with a sawed-off .22 caliber rifle. There were two other bullet holes in the room, one in the wall and one through the ceiling. Neighbors I interviewed later, claimed they heard three shots.

Beside the bed stood an old wooden dresser, with some beat-up stereo gear and some old records collecting in a dusty pile on the floor. The dresser was full of Manning's clothing: clean socks, underwear, and tee shirts folded neatly. In the top left hand drawer were some cigarette rolling papers, a plastic baggie with a small amount of marijuana, and a homemade smoking pipe made out of aluminum foil. Before I had the body removed to the coroner's office, the ID technicians came up the stairs and took numerous photos of the deceased. The whiskey bottle and the glasses were also all fingerprinted by ID, photographed and placed into evidence. A few minutes later the men from the morgue took the body carefully down the narrow wooden stairs and out to the waiting van.

After they had left with the body, I went back to the room to search, to see what else I could find. That's when I found three car titles. One car was registered to a person living in St. Johns. At that point, I knew that the car titles were being used as collateral for drug money owed by previous drug buyers. Later, when I interviewed Annie Mae, Zebedee's mother, I asked her, "Tell me about your son. What kind of person was he?" Annie Mae paused for a moment, struggling to gain her composure and wiped her eyes with a Kleenex. "He went to high school and was a pretty good boy," she began hesitantly. She was insistent that he was a normal boy and didn't use drugs or alcohol, to her knowledge.

She had no idea whose alcohol was on the kitchen table or who might have been drinking, as she was adamant that no alcohol was in the house or would ever be *allowed* in the house. I didn't tell her about the marijuana I'd found in his bedroom, but I did mention the three car titles. She told me he didn't own a car and had no idea where they'd come from.

Around this time in my career, I'd decided to make a point of arriving late for all the autopsies I was required to attend. I wanted to spare myself the horror of having to see another head or chest cavity cut open and gutted out. By the time I arrived at the morgue, the medical examiner, Dr. Brady, was already talking into the Dictaphone, recording a detailed description of the bullet hole in Manning's forehead. It was a small, bluish hole, in the center of the forehead, with a clear and visible circular imprint of the gun barrel. When a gun is fired, the exploding powder comes several inches out of the barrel, as well as the slug. You can tell exactly how far away the barrel is from the skin by reading the pattern of burned powder called stippling that is imprinted on the flesh. In this case, there was no stippling, because the barrel of the gun had left a clear imprint after being fired. It appeared that this sawed-off .22 rifle had been fired while pressed directly against Manning's forehead. Though it was a sawed-off gun, it would have been clearly impossible for Manning to hold it flush against his forehead and pull the trigger. It was simply too long. Someone else had to have pulled the trigger.

Dr. Brady felt the back of Manning's head looking for an exit wound. There wasn't any, nor had there been any blood splatter at the crime scene, which meant the bullet was still in the brain. Because it was a .22 short—a very small cartridge—it hadn't come out. The bullet went in, straight through the brain, and cracked the back of the skull, leaving a small protrusion, just as if a chicken had been pecking from the inside of an egg. Upon further examination of the body, we could see that the boy's arms and legs were covered with small red bumps.

"Those bumps, what are they? I asked.

"They look something like bee stings," I continued.

"They are bee stings, sort of," said Dr. Brady thoughtfully.

"What do you mean? What are they caused from?"

"This kid's been skin-popping. Injecting small amounts of dope just under the skin."

"Why do they do that?" I asked, perplexed.

"Some people just can't stick a needle into their veins at first. They kind of work up to it by skin-popping first," Dr. Brady said. "Or if they've been shooting dope a long time, their veins collapse and it's the only way they can get high." Again I closed my eyes and turned away when Dr. Brady reached for the linoleum knife. I just couldn't watch that part of it. All the organs were cut out and examined. Everything appeared normal and they were piled one on top of the other, in the big plastic bag. Next the head was positioned on the wood block ready for cutting. There was something about the sound of the high speed surgical saw cutting open a skull that just ripped through me every time, It was like fingernails on a chalk board, only a lot worse. Dr. Brady carefully lifted out the brain to examine it under the harsh light, finally placing it on an adjoining table. Small bits of bone were embedded in the brain from the entry wound. The .22 slug was in the back of the skull stuck there, after having gone clear through the brain. When Dr. Brady cut the top of the cranium off, that's where he found the bullet lodged, in the back of the skull there. Dr. Brady dug the bullet out of the empty cranium with his fingers and handed it to me. I took the bullet from him and dropped it in an envelope, to place into evidence. I had seen enough. I already knew Manning died from the gunshot wound, but for the full story, I would have to wait for the lab results on the drug and alcohol toxicology reports, so I thanked Dr. Brady for his help and quickly walked out of the morgue.

When I read the coroner's report the next day, I couldn't believe my eyes. Manning's death had been temporarily ruled a *suicide*. Since Manning had been found home alone and shot in the head at close range, Dr. Brady ruled the death suicide by self-inflicted gunshot pending further investigation by detectives. The fatal gunshot wound in the head could have been self-inflicted, Dr. Brady concluded, in the written autopsy report, due in large part to the short size of the sawed-off rifle. However, at no time did Dr. Brady actually have the opportunity to examine the rifle and come to a more informed conclusion, as I was able to do. I had placed the rifle into evidence at central precinct, but Dr. Brady never requested that it be delivered to him so he could examine its dimensions and arrive at a proper conclusion. This was no suicide. If Manning was planning suicide, he might have poured himself two or three stiff drinks first, but what about the other three people in the kitchen? Who drank from the other three glasses? Who brought over the bottle of whiskey? And since no firearms were allowed in the home, who brought the rifle to the house?

And how about the car titles in Manning's dresser drawer, that his mother didn't know about? It was common at that time, in the dope business, to hold a car title as security against money owed. And what about the first two shots that were fired in the bedroom? Was that to scare Manning? What did the killers *want* that they were trying to scare this boy in such a violent way? Suicide? No, Dr. Brady, it wasn't that simple or neat. When I went to work the next day, I found that my case had been erased from the status board and filed away as a closed suicide, by the lieutenant. No problem, I thought. I'll just go and talk to the lieutenant about it. When I got to his office, I explained that the dead boy had been using drugs and alcohol and had been drinking with three other people before his death. The toxicology report also stated that Manning had been both high on drugs, and legally drunk when he died from the gunshot wound.

I told the lieutenant about the three car titles I'd found in Manning's bedroom and the significance of the car titles and what they likely implied, something the lieutenant well understood. I told him there was no suicide note and that the mother said her son was not depressed or suicidal in any way before the unexpected death, and that he had been planning to do things in the future, like travel to visit relatives. I also asked him, "How do you shoot yourself and then fold your arms afterward? And why didn't he leave a suicide note for his mother?" I explained to the lieutenant that Manning was more than likely the victim of a dope deal gone bad rather than a simple suicide.

To my surprise, the lieutenant shook his head no. He had already made up his mind. He told me to forget about the case. "It's over, DuPay. Go work on something else," he told me nonchalantly. Dr. Brady's report claimed Manning's death was a suicide and that was good enough for the lieutenant. He stood behind his desk and with an air of complete indifference said, "He's just another nigger dope dealer who cashed in his chips—so what!" I stood across from him, speechless. I was amazed that he would say something so callous about a 15-year-old boy. And I further wondered what made him think I would drop a murder case. This bullshit was starting to remind me of my old days working North Precinct. I hadn't let Captain Jim Purcell tell me what whorehouses to leave alone, so why did this lieutenant think he could tell me *not* to investigate a coldblooded murder? Fuck him too, I thought to myself.

So, I worked the case on my own time, which was a lot harder to do because I was working in secret. I checked the name on the three car titles through criminal records. The car owner had a drug record, but then I already knew he would. I drove by the house in St. Johns where the car was registered and knocked on the door. I identified myself to the person who answered, as a homicide detective with the Portland Police Bureau. They refused to give a name and I got a bunch of double-talk about the car. It hadn't been running, they said. Maybe it had been towed, they said. No, they didn't know any Zebedee Manning or have any idea how he got their car title. I went back to talk to Manning's mother, Annie Mae. I felt so sorry for her. She seemed to be a poor but good Christian woman and in many ways, a typical single parent who had wanted to raise her son well. Obviously her son had a life she hadn't known about. He had used both alcohol and drugs within hours of his death. She turned out to be completely unaware of his drug activity or drinking, and unfortunately, she couldn't shed any light on his death either.

But then something interesting happened. A couple of weeks after Manning's death, and my continuing investigation, both Annie Mae and another family member received threatening phone calls from a man who, according to both of them, "sounded white." The caller told them to cool it with the police investigation.

"Call off the police or we'll get you too!" the caller warned.

We'll get you too. I kept thinking about that threatening phrase. If they were going to get his relatives "too" it told me they had gotten Manning first. Now, there was no doubt. Zebedee Manning had been murdered. Once again, I approached the lieutenant and we argued for over ten minutes. "Damn it Lieutenant, the boy was murdered!" I stated flatly, "And we *both* know it." There was a lot of shouting back and forth. I paced the room and tried to reason with him, explaining what I knew and what I suspected. In the end, I was ordered once again not to investigate the case. Not even on my own time, I was told. From my end, I couldn't understand it. How in hell could a homicide commander refuse to investigate a blatant homicide and maintain *any* kind of integrity?

"You know the boy was murdered! What's the fucking problem here?" I shouted. "Why can't I investigate this case?"

"There is no case, DuPay! I told you it's over! It was ruled a suicide."

"It wasn't a suicide and you know it!"

"You're not investigating it!"

"Are you serious?"

"In fact you don't work homicide anymore. You've been transferred back to burglary!" the lieutenant told me, with a smirk. The perfect crime had just been made possible by my police lieutenant.

I believe Zebedee Manning was murdered by low level police officers in a botched drug robbery. I base this belief on my experience of what goes into working vice, the negatives of police work in general, and various things I heard through the active police bureau grapevine at the time. Some of the law enforcement men I knew, who worked the narcotics detail, were known to use cocaine before they went out on raids. They'd get high and go out and fuck with people. Sometimes just everyday Portland citizens. It brought out the aggression in them and quickened their responses. It also made kicking down doors more exciting and made it easier to point the gun. But ultimately, it made them more dangerous and less effective as police officers.

When I worked vice, in the middle 1960s, we were expected to not only drink alcohol, but also to pass around the marijuana joint, in order to dispel any suspicions that we were undercover cops. I remember a particular poker game, over in the North End, that my partner and I were trying to bust, with about six men around the table. One of the players lit a joint and passed it around. When it came to me, I looked across at my partner and our eyes locked. We both knew we'd have to smoke it.

I had never smoked marijuana before but I knew I'd have to this night. I took two hits, and tried to play it cool, like I was an old hand at it. It went around the table and my partner took two hits. Later that morning, after I got off shift, I remember thinking about the job and how we had to lie to everyone about what we were really doing. It was that part of the job, working vice, that I hated the most. With men working vice, in the 1970s, and currently, while going on cocaine raids, the expectation was and is today, the same. Vice cops are expected to use cocaine to create an illusion of legitimacy among the criminal drug dealing elite. What happens, obviously, is these police officers become tragically addicted to cocaine. And a cocaine addicted police officer is no different than any other cocaine addict. They will lie, cheat, steal and kill to get more of the drug. It can happen to vice officers or even the common patrolman, when and if they decide to dabble in the powder.

Henry Johnson was well-known to the Portland Police all during the 1970s. He was an active drug dealer, who drove around town in a Rolls Royce, wore fancy suits and lived the fast life, with plenty of cash to throw around. He was also Zebedee Manning's uncle by marriage, as Johnson had married Manning's older sister. After Johnson got Manning hooked on heroin, he used him to sell dope, along with other relatives. This occurred despite Manning's mother, Annie Mae and her best attempts to shield him from that kind of life and provide Zebedee with some stability. Manning's killers must have surmised there was a large stash of heroin in his possession, because Johnson had been arrested by police, two weeks before Manning's death on a *humbug*, which is an old term for a "made-up arrest." I heard this from an old informant who claimed the police wanted to intimidate Manning, so they could get to one of Johnson's heroin stashes, which they believed Manning had been holding for him until Johnson could be released from jail.

But foolishly, the killers got drunk themselves, while in the process of trying to get Manning drunk. In my estimation, they were hoping he'd talk and tell them where the drugs were. When Manning refused to give up his uncle's heroin and would not cooperate, they became frustrated and angry and shot him to death instead. These corrupt patrolmen never did find the heroin. But Annie Mae, Manning's mother, did. As I learned later, she found it shoved into a crawl space, hidden in a crevice in the wall of Manning's bedroom. She flushed it down the toilet, eager to get rid of it and probably unaware of how valuable it would have been on the street. After the trauma of losing her son, and then being threatened by the man who called on the telephone, I heard that Annie Mae left town, and may have moved to Texas for a while. She finally died October 19th, 2008 in Portland, Oregon, about a month or so after the 33rd anniversary of her son Zebedee's death in 1975.

Every fiber in my cop being told me that Zebedee Manning had been murdered and what you have just read here are some of the reasons why I believe this to be true.

In the early 1980s, I requested Zebedee Manning's records regarding his death, from the Records Division at the Portland police Bureau. I was told no Zebedee Manning records existed, and that his death was ruled a suicide. I was shown *one* record card that indeed listed the death as a suicide. I knew complete death records had to be kept indefinitely. Where were the reports that I had originally written? What about the autopsy report, where I'd been present? I had to ask myself, why were there no records or photos of the dead body? Where was the main file? Why were there no records of the fingerprints that were done on the glasses and whiskey bottle? Where *were* the glasses and the whiskey bottle? Where had they gone? Where were all my written investigative reports, typed up by the secretarial pool? Again, I had to ask myself, *who* wanted this case to disappear? My initial belief that Zebedee Manning was murdered in a botched drug deal by corrupt Portland police officers was underscored when I heard, through the bureau grapevine and from Manning's own family members that he had been killed by a low-level patrolman. This man had a serious drug problem and a reputation as a young officer who had gone nuts with the power that being a police officer afforded him. He wasn't very bright, I learned, but rather a badge-happy, aggressive, control freak who had gotten completely taken in by the fast life of booze, cocaine, prostitutes and violence.

Over the years, I continued searching for the truth, and I feel that I have done everything humanly possible to find Zebedee Manning's killers. I did my best but was not successful. And I did so because I cared. Zebedee Allen Manning was a 15-year-old boy who deserved more life than he got. And though Zebedee Manning's death is still classified a suicide, which I know to be incorrect, I hope I am remembered for having done everything I could do to get him justice.

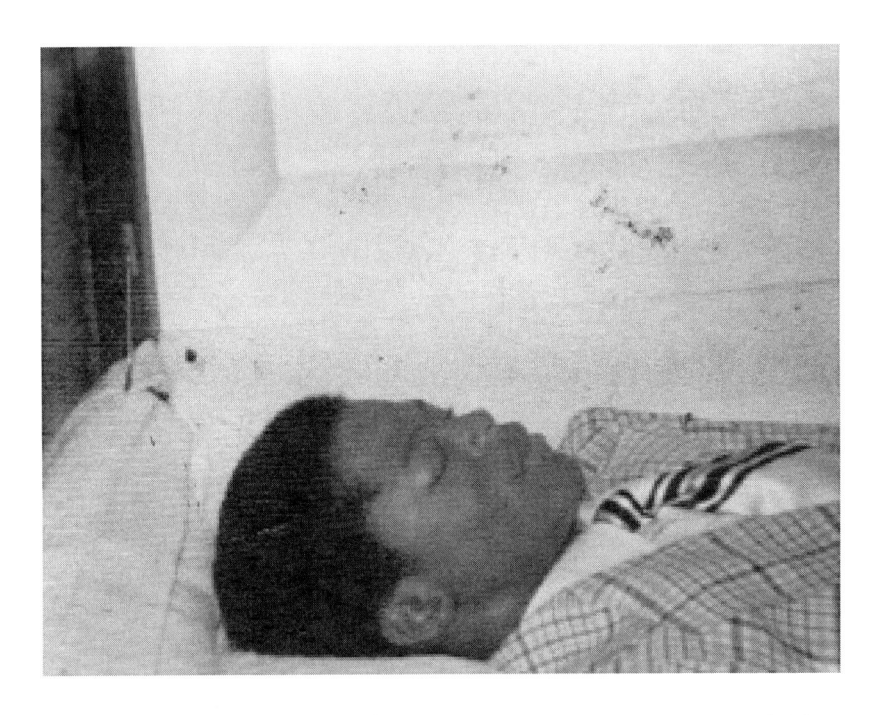

Zebedee Manning, aged 15 1/2, lying in state at his funeral. A child, murdered by corrupt vice officers with the Portland Police Bureau. September 1975. Photo provided by Zebedee Mannings best friend in childhood, Mr. David Wayne, of Portland, Oregon.

Epilogue

AFTER BEING FORCED OUT OF homicide by my racist lieutenant, I stayed around for another three years, working for the bureau. I was reassigned to work burglary cases and coach new detectives. Height, weight, and sex limitations had been relaxed. The length of service time required to be eligible for detectives was cut from five years to only three. I personally did not approve of that change because I don't believe that three years working the streets gives the officer enough experience to advance to detective. The average patrolman, to advance and comprehend the demands of the various details, needs more than just training transfers, in which he or she spends only brief periods of time at one task. They need more overall experience to become skilled, adequate detectives. I don't believe that three years on the street provides that experience in *any* capacity. Three years on the force does not create a veteran cop, and only a veteran should be eligible for promotion to detective. Police officers need at least five years experience working the streets, to get an adequate understanding of crime and criminals, the human condition and other social factors that are linked to criminal causation—before being promoted to detective. I still have this opinion today.

Younger people were coming through for training and I was able to see exactly how burnt-out, cynical and frustrated I had become with my career in law enforcement. How do you tell the young idealistic faces sitting in the police academy that they will likely never make a difference? How do you explain that no matter how many burglars, thieves and killers they arrest, they can't stop crime? How do you stop the dead bodies from piling up in the morgue? How do you end the daily butchery of human bodies by the medical examiners?

The answer is simple. There is no way.

There is no way to explain to recruits that their life's work will be the ultimate exercise in futility. Not only will most civilians not remember your name, neither will most cops you worked with either. Who remembers *my* name or the sacrifices I made while putting my life at risk every day that I strapped on my gun-belt?

It's not that I'm anti-police, because I'm not. Police work *is* an honorable profession and necessary. I must have helped lots of people in my time, but after so many years on the job, I felt overwhelmed by the stress and the relentless, depressing negativity. To such an extent in fact, that I felt the end result was pointless and my contribution irrelevant.

When it comes to police work, I'm anti-abuse and pro Constitution. Too often the Constitution fell by the wayside in the detective division during my time there. More than once, uniformed patrolmen would visit me attempting to get a search warrant for a bad guy they were after and they weren't too particular how they got it either. I was always happy to look over the work they had done, to see if there was enough information to legally obtain a search warrant, but too often they had not done their homework and needed to go back and do more thorough investigative work. More than once they went around me to another detective in a different detail, who would just rubber stamp their search warrants and send them on their merry way to violate someone else's right against unlawful search and seizure.

Once, in 1973, when I was a burglary detective, a patrolmen from North Precinct came to my office, asking me for help to obtain a search warrant that he wanted. I looked over his paperwork and saw that it was not sufficient. Having taught search and seizure at the police academy, I knew he didn't have enough information to get a legal search warrant. "Is this *all* you have?" I asked him. He stood in front of me defiantly, his chin high, arms folded behind his back and said nothing, waiting for my decision. The patrolman hadn't performed adequate surveillance and had not developed his informants sufficiently, so I explained to him that I could not help him because he lacked the proper information. "I can't help you with this. It's not enough." I told him. With a scowl on his face, he mumbled "Oh, fuck you!" and stalked off down the hall to find another detective who didn't care so much about the constitution. There were two detectives who were notorious for "rubber stamping," search warrants and it used to piss me off. Their names were Harry and Bill and they worked together. It never seemed to matter why or who wanted search warrants. They'd give them to anyone. I've wondered since then, if I should have made more of an effort to put a stop to it. Should I have followed the patrolman down the hall? Should I have objected more vocally? The truth is, it would have been like spitting against the wind and I knew it. These illegal search warrants happened all the time while I was employed with Portland Police Bureau. But they didn't happen with *me*.

*Since you have no idea about the moral integrity of the cop behind the badge, you have to protect your own interests. If a cop tells you that you have the right to remain silent, believe it and keep your mouth shut. Call a lawyer. There is absolutely no reason you have to talk to a cop about anything. If the cop has a right to search your home or vehicle, he may then get a search warrant. Make him do so. A lot of Marines died face down in the mud protecting those American rights. Don't bother telling a cop, "I'll see you in court!" The officer is a professional witness. That is where he makes his living, and you're entering *his* environment. He'll make his case on paper and nine times out of ten, the judge will believe *him* over you. If you need a lawyer, get a good one, but make damned sure he's working for *you* and not just pleading out your case, getting paid and going onto the next case. If he's not committed to your best defense, fire him and find one who will work for you. Remember, every person sitting in the jail house was defended by a lawyer who got paid to defend him.

*If you notice a police car in traffic with you, stay behind him, if you can. If a cop gets behind you, he may pull you over just to fuck with you about your seat belt. Maybe he needs one more ticket for his quota. Watch the cop, don't let the cop watch you.

Officer Friendly? Don't raise your kids to think that cops are their friends. Officer Friendly is a myth. The *us/them* dynamic is as alive today as it was in 1961 when I was a young recruit. The police being the *good guys* and everyone else, as in civilians being the *bad guys*, even law abiding citizens who might find themselves in the wrong place at the wrong time; that dynamic is as alive today as it was fifty years ago.

Big city police work is high stress work. Ordinary men get dressed in front of their mirror and go to work in an office, restaurant or construction site. Police officers get dressed in front of their mirror, strap on a gun, and go to war. It's a different war every day but it's still a war. Working in law enforcement is a lot like military combat, with the daily death and dying. Human beings cannot survive twenty five or thirty five years of it without dire consequences to their health and mental and emotional well-being. Most cops have had it after about fifteen years. They become cynical, burnt-out and non-productive. They disengage. Police work is a young man's profession, particularly working the streets as a patrolman. Retire them early and pay them well.

And finally the poor citizens, when they see a cop, all they see is the uniform. All they see is the badge. There is no integrity in the shiny metal itself, you have to look behind the badge. They are both dazzled by the bright shiny metal and frightened and intimidated by its authority, and what that authority may represent. They never see the man *behind the badge* or beneath the uniform. Some of the police I knew wore that badge with pride and respect, understanding that it did not give them greater rights, but rather made them carry the weight and obligation of protecting *all* people's rights.

These were the good men I worked with, who had integrity and concern for the members of their communities. But many others used that badge as a cover, a shiny intimidator that covered the drinking and the drunkenness, the sleeping and the lying, the stealing and the dealing. And the priorities that put lunch appointments ahead of criminal investigation. They used that badge to protect the corrupt captains, the incompetent patrolman, the alcoholic sergeants and the racist and bigoted lieutenants.

They were the power, they were the police.

Authors Note

It was not without trepidation that I decided to resign from the police bureau, in 1978, for it had been my life for many years. The constant stress of police work, the racism and the blatant dishonesty of the command structure had taken its toll on my well-being, a toll I was no longer physically willing to pay. The constant stress of trying to solve horrendous crimes, the bodies of those killed, those maimed, the rape victims—*those* images accumulate in your head, until you can think of nothing else. That is why I ultimately resigned. I would have died from the stress, had I remained on the job.

Resigning was not done in a fit of unplanned anger. There were many papers to sign and I had to find and return the Police bureau manual I had been assigned years before.

During my last year with the Portland Police Bureau, I counseled with Police Chaplain Ed Stelle, on several occasions, and together we talked about the possible impact of my resigning. But in the end I kept hearing my doctor's advice in my ear, "Someday Don, you're going to have to make a decision; your job or your health."

A couple of years after I left the bureau, I heard through a personal friend and Bureau associate, that a rumor began circulating through the police grapevine, that I'd left the job suddenly in a "fit of rage," over some perceived slight, only to come back the following day to request my job back. Many of the details of this rumor were and are patently false. I would never have behaved so erratically. I thought long and hard about resigning, simply to save my health and emotional well-being. And I planned for any possible complications.

The rumor that had circulated described a scenario in which my commanding officer had smelled marijuana one morning, as I entered his office in early April 1978 to begin the working day.

He questioned me about it accusingly and I was supposed to have flown into a rage and thrown my badge on his desk, saying I was through with the bureau, then stalking off out the door.

The reality was, for almost ten years, my health had been suffering in a myriad of ways because of the constant stress of police work and I was tired. Because, ultimately, the most frustrating part of the job was not dealing with the public or the crimes I had to investigate but the command staff that routinely demonstrated their lack of integrity and their lack of concern for me personally. Over the years, I either worked for or with no less than three cops who were captains or became captains, and I look back now, wondering if too often the rank of captain was reserved for those men who had sold their integrity, as those three demonstrated to me time and time again.

The rumor went on to suggest that I'd come back the following day to beg for my job back. I never would have done so. I had far too much personal pride to slither back the following day and beg for something I didn't want.

Let me tell you what really happened: I came into work that morning and my commanding officer and I got into a heated argument. He accused me of smelling like marijuana and was very condescending. I resented his attitude and his questioning of me. I'd been introduced to marijuana during several vice operations over ten years before and that introduction was not something I could undo. Passing around and smoking the marijuana joint was part of the job. At the time, though we hated the idea of having to do it, we felt we had no choice and did it out of a sense of duty to our profession and the *greater good*. After experiencing the effect and realizing it was not this horrible drug that made people crazy, and that it actually lessoned my dependence on alcohol, and calmed me, helping me to relax, I continued using it, secretly, in a therapeutic manner. I was after all, a police detective with an image to protect. So, like many other officers at the time, who also used marijuana, and for many of the same reasons, I told no one, other than my wife and my oldest son.

At one point in the argument, I tossed my badge on the captain's desk, telling him that I was sick of the job and tired of the hypocrisy of people just like him. I told him my health had been suffering and I hated the work, only because I hated some of the people I was forced to work with. I also hated being told I could *not* investigate a particular 1975 *suicide* that I knew to be a murder. I told him I would be resigning. I walked out of his office and returned the next day with the manual I would need to return and sat down to sign the several resignation forms. I was still *very* angry but also oddly relieved. I was finally getting out.

During this argument, I *was* angry but not in a rage. I *did* toss my badge down on the table and I *did* resign. At no time however, did I ever beg for my job back. Not the following day or any other day. The slow evolution of the rumor and how it changed and altered is typical, classic cop gossip. I imagine with the passing of this rumor from one person to the next, my behavior became more diabolical and my actions more degraded and exaggerated over time. That tends to be how gossip and innuendo work in most police departments. The facts are often warped with the passage of time, and become more absurd with each inaccurate re-telling of the story.

Within a week of resigning from the Portland Police Bureau, in early April of 1978, I applied for unemployment benefits. I was later informed by the unemployment office, that the police bureau was attempting to deny any unemployment benefits to me. I had planned ahead however. I had spoken with my family doctor several weeks prior to my resignation about my plans to leave the force. I had asked my doctor, due to my health, that he furnish me with a typed letter. In the letter, he explained that because of my ongoing issues with a bleeding ulcer, high blood pressure, and serious recurring episodes of depression, I would need to find another line of work and would be resigning. My family doctor was more than happy to write this letter sharing his professional recommendations in this regard.

Because of the existence of the letter, and what it meant legally,

I was later awarded full unemployment compensation benefits for several months. I had been able to prove that I'd resigned under a doctor's orders and for health reasons, and the bureau was forced to comply and pay their portion. They had tried to deny me simple unemployment benefits so that I might survive after almost twenty years of exemplary service as a police officer and detective, and they had lost. I heard from another bureau associate that the higher ups were damned mad about it, but I didn't care. I needed to reclaim my health *and* my life.

I was further shown the extent of the rumor and the apparent desire to smear my name. In my subsequent position as director of security for the Benson Hotel in downtown Portland, in the early 1980s, I came across a Multnomah County sheriff's detective I had known and worked with. He approached me at a dinner function at the Benson and said hello. As he slapped me on the back he asked, "Hey, DuPay, I heard you went crazy?!" I laughed and asked him, "Is that what they're telling people now?" We continued to chat, laughing about old times, but I was left with the distinct realization that people were trying to discredit me, and make me look like some kind of "mental." What motive would anyone have to do that? What would they be trying to hide by spreading false rumors about me or the kind of detective I'd been? What did they have to gain? Or perhaps I should ask, what did they have to *lose?*

This book represents many of the highlights of my career with the Portland Police Bureau. It recounts certain incidents, both comic and tragic, inspiring and shameful, that I can recollect with the most clarity. But this book and the narrative it contains represents only a fraction of the events and experiences I was able to survive as a policeman and later, as a detective. It provides only a few transitory glimpses into a long and demanding career, but is *not* the sum total of what I experienced and was able to recollect and overcome.

Due to the choice I made, to leave the force, I am in reasonably good health today and have outlived most of the miscreants mentioned in my book. I was able to walk away without looking back. My integrity is intact and I have *never* regretted my decision.

—Don DuPay, September 2nd 2012

Final Editors Reflection

Before I first became acquainted with Don DuPay in February of 2011, I had been warned about him by no less than three retired Portland police officers. One told me he was a "mental," and that I shouldn't interview him for my growing collection of law enforcement interviews, because he might go crazy on me. Another told me he was an "addict," and still another told me he was "crazy," and a "degenerate." Instead of being frightened, I was intrigued. I contacted Don and went through with the interview anyway. I interviewed him three times over a period of several months during 2011. During this process, I found Don to be none of the things these people had told me he was. It made me wonder why anyone would attempt to defame or vilify him so callously. Did these people have something to hide or were they simply misinformed? The characteristics I found Don to possess in full measure were good manners, thoughtfulness, generosity and a calm emotional stability that made me feel safe. We developed a friendship and slowly got to know each other. I found him to be gentlemanly in the old-world way; courteous, witty, protective and incredibly patient.

After agreeing to work on his original 1991 manuscript, entitled "A Look Behind the Badge," detailing his career in law enforcement, which later became *this* book, I often struggled with that shred of doubt that still existed in the back of my mind, remembering what I'd been told. One aspect of the warnings I'd received from these people, the significance of which was never lost on me, was the fact that after asking these individuals if they *knew* Don, they informed me that not only did they not know him, but most of them had never met him, worked with him or even spoken with him. This new awareness confirmed the fact that they were relying exclusively on rumor, gossip and innuendo to come to a determination about a man they had no concrete experience with.

Don shared many experiences with me, during our extensive creative collaboration. He shared intimate details of his time working the streets as a patrolman for the Portland Police Bureau and later as a burglary and homicide detective. At no time in my working relationship with Don did he ever appear emotionally unstable, mentally fragile, or in any way mentally unbalanced. And yet, to maintain a sense of rational distance, there always existed that shred of doubt in my mind, as to the claims he made regarding his long career. All Don could offer, to support his various claims, were his own recollections from fifty years of previous life lived. I hoped for more, for some kind of documentation perhaps, to corroborate his statements. That documentation arrived, in early August of 2013 when, after a little digging, I found his original PPB personnel file. After examining the original copy, (with many fragile documents and original signatures that were well over fifty-years-old) I was able to secure a complete photo copy of the file for Don's personal records. This included 166 pages of documents, in the form of crime reports, records of arrests made, and statistics on hundreds of stolen cars and other stolen items he'd been able to return to owners. There were also letters of commendation, including one from the FBI commending him on solving a 1973 diamond heist that resulted in the return of $17,000 worth of stolen diamonds taken across state lines.

There were performance evaluations, (written twice, yearly) and letters of appreciation from citizens which would provide a rare glimpse inside Don's career; a perspective I had not been privy to before that. I was also allowed free access to numerous other police personnel files from the Portland City Archives and Records Center. As a result, I was able to corroborate other pertinent facts regarding Don's career with PPB. I was soon to discover that each claim Don had previously made to me about various cases, positive performance evaluations, number of arrests, and other highlights of his career were indeed *factual*. The file offered a veritable gold mine of useful information which provided insight on particular cases and events, some of which Don had forgotten over the intervening decades. I was able to record dates, times, and details of specific incidents and crimes that were noteworthy and memorable, and include that valuable information in the memoir manuscript.

Most interesting to me were the numerous performance evaluations, for obvious reasons. These documents mapped out Don's entire career. The first performance evaluation was conducted shortly before he became a detective. The document is dated April 1st, 1967. Still working as a street cop, Don is described by the evaluator: "Officer DuPay is an excellent police officer. He has a talent for handling problem areas and problem establishments. He is one of the hardest working men on the relief. He has qualities that will make him a good supervisor. DuPay has completed a number of police courses at Portland State College. DuPay has a strong interest in vice activities and has shown his effectiveness in this area." (Official personnel file records).

These evaluations provide clear and concise information about the type of officer and detective Don demonstrated himself to be through his work ethic and his conduct. After examining all 166 pages of the personnel file, I became convinced that Don had been completely truthful in confiding various details of his career. Don had never exaggerated, if anything he had been far too modest in his recollections. In one evaluation after another, he is rated at "Superior" and "Competent" and never, at any time, anything below that. Also documented in the personnel file is the slow arc of his deteriorating health, which began after approximately ten years on the job, beginning when he was only thirty-five.

In April of 1971, his evaluator comments: "Detective DuPay discovered that he was suffering from High Blood Pressure which was partially the result of his reduced efficiency during the past rating period. This ailment is currently under control. Detective DuPay has been hospitalized with a major stomach ailment. Since our last discussion, Detective DuPay has done an excellent calibre of work and I am sure that this will continue." (Official personnel file records).

Due to the relentless high stress level of working first as a street cop and then later as a detective (without any form of counseling available at the time to relieve stress) and due to conflicts within the command structure, Don began to experience high blood pressure, along with a bleeding ulcer. His deteriorating health also had consequences to his emotional well-being and resulted in episodes of serious depression and a feeling that his work in law enforcement was futile and meaningless. It was clear, Don was experiencing serious burn-out. However, in one performance evaluation after another, throughout his entire career, the reviewers offer glowing insights into the dedication, professionalism and commitment that Don demonstrated in his career in police work. In a performance evaluation from 1967, immediately after Don was made detective, the reviewer states: "Detective DuPay seems to be an interested precise police officer who is willing to do anything asked of him. Although observed only a short time, he seems to be trying to grasp the procedure of his new duties as rapidly as possible." (Official personnel file records).

In another performance evaluation, dated September 5th 1968, the reviewer states: "DuPay does excellent work in all his assignments and through his own initiative has cleared numerous cases and recovered large amounts of stolen property." (Official personnel file records). In 1969, another reviewer states: "Detective DuPay is assigned to the Investigation of Commercial Burglaries and also the care and handling of equipment used in burglary investigation. DuPay is exceptionally good at interrogation and interviewing. He consistently obtains excellent tapes and statements regarding the crime investigated. DuPay is responsible for a large number of clearances and the recovery of property." (Official personnel file records).

In yet another 1969 performance evaluation, Don is described by his reviewer: "Detective DuPay displays outstanding ability in the field of burglary Investigation. He has developed his ability in the field of interrogation which has resulted in many confessions. In conclusion DuPay is an outstanding Detective and does an outstanding job. DuPay is currently active in preparing teaching material for the Burglary School at the academy. He is very interested in the progress of our new officers." (Official personnel file records). Don's leadership abilities and his desire to be proactive are also illustrated when one reviewer writes: "Detective DuPay continues to handle his responsibilities in a professional image that reflects the best interests of the Bureau. Detective DuPay consistently strives to change those procedures or areas that hinder investigation, and in doing so saves not only time and resources, but reflects a better professional image of the Detective Division. Detective DuPay also coaches new detectives and does so in a very competent manner." (Official personnel file records).

In another flattering performance evaluation, the reviewer writes: "I. Personal appearance; Detective DuPay's appearance is in keeping with the highest expectations of the Bureau and Detective Division. II. Professional Demeanor; Detective DuPay always portrays a professional image that reflects his image as a detective. III. Knowledge of procedures; Detective DuPay has a superior knowledge of Laws, Rules and Regulations. IV. Report writing; Detective DuPay's reports are always concise, complete, accurate and on time. V. Interviewing; Detective DuPay does an excellent job of interviewing." (Official personnel file records).

In one performance evaluation after another, Don's dedication to duty, his thoroughness, work ethic, promptness and excellent grooming and appearance are all recorded and these records present a consistent image of a man seriously dedicated to law enforcement and to his career. The last performance evaluation of his career would also be positive, offering the previously mentioned areas of expertise and dedication commonly attributed to him, as a working detective. This was an exceptional police officer and detective, who maintained levels of professionalism and dedication that were often missing in other officers of his generation. Don's career was not without some unanticipated consequences though. By his own account and in his own words he admits to inadvertently breaking a man's collar bone who was resisting arrest, knocking out several teeth, with a sap, of a man who was violently assaulting one of his older sergeants, and fracturing the skull of another man who was also violently resisting arrest.

And in all fairness to accuracy, there is one significant incident in his personnel file that details an accusation of excessive force while he worked as a patrolman. On October 7th, 1963, Don arrested a man for speeding while crossing the Ross Island Bridge. A man named "Thomas," of SE 174th place accused Don of excessive force and had a Milwaukie, Oregon attorney write a letter demanding an investigation. In the letter, Ralf Erlandson writes, "As I understand the facts, Officer DuPay was extremely aggressive and belligerent when he stopped my client and charged him with violating basic rule, alleging a speed of 64 miles per hour on the Ross Island Bridge. In response to my client's questions, Officer DuPay retorted "Shut your God damned mouth!" On this charge of violating the basic rule, my client was arrested and a paddy wagon called. When "Thomas" wanted to get his car keys, Officer DuPay grabbed him from behind, man-handled him and threw him into the paddy wagon, causing bruises to his legs and tearing his clothing. I think there is some reason to be concerned about the conduct of this police officer and I respectfully request that an appropriate investigation be made." (Official Personnel file records).

In Don's written report, dated October 22, 1963, he states, "While on routine patrol at approx 3 am on 10-7-63, I observed a two-tone green 1954 Olds, Eastbound across the Ross Island Bridge at a high rate of speed. I pursued the vehicle and obtained clock speed of 64 mph, as it reached the peak of the bridge, heading downhill on the East side, the car continued at a high rate of speed." (Official Personnel file records). Don goes on to detail the physical altercation, explaining that it happened after repeated warnings were ignored by the defendant. "When the patrol wagon arrived, the Def was searched in the presence of the other officer and I asked the Def where the keys to his vehicle were. He stated at this time that they were in his car and he was going to take them out. I told him that he could not take his keys out as the tow truck driver had to have them. He stated adamantly that he was not going to leave his keys in the car & pulled away from my grasp & walked forward to his vehicle. I told him at this time again to leave the keys in the vehicle, again explaining why. He again repeated adamantly that they were not going to be left in the vehicle & that he was going to take them out and take them with him. At this time he stuck his head and shoulders inside the open window of his vehicle to remove the keys. At this time, I walked up behind him, placed my arms around him in a bear hug fashion, lifted him bodily off the ground & carried him partially approx ten feet back to the patrol wagon & where the driver, Ofcr Traver had the door open. He was placed, not thrown into the patrol wagon & the doors were shut. At this time, Ofcr Traver remarked, "You sure have a lot of patience DuPay." (Official Personnel file records).

Later, a letter was written, October 25th of 1963, in defense of Don's conduct, by Chief of Police David Johnson, who went on to explain, "The actions of Officer DuPay, which were witnessed by the patrol wagon driver, were no more than were necessary under the circumstances to maintain custody of an arrested person and to transfer that person to the custody of the jail. It might be of interest for you to know that your client was arrested for speeding in February of 1961, in May of 1962, and now again in October of 1963. Thank you for the opportunity of allowing the other side of the case to be presented before reaching a conclusion that the police officer was all wrong and your client completely in the right." (Official Personnel File records).

What the personnel file does demonstrate with consistent regularity is that Don was a dedicated and committed police officer and detective, who took his job very seriously. He was a hardworking professional who tried to maintain fairness and consistency with all those he had dealings with. But he was also able bodied enough to put *hands on* when the occasion and need presented itself, as it always will in law enforcement situations in which criminals and or citizens decide to resist arrest.

The most incongruous aspect of Don's personnel file, however, is the resignation form that was completed April 11th, 1978. After a career noted for excellence and devotion to duty, two boxes are checked off on the resignation form which seem to suggest otherwise. Both boxes are initialed by the captain who signed the form. In two areas of the form, where the commanding officer can indicate if the officer was "satisfactory" or not, and would be "considered for rehire" or not, the captain has marked off, "was not" and "would not." This means that in this captain's mind, Don was *not* satisfactory and would not be considered for rehire. The question begs why, after such an outstanding career, would this detective, who had worked in the burglary, safe and homicide details be considered unsatisfactory and not available for rehire? In another section of the form, under "Notes" the space is blank. The captain had the opportunity to include details regarding the resignation and why he would indicate that Don was not "satisfactory" and would not be "considered for rehire" but chose to leave that section blank. Why?

Could it have been Don's habit of smoking marijuana that predisposed the captain to come to that conclusion? At a time when many other police officers with PPB also smoked Marijuana, it seems unlikely that that would provide sufficient reason. There is one last performance evaluation quote I'd like to share. In July of 1975 Don had been transferred to the homicide detail, which is generally considered the most prestigious of the various details in police departments nationwide. He had done well there, and in a performance evaluation from that period, dated October 10th of 1975, the reviewer has written: "Detective DuPay was assigned to the Homicide Detail in July of this year. Since that time he has worked closely with a detective more experienced in Homicide investigation to obtain the specialized training required in homicide detail. Although I have personally supervised him for only about six weeks, it has been my observation that he has adjusted well to the demands of this detail. He has shown interest in working person's crimes. Detective DuPay is an experienced investigator and has a good working knowledge of laws, rules and regulations. His reports are well written and follow prescribed format. He has used 7 days of sick time this evaluation period, however only one day since assigned to this detail." (Official Personnel file records).

This last performance evaluation quote is quite revealing, if you look at the subtext. Police work was Don's forte. It was something he loved and something he lived for. He was a well-known stickler for details and even a little rule crazy, which made him an excellent investigator and occasionally something of a problem for other detectives who bent the rules more easily. At a time when illegal search warrants were commonplace, and by some accounts even rampant, Don refused to grant younger officers the search warrants they requested if they had failed to do the proper investigative work to obtain one. Because of this, I believe he stood out as inflexible and perhaps even dangerous to other officers who may not have been as honest and forthcoming with the truth and with observing proper procedural correctness.

In 1975, Don, working in the homicide detail, burnt-out by police work but at core still an idealist, was called to investigate a death in NE Portland. The death of Zebedee Manning was ruled a "suicide pending further investigation," when Don, by virtue of specific red flag clues believed the death to be the result of a homicide. Not only did he believe the death to be a homicide but he also believed that corrupt drug addicted Portland police officers working in the vice unit may have been responsible for the murder of Zebedee Manning. Don argued with his lieutenant about the conclusion of the death investigation and was vehemently ordered to stop investigating it by that lieutenant. Don was told that the deceased 15-year-old, minor boy was only, "another nigger dope dealer," and apparently, didn't matter as a result. When Don continued to investigate the murder on his own time, he was thrown out of the homicide detail and transferred back to burglary. The transfer being a clear punitive repercussion to anyone in the know in law enforcement circles.

The later rumor that was circulated by individuals from the bureau who claimed Don was "crazy," was likely not happenstance. It was likely intentional. There was a need to discredit this man, described recently by a former PPB colleague and old friend as a man who had been "a great detective." But the question begs; why? What could be gained by discrediting Don DuPay and smearing his reputation? And why would anyone want to do that? Does it have something to do with the death of Zebedee Manning? And if so, are the players still alive? Is the shooter of Zebedee Manning still alive? And what is this man *still* attempting to conceal?

Theresa Griffin Kennedy,
2013

About the Editor

THERESA GRIFFIN-KENNEDY IS A WRITER, interested in social activism. She is also a confessional poet, creative writing instructor, painter of abstract art, and a lifetime resident of Oregon. She lives in Portland with her husband, writer and retired police detective, Don DuPay, where she continues to write and be published. Her website can be found here
https://sites.google.com/site/theresagriffinkennedy/

Acknowledgements

WHEN I SET OUT TO write a book about my years working for the Portland Police Bureau in the early 1960s and into the late 1970s, like any novice I thought "This will be easy. I can do it alone." Starting the book back in 1991 was a fairly smooth process. Once into it, however, I realized that writing and completing a manuscript and seeing it polished to the point of being accepted by a well regarded publisher, would not be an easy task, particularly in the modern world of publishing.

Firstly, I need to acknowledge and thank those law enforcement men who taught me about police work. The good cops who demonstrated their integrity every day. Detective Lieutenant Myron Warren took me under his wing in the burglary detail and showed me how good detectives became better detectives. I was one of the youngest detectives at that time, to work the burglary and then later the safe detail, this being the late 1960s, and I came to find out later that Myron had handpicked me for the safe detail. Myron was impressed with my drive, work ethic, and serious commitment to doing good police work. I found him to be one of the most dedicated, honest police officers working in the bureau and the impact he had on my life and my career cannot be measured.

I want to thank my early officer coaches, Fred Brock and Charlie Mayhew out of East Precinct, who showed me the ropes of how street police work was really done. Officer Paul C.L. Peterson, my coach in the traffic division taught me about skid marks and estimating vehicle speed with a complicated formula for the "co-efficient of friction" on asphalt which I never adequately understood. I want to thank Sergeant Bud Rowley, the second night traffic supervisor, who let me work alone, roaming the city at night making "the good arrests," for DWI and for speeding.

In my time as a street cop and detective, I learned that police officers are just human beings with all the frailties of lesser mortals.

Most men cannot handle the power given to them by the badge or the gun on their belts. Too much alcohol consumed, too many women to play with and the drunkenness that too much power brings will take its toll.

I'd like to acknowledge the memory of two good friends I had within the bureau, men who later killed themselves: my longtime partner Frank Jozaitis and my friend and supervisor in traffic Leo Miller. Although we were friends, I never understood why they decided to end their lives until many decades later and the reality and heartbreak of their suicides never left me. I thank them for the positive impact they had on my life and on my career.

I want to acknowledge the infamous Captain Jim Purcell Jr., from whom I learned the meaning of true corruption. I had the misfortune of working for Purcell after his exile to North Precinct. He was ousted as police chief in the late 1950s and we famously clashed, to the chagrin of many of my colleagues who were afraid of him. I never was.

Writing is not something one can do alone. Others must read, edit, rearrange and alter mischosen words. I would like to offer my gratitude to Editor Jonathan Stark for performing a professional developmental edit on this project. Jonathan provided input regarding the importance of, time, place, sequence and chronology, as well as opinions on various stories and how they might be fleshed out. Jonathan's involvement in this project made the final manuscript far richer than it would have been otherwise and for that I am very grateful.

I would like to thank writer, editor, and longtime newspaperman, Timothy Martin Flanagan for helping with preliminary, grammar and final edits throughout this process. Furthermore, I would like to thank Tim for the friendship, good humor and patience he has always generously offered during this process of collaboration.

I would like to thank Jim Huff, former curator of the Portland Police Museum for his generous help in providing me with a complete copy of my original personnel file documenting the seventeen years I worked with the Portland Police Bureau. After coming under heavy pressure and criticism for assisting me, Jim provided me with the file anyway and for that I am very grateful.

I would like to offer my sincere thanks to Mary Hansen and Brian Johnson of the Portland City Archives and Records Center, for generously assisting with historical research for this book and for providing copies of needed documents and numerous scanned photos of the men I worked with in the bureau. They were both extremely helpful and patient during this time consuming, tedious and very necessary process.

I would like to thank Ms. Joyce Boles, retired Journalist, social activist and fearless fiction and creative non-fiction writer. Joyce provided keen proofing skills and made many sound suggestions regarding areas that needed additional development in the manuscript. Her deep understanding of the social challenges of the times covered in the book, the geographical areas, along with having known some of the specific players was an added bonus. Joyce brought to light important issues regarding the readership and audience that I had not considered before, and for this I am very grateful.

I would like to thank Pfc. John McF. Mood, retired police Officer with Charleston South Carolina, Police department. John read the manuscript and provided insight and advice on how topics and sections could be fleshed out. He provided valuable proofing of the manuscript and assisted in the process of finding and addressing inconsistencies and errors. John also provided wonderful encouragement during this process, cheering me on and offering his support for the project and all that it entailed, and for this I am extremely grateful.

I wish to offer my sincere thanks to retired Portland Police Officer Bert Combs. Bert was kind enough to read and proof the manuscript in its preliminary stages, providing helpful and creative insight from a fellow law enforcement man and retired professional. Bert offered me a cop's point of view, and though he served the Portland citizens in a different time period, his perspective on my memoir was important and appreciated. Bert disagreed with some of the perceptions and assertions I make in my book, but he was always understanding and friendly in expressing his valued viewpoints, opinions and suggestions for how I might make the book stronger with a more nuanced view of law enforcement. I thank Bert very kindly for his invaluable assistance.

I would like to extend my sincere thanks and gratitude to Ms. Sheila Ahern, for her wonderful friendship, encouragement and support all during the demanding process of writing, rewriting and the seemingly constant process of revision and then more revision.

I would like to thank crime writer, JD Chandler, for his wonderful assistance with research and important fact finding. JD helped to resolve and correct several sections of the manuscript that were still unclear and slightly factually inaccurate. JD helped make the manuscript that much clearer and historically accurate by finding articles and news stories that corroborated my memories and helped flesh out my law enforcement recollections from some fifty years ago.

I would also like to thank renowned Portland crime writer, Phil Stanford, for generously writing the foreword to my book and for his support, encouragement and friendship over the years. Phil was one of the first people in Portland to take my perspective as a former police detective seriously and to listen to me, (going back to before 2004) and ultimately value my experience and history as I shared my memories of a very different police department and a very different city. Thank you Phil.

And finally, I would like to thank Theresa Griffin-Kennedy, who is also my wife. Theresa acted as my main editor, creative collaborator and overall helper on this formidable project. She scanned my original and only surviving manuscript hard copy and sat with me during eight laborious and emotionally difficult line-by-line edits. She encouraged me to tell the stories as they really happened, sharing details I might just as easily have left out.

She helped me make the officers, crime victims and criminals real. I wept on more than one occasion, as she patiently questioned me, prying details that were painful to remember. Too many years of death and destruction, buried away in my memory have been brought out and are here for all to read. The hard work Theresa contributed to this project is simply immeasurable. If not for Theresa, the manuscript would have remained in a suitcase under my bed, forgotten. To all of these people I offer my profound, sincere and grateful thanks.

Don DuPay,
December 24th, 2012

ABOUT THE AUTHOR

Don DuPay was born in Wenatchee Washington, spent several years in Montana and finally came to Portland Oregon in 1947, at the age of eleven, to live permanently. He graduated from Grant High School in 1954, and then studied for two years at Lewis and Clark College. DuPay went on to spend three years active service in the US Navy as a Communications Technician, performing top secret radio surveillance on the Baltic Sea. After completing military service he joined the Portland Police Bureau in 1961. Promoted to detective in 1967, he remained with PPB until 1978, when he resigned from the force for documented health reasons. Mr. DuPay subsequently became the director of security for The Benson Hotel in downtown Portland for several years during the 1980s. Years later, he co-hosted a cable access television program called Cannabis Common Sense, for almost five years. The show continues to run today and is devoted to the medical marijuana movement. DuPay currently resides with his fourth wife, writer, Theresa Griffin-Kennedy, in Portland, where he continues to write and be published.